BEST GREEN CAREERS

Titles of Additional Interest

Best Careers for Veterans

Best Careers for Teachers

BEST GREEN CAREERS

Explore Opportunities in this Rapid Growing Field!

LearningExpress®

NEW YORK

Library of Congress Cataloging-in-Publication Data:

Best green careers : explore opportunities in this rapid growing field!
    p. cm.

  ISBN-13: 978-1-57685-743-4 (pbk. : alk. paper)
  ISBN-10: 1-57685-743-3 (pbk. : alk. paper)

    1. Vocational guidance—United States.   2. Green movement—Vocational guidance—United States.   3. Environmental protection—Vocational guidance.   I. LearningExpress (Organization)

    HF5382.5.U5B476 2010
    331.702—dc22   2009051754

Printed in the United States of America

9 8 7 6 5 4 3 2 1

First Edition

ISBN-10 1-57685-743-3
ISBN-13 978-1-57685-743-4

For more information or to place an order, contact LearningExpress at:
  2 Rector Street
  26th Floor
  New York, NY 10006

Or visit www.learnatest.com

ABOUT THE AUTHOR

Jeffrey Dinsmore is a freelance writer based in Los Angeles, California. This is his third book for LearningExpress. Dinsmore is the founder of the independent fiction publishing houses Awkward Press and Contemporary Press. Through Contemporary Press, he authored two comedic novels: *I, an Actress, the Autobiography of Karen Jamey* (2005) and *Johnny Astronaut* (2003). Through Awkward Press, he edited and contributed to *Awkward One* (2009), an anthology of imaginative fiction.

CONTENTS ||||||||||||||||||||||||||||||||||||||||||||||

INTRODUCTION ||||||||||||||||||||||||||||||||||||||||||||||||

In 1994, carpet manufacturer Ray Anderson had an experience that changed his life forever. Throughout his first 21 years as founder and chairman of Interface Inc., the world's largest manufacturer of modular carpets, Anderson had never given a passing thought to the environmental impact of his company's products. However, as a new form of environmental consciousness began to move into the mainstream, Anderson found himself having to answer customers' questions regarding the sustainability of Interface carpets, questions that he had never even considered.

That summer, a group of Anderson's employees launched a task force to examine Interface's environmental policies. They asked Anderson to give a kick-off speech to the task force that articulated Interface's environmental vision. There was only one problem—Interface *had* no environmental vision. "I did not want to make that speech," Anderson says in the 2003 documentary *The Corporation*, with a chuckle.

Desperate for inspiration, Anderson began flipping through Paul Hawken's book *The Ecology of Commerce*. Reading the book, Anderson says, was like "a point of a spear into my chest. As I read on, the spear went deeper, and it became an epiphanal [sic] experience." Not only did Anderson have material for his speech, he had a newfound sense of his company's place in the world.

Within months, Anderson had set a goal of eliminating "any negative impact Interface [had] on the environment by 2020." To many within the company, the goal seemed impossible—the majority of carpets at the time were made from oil-based synthetic materials. In order to meet their new goals, Interface would not only have to adapt their business model to a new philosophy, they would have to recreate the way they manufactured their products from the ground up.

Although he assumed his decision would have an impact on company profits, Anderson felt he had no other choice if he hoped to leave behind a legacy of which he could be proud. Soon after Interface started working toward its new goals, Anderson discovered that he was right; their new business methods did indeed have an impact on company profits. However, he was astounded to find that, contrary to his assumptions, the financial impact was almost entirely positive. By eliminating waste, Interface cut costs, increased sales, and boosted profits. Today, Interface has cut landfill waste by more than 50%, has cut water usage by 75%, and has planted almost 87,000 trees. Even more impressive, seven of the company's facilities are powered by 100% sustainable sources of energy—a rarity in any industry.

Interface learned early on what many corporations are just starting to realize: *going green* is not only a smart environmental decision, it's a smart *financial* decision. Today, there is near-unanimous agreement that human activity has a negative impact on the environment. A 2007 survey conducted by Yale University, Gallup, and ClearVision Institute found that 62% of Americans "believe that global warming is an urgent threat requiring immediate and drastic action," and a 2006 survey by *Time* magazine found that 88% of Americans think "global warming threatens future generations." It is no longer possible for corporations to ignore the impact they are having on the environment, for the sake of Earth, and for the sake of their bottom lines.

Aware that a tremendous cultural shift is taking place, corporations across the United States are scrambling to remake themselves Earth-friendly. A 2009 report by the Pew charitable trusts found that green jobs are growing at a rate of more than *double* that of any other type of employment. There's no doubt about it: For people seeking employment, the future looks very, very green.

Some of the industries that fall under the green umbrella have existed for years, such as solar panel manufacturing or sustainable architecture. Other industries, like fuel cell manufacturing and ecotourism, are in their infancy. No matter what your interest and experience, however, it is a safe bet that there is a green job out there for you.

Best Green Careers is designed to help you find employment in the rapidly growing field of green and green-collar jobs. Our interviews with representatives from a variety of different occupations in the green economy will give you the inside information you need to start planning your new career. Whether you're a student just entering the workforce or a seasoned worker looking to make a career change, this book will help you find the career that's right for you. I take you through each step of your job search, from building your resume to networking to making a great impression in interviews. In addition, I point you to valuable resources you can use to get the jump on the competition and finally land that job of your dreams.

Here is a brief overview of each chapter.

Chapter 1: The Greening of the Workplace explores the history of the environmental movement and tackles the question that has been confounding Americans for the past few years: What exactly *is* a green job?

Chapter 2: The Green Horizon takes a look at why this is a great time to pursue a green job. In this chapter, I also discuss how government policy is shaping the jobs of the future and give important information about government incentives for green workers.

Chapter 3: Green Industries contains detailed information about nine major fields for green careers: Renewable Energy; Building; Transportation; Food and Agriculture; Recycling and Waste Management; Advocacy; Conservation; Nonprofits, Policy, and Research; and Entrepreneurial Opportunities.

Chapter 4: Learning the Ropes: Getting a Green Education talks about schools, programs, and certifications that can help you prepare for the jobs of tomorrow.

Chapter 5: Building a Green Resume gives expert advice on building resumes and cover letters that will help you break through the clutter.

Chapter 6: Networking and Making Connections talks about the most important tool for getting your foot in the door: networking. Included are valuable tips for using the professional networking site LinkedIn to connect with employers.

Chapter 7: Mastering the Interview Process shows you how to make the kind of lasting impression in an interview that will get you hired.

Chapter 8: Changing Careers: Advice for Experienced Job Seekers explains how your previous job experience can help you transition into a fulfilling green career.

Chapter 9: Online Resources for Green Job Seekers provides a list of useful resources that you can use to conduct your job search and keep up to speed with the latest developments in green jobs and technology.

BEST GREEN CAREERS

CHAPTER ONE

THE GREENING OF THE WORKPLACE

Chapter Overview

The move toward green jobs has the potential to transform the way we do business. In fact, many are predicting that the development of green energy will have as big an impact on our lives as the Industrial Revolution had on people of the eighteenth and nineteenth centuries. This chapter shows you the roots of the environmental movement and the ways in which it might impact our working lives.

Section 1: Terms of the Trade
Listen to any discussion of the economic future of the United States and you'll be certain to hear terms like *factory farms*, *sustainability*, and *carbon footprint*. In this section, you'll be introduced to some of the important terms that are used throughout the book.

Section 2: A Brief History of the Environmental Movement
Although the move toward a sustainable future has exploded in recent years, the environmental movement has been growing for more than a century. In this section, we take a brief look at the people and events that made the environmental movement what it is today.

Section 3: What Are Green Jobs?

Before you can identify whether a green career is right for you, become familiar with what we mean by *green jobs*. In this section, we look at the history of the term *green jobs* and talk about where this field is heading.

Section 4: Rethinking How We Work

As we move toward a greener future, many believe this is a perfect time to reexamine our entire system of labor. In this section, we explore some of the ways that the green revolution is changing the way we do business.

In Their Own Words: Gabe Ayala, Co-Founder Enovative Group, Inc.

Gabe Ayala is one of the principal founders of Enovative Group, Inc. (EGI), a company in Southern California that develops and manufactures energy-efficient technologies.

How did you get started doing what you do?

I started out working for 3M in Minnesota as a sales guy. As an added value for our customers, we'd look at their manufacturing processes and try to eliminate inefficiencies. I became interested in energy sometime after September 11, when I started thinking more about the relationship between our energy policy and national security. And then 3M transferred me [to Los Angeles] to manage the sales territory.

I ended up leaving 3M to get my real estate license and went to work with a buddy from Minnesota, a real estate developer who's out here. His company had all these different properties, and this guy who worked in HVAC (*heating*, *ventilation*, and *air-conditioning*) owed them a bunch of money. One of the things he gave the company to settle his debt was the rights to a new technology, the water pump. Greg, the guy I was working with, came to me and said, "Gabe, tell me if you can sell this." I started looking at it, and I thought, This is pretty cool. So I started thinking more about if I were to start a company with this new technology, how I would penetrate the market. How much money is being set aside to incentive people to adopt energy-efficient technologies?

And I'm guessing it wasn't nearly as much then as it is now.

No, this is pre-*Inconvenient Truth*. So it was still very much on the periphery. I think it's still . . . I don't think it's gone totally mainstream, but we're definitely getting there. So, yeah, I was kind of on the beginning curve, when everything started to move in that direction. And then we started building this business. We realized pretty quickly that we'd need to do a lot of testing before we could convince people to buy it.

How did you go about doing that?

Well, one of the best things we did early was in order to secure the intellectual property from the inventor, we made an exchange in shares of stock. So he's a part owner of our company, and he's been in the industry for 20 years. He has a ton of contacts. Another investor in our company is a guy named Gary Klein, who spent 30 years with the California Energy Commission. His area of expertise is the water–energy relationship. Having those guys as part of our company has opened a lot of doors for us. We have an inside track that we never would have had by ourselves. So that puts us in touch with a lot of energy engineers. We've learned a great deal about how to effectively evaluate something and how to test something for energy savings. It's a tough science, though. I think any energy engineer will tell you the toughest part of their work is trying to get the numbers exact. It's virtually impossible.

Why is that?

Every building is completely unique. There are so many factors that it's hard to isolate all the variables and get an accurate reading. We've done studies on buildings that were side by side, exactly the same, and we got two different sets of data coming back to us. So sometimes it's very difficult to pinpoint what's going on. Therefore, if you're asking about where the best job opportunities are, I'd put energy engineers pretty high up on that list. We need more of those, because we need to be able to quantify this stuff. It's really difficult to do that right now.

What do you think is the most important step we can take toward sustainability?

In my opinion, energy efficiency represents the best bang for our buck in terms of reducing our energy consumption. Something like 40% of our energy pie goes to buildings. And that's the low-hanging fruit. That's where we need to focus our efforts: how to make buildings work better, smarter, more efficiently. And when you look at what in a building is hogging up all that energy, they're all the components that go into making them livable spaces: lights, fans, pumps, chillers, boilers . . . lighting, and HVAC, basically. There are a lot of things that need to be retrofitted, replacing old technology with new, smarter technology.

Energy efficiency means putting lights on a schedule. Or modulating the speed of an air handling fan or AC unit so it isn't pumping as hard. Things like that. This is stuff that anyone can do right now. And the cost benefit is very favorable.

One of the things I've heard as I've been talking to people is that the reason the green economy is not growing faster is because they can't find enough qualified workers.
You hit the nail right on the head. There are not enough qualified workers to go out and do this work. We look at a lot of energy engineering firms, and they have more work than they know what to do with. The problem for them is hiring people who have some qualifications, so they're stealing talent from one another.

What would you say to someone who is going to school right now, or who is looking to change careers . . . what are some of the biggest opportunities?
Engineering is one of the biggest ones. I think any of the traditional business courses are good, because we will need people trained in business in order to make the companies of the future or to take our market and sell our products. We need salespeople. We also need lawyers. I think that green careers will be so all-encompassing that pretty much all of the more traditional curriculum will be somehow used.

But what we really lack right now are the new technologies and that's really what we need most. We need people to think about how to remake our infrastructure. A perfect case is the *smart grid*, a project that is so ambitious that people don't even quite know how to define what it is. But you know when we figure it out, we're going to need a hell of a lot of engineers to develop the necessary technologies to make this thing real.

Are you encouraged? Do you think we're heading in the right direction?
Yeah, I do. I think the fact that we have so much money committed to this is a very positive thing. I look at what I'm doing and I think that there are so many other opportunities for entrepreneurialism. I look at the American spirit as being an entrepreneurial spirit. As long as we provide a breeding ground for opportunity, people will go out and do it for themselves. And I think that's part of why we're so successful. The hardest part is to change hearts and minds, and it seems like we're doing that.

Section 1: Terms of the Trade

Before you can walk the walk, you should learn how to talk the talk. Listed below are some of the most crucial terms and words to know as you embark upon your search for a green career.

Alternative energy   Any source of energy that is more sustainable to the health of our planet than current sources of energy, such as coal or oil. These energy sources can come from technology that has been in existence for centuries, such as wind or water power, or from new developments, such as hydrogen fuel cells.

ARRA   The 2008 American Recovery and Reinvestment Act, otherwise known as the *stimulus package*. Much of the money that is going into green training and green job creation is coming from ARRA.

Baseload energy   Energy sources that produce constant power, such as geothermal heat.

Biodegradable   Any material that decomposes naturally and can be reabsorbed into the ecosystem.

Brownfields   Sites that are difficult to develop or underutilized due to industrial pollution or hazardous substances.

Cap and trade   A system whereby companies are given an *emissions permit* for every ton of carbon dioxide they release into the atmosphere. If companies emit *less* carbon dioxide than expected, they are allowed to trade the remainder of their emissions with other companies, giving those companies permission to overpollute. Over the course of time, the amount of emissions allotted to companies will become stricter, with the ultimate goal being a drastic lessening of the amount of greenhouse gases released by corporations.

Carbon footprint   One of the major hurdles we face as we look at the future of the planet is reducing the amount of carbon dioxide we release into the atmosphere. A *carbon footprint* is a measure of the amount of carbon dioxide that an individual or a company produces.

Carbon neutral   There has been a movement in recent years on the part of companies and individuals to become *carbon neutral*, which means ensuring that every amount of carbon dioxide you release into the atmosphere will be absorbed. In most cases, this involves both lessening the amount of carbon dioxide one releases (through greener means of production, transportation, etc.) and planting enough trees to absorb any additional carbon dioxide. Although the effects of carbon neutrality are not immediate, if enough people and organizations became carbon neutral, they could theoretically slow or stop the processes that lead to global climate change.

Clean coal   A euphemism for carbon capture and storage (CCS) technologies. CCS is a process by which coal is "washed" to reduce carbon dioxide emissions. The excess carbon dioxide is then stored underground in rock formations. Although the U.S. government is investigating clean coal technology (President Barack Obama included $3.4 billion for clean coal projects in his 2008 economic stimulus package), many argue that investing in clean coal technology is a quick fix for a problem that requires longer-term solutions.

Ecosystem   Used to describe how the totality of life on the planet interacts with the environment. For example, if you say that high mercury levels in fish are bad for the *ecosystem*, this means that high mercury levels affect more than just the fish themselves; anything that eats the fish will be affected, as will the environment in which the fish live.

Environmental Protection Agency (EPA)   The government agency tasked with setting and enforcing rules that protect the environment and control pollution. Although the EPA is considered an independent agency, the president appoints its administrator, which has led to charges of bias in previous administrations.

Factory farms   Most of the meat and vegetables consumed in the United States today come from *factory farms*, which are large farms that are devoted to raising a single type of livestock or agriculture. Factory farms, particularly cattle farms, often generate large amounts of waste that can contaminate water sources and the atmosphere.

Fossil fuels   Coal, petroleum, and natural gas are all *fossil fuels*. These are fuels that have been created over millions of years by the decomposition of plants and animals. We all use fossil fuels every day to heat our homes, generate electricity, and power our cars.

Global warming/global climate change   For years, the term *global warming* was used to refer to an increase in the average temperature of Earth's surface. In recent years, the term *global climate change* has become more acceptable as a means of describing the total effect of increased greenhouse gases on the environment.

Greenhouse effect and greenhouse gases   In a greenhouse, panels of glass let light in but do not allow heat to escape, which makes the temperature inside the greenhouse rise. The atmosphere operates much like a greenhouse, except instead of the sunlight passing through panels of glass, it passes through a layer of *greenhouse gases*. These gases, which include carbon dioxide and methane, trap the sunlight and cause the atmosphere to heat up, a process known as the *greenhouse effect*. Thus, the more greenhouse gases there are in the atmosphere, the more heat will be trapped—and the warmer Earth will become. It's important to note that the greenhouse effect is not a negative thing that needs to be stopped; the term is simply used to describe a natural process. The overabundance of greenhouse gases in the atmosphere is a problem, but the greenhouse effect itself is just the way Earth works.

Greenwashing   The process by which corporations or industries attempt to make themselves seem more environmentally friendly than they actually are.

HVAC   Heating, ventilation, and air-conditioning. The heating, ventilation, and air-conditioning systems in a building are collectively referred to as HVAC systems.

Intermittent energy   Energy sources that are available only at certain times or under certain environmental conditions, such as solar or wind power.

LEED   Leadership in Energy and Environmental Design. LEED is a rating system designed by the U.S. Green Building Council to measure the environmental impact and energy efficiency of new construction projects.

Organic   Technically, anything living is *organic*, meaning it is composed of carbon. In agricultural terms, *organic* refers to anything grown without the use of manufactured chemicals. In recent years, as corporations have come to realize that there is money to be made with organic products, the U.S. Department of Agriculture has come under fire for loosening the standards of what kinds of foods can be considered organic.

Pre-consumer waste Waste that is created before a product has been used, such as the waste pulp that is created during the process of manufacturing paper.

Post-consumer waste Another word for trash: hamburger wrappers, cigarette butts, potato chip packages, and so on.

Renewable resources/nonrenewable resources Any type of natural resource that is either limitless or easily replaced, such as wind, the sun (solar power), or wood. Metals are also considered *renewable*, as they can be recycled. *Nonrenewable resources*, by contrast, are sources of energy that are not easily replaced, that is, fossil fuels. A major part of the growing green jobs movement is companies that are working to find renewable alternatives to nonrenewable resources.

Smart grid An energy-efficient electricity grid controlled by digital technology. In 2009, the Obama administration kick-started the building of the U.S. *smart grid* with $3.4 billion worth of grants. When installed properly, smart grid technology gives power providers and consumers more control over when, where, and how electricity is generated and distributed.

Sustainable A process or practice that can be repeated indefinitely without negatively impacting the environment. In *sustainable* agriculture, for example, crops and animals are rotated in such a way that the waste of one process is absorbed into another process.

Section 2: A Brief History of the Environmental Movement

The sudden mainstream acceptance of the environmental movement may make it seem as if concern over the environment is a recent phenomenon. In fact, as long as there has been industry in the United States, there have been people fighting the effects of waste and pollution. In 1739, for example,

Benjamin Franklin and a group of Philadelphians petitioned the Pennsylvania Assembly to disallow leather factories from dumping their waste in Philadelphia's commercial district. The petition cited problems such as "foul smells" and "disease" that were caused by the leather waste. Even back then, people recognized that industrial waste was something that could cause health problems and harm the environment.

The Birth of the Environmental Movement

To discuss everyone who played an important role in the birth of the environmental movement would take more room than we have to spare. However, three key figures must be mentioned in any history of the modern green era. The first is Henry David Thoreau. In 1845, Thoreau, a writer and civil activist, built a small cabin near Walden Pond in Concord, Massachusetts. He spent the next 26 months living there in relative isolation, attempting to get back in touch with the natural world that humans were beginning to leave behind. Nine years later, Thoreau published an account of his experiment entitled *Walden, or Life in the Woods*. The book challenged readers to take a close look at the results of "progress" and to determine whether that progress was making their lives healthier or happier. The book took several years to catch on, but today it is considered a classic of American literature that is often referred to as the bible of the environmental movement.

A little less than 40 years later, a conservationist named John Muir became the second key figure in the environmental movement when he founded a group called the Sierra Club. The Sierra Club's motto is "explore, enjoy, and protect the planet." Muir's club was instrumental in the establishment of several national parks, including Glacier and Yellowstone, as well as the founding of the National Park Service. The Sierra Club was one of the first national advocacy clubs to promote appreciation of the environment, and it continues to be a crucial voice in support of America's wild lands and national parks.

The third key figure was a writer and scientist named Rachel Carson. To many, the real catalyst of the modern environmental era is Carson's 1962 nonfiction book *Silent Spring*. Originally serialized in *The New Yorker* in 1962, *Silent Spring* took a thorough and chilling look at the effects of pesticides on the environment. The book hit America like a slap in the face, becoming an instant bestseller and awakening many Americans to the negative consequences of industrial progress, much as *Walden* had 100 years earlier. As Jack Lewis wrote in a 1985 issue of the *EPA Journal*:

> Silent Spring *played in the history of environmentalism roughly the same role that* Uncle Tom's Cabin *played in the abolitionist movement. . . . The influence of her book has brought together over 14,000 scientists, lawyers, managers, and other employees across the country to fight the good fight for 'environmental protection.'*

After *Silent Spring*

Carson's book was released just as a new generation of Americans was beginning to come of age: the *baby boomers*. The product of high post–World War II birth rates, the baby boom generation grew up with a newfound concern for the planet and a suspicion of the old ways of doing business. The boomers took Carson's message about the dangers of corporate farming practices and adapted it into a full-blown movement. Carson's book helped usher in what green jobs activist Van Jones calls "the regulation wave" of the environmental movement. The period of ecological awareness that grew from *Silent Spring* led to such important pieces of legislation as the 1963 Clean Air Act and the 1967 Air Quality Act.

In 1968, the burgeoning environmental movement rallied around another publication: Stewart Brand's *Whole Earth Catalog*. Equal parts shopping guide, how-to book, and political manifesto, the *Whole Earth Catalog* was an attempt to create a complete listing of "tools" that readers could purchase to benefit themselves and the world around them. Although the *Whole Earth Catalog* was not just centered around environmental concerns, the ideas of sustainability and human's connection to nature were an important part of the catalog's mission. The motto listed at the beginning of each issue describes this mission in colorful detail:

Green Quotes
Henry David Thoreau's writings were a huge inspiration to John Muir. However, in Muir's opinion, the solitary Thoreau stuck a little too closely to the city: "Even open-eyed Thoreau would perhaps have done well," Muir wrote, "had he extended his walks westward to see what God had to show in the lofty sunset mountains."

We are as gods and might as well get good at it. So far remotely done power and glory—as via government, big business, formal education, church—has succeeded to the point where the gross defects obscure actual gain. In response to this dilemma and to these gains a realm of intimate, person power is developing—power of the individual to conduct his own education, find his own inspiration, shape his own environment, and share his adventure with whoever is interested. Tools that aid this process are sought and promoted by the WHOLE EARTH CATALOG.

The *Whole Earth Catalog* was published only regularly for four years, but during that time, it was enormously popular, introducing readers around the country to concepts like organic farming, alternative energy, and the costs of pollution.

Green Quotes
In Apple founder Steve Jobs' 2005 commencement
speech at Stanford University, he discussed the
effect that the Whole Earth Catalog *had on him:*
"When I was young, there was an amazing publication called
the Whole Earth Catalog, *which was one of the bibles of my*
generation. . . . It was sort of like Google in paperback form, 35
years before Google came along. . . . On the back cover of their
final issue was a photograph of an early morning country road,
the kind you might find yourself hitchhiking on if you were so
adventurous. Beneath it were the words: 'Stay Hungry.
Stay Foolish.' It was their farewell message
as they signed off. Stay Hungry. Stay Foolish.
And I have always wished that for myself."

Meanwhile, the outcry created by *Silent Spring* continued to reverberate around the country, leading to a 1969 bill known as the National Environmental Policy Act

(NEPA). NEPA marked the environmental movement's final leap into the mainstream. As stated in the preamble, NEPA's goals were:

> *To declare a national policy which will encourage productive and enjoyable harmony between man and his environment. To promote efforts which will prevent or eliminate damage to the environment and biosphere and stimulate the health and welfare of man. To enrich our understanding of the ecological systems and natural resources important to the Nation.*

In a symbolic gesture, the bill was signed into law by President Richard M. Nixon on New Years' Day, 1970—the first legislation of the new decade.

Two months after that, the first Earth Day celebration was held. With an estimated 20 million Americans attending Earth Day festivities around the country, Washington now recognized that the pro-environment forces were getting too big to be ignored. A few months later, the Environmental Protection Agency (EPA) was formed to "establish and enforce environmental protection standards," "conduct environmental research," and "provide assistance to others combating environmental pollution." By the end of 1970, the EPA had helped pass an updated version of the Clean Air Act, which remains, to this day, one of the most substantial pieces of environmental policy ever passed.

One Step Forward, Two Steps Back

After the dramatic gains of 1970, it seemed like the United States was on track to lead the world in progressive environmental policy. Unfortunately, this wasn't to be the case. As the seventies wore on, a presidential scandal, an unpopular war, and an economic recession turned American attention inward. Although many Americans remained passionately concerned about saving the Earth, for many years following the 1970 victories, political progress was incremental at best.

In the 1980s, industrial pollution went nearly unregulated, even as environmental news became increasingly more dire. This decade saw such environmental catastrophes as the Chernobyl nuclear disaster (1986) in the U.S.S.R. and the *Exxon Valdez* oil spill (1989), which remains among the largest environmental disasters in United States history.

Progress remained stalled throughout much of the 1990s in America, although other countries were beginning to accept that drastic steps needed to be taken to combat climate change. In 1992, 150 countries signed a treaty with the unwieldy name of the United Nations Framework Convention on Climate Change, known by the only slightly less unwieldy acronym UNFCCC. The treaty basically said that although we may not be 100% certain that global climate change is a result of human activity, the threat of irreversible damage is reason enough to curb greenhouse gas emissions. The treaty also distinguishes between "first world countries" (Annex I) and "developing countries" (non-Annex I), with the Annex I countries agreeing to make larger cuts than the non-Annex I countries. The UNFCCC was a step in the right direction, but it was not very specific; it did not specify any goals, nor did it put any requirements on its members to follow through on their promises.

The UNFCCC nations decided that if progress were to be made, they had to impose stricter requirements on industrialized countries. In 1997, the leaders of the industrialized countries in the UNFCCC met in Kyoto, Japan, to try to find common ground. President Bill Clinton, wanting to change the U.S.'s image as an opponent of environmental regulation, announced before the meeting,

We will bring to the Kyoto conference in December a strong American commitment to realistic and binding limits that will significantly reduce our emissions of greenhouse gases.

Did You Know?
The 1989 Exxon Valdez oil spill was one of the worst ecological disasters in U.S. history. The spill made headlines around the world and sparked a national discussion about the ecological effects of our dependence on oil. Nonetheless, in 2008 the U.S. Supreme Court reduced Exxon's punitive damages from $2.5 billion to $500 million. The amount of the fine is equal to four days of Exxon's profits.

Unfortunately, the members of Congress weren't quite as excited about imposing regulations on the industries in their states. Senator Robert Byrd introduced a Congressional resolution demanding that President Clinton agree to stricter greenhouse gas emission standards only if developing nations were required to meet the same criteria. In a move that foreshadowed the United States' path on climate change for the next 10 years, the resolution passed 95–0.

At the Kyoto conference a few months later, representatives from 84 countries signed a bill stating their intentions to reduce greenhouse gas emissions, with the European Union agreeing to an 8% reduction below 1990 levels by 2012, and the United States agreeing to a 7% reduction. Developing nations, who typically emit far lower levels of greenhouse gases than developed nations, would be asked to reduce their emissions on a purely voluntary level.

Although the Kyoto Protocol, as it came to be known, would reduce emissions only by about 5% worldwide, it was an important step on the path to victory over climate change. The United States rolled up its sleeves and got to work, global greenhouse gas emissions dropped dramatically, and the planet was saved from almost certain peril.

Wait . . . Really?

Sadly, no. The Kyoto Protocol was signed by Vice President Al Gore on November 12, 1998. However, in order for the Protocol to become binding, it would have to be passed by Congress. Congress had made no attempt to hide its opposition to the Protocol, so President Clinton did not even bother to pass the treaty along.

After the Clinton administration had left office, the Kyoto Protocol was basically dead in the water. President George W. Bush wrote in March, 2001:

> *I oppose the Kyoto Protocol because it exempts 80 percent of the world, including China and India from compliance . . . there is a clear consensus that the Kyoto Protocol is an unfair and ineffective means of addressing global climate change concerns.*

Instead, the Bush administration proposed a Clear Skies initiative with emissions limits that were strictly voluntary. Meanwhile, for every year that the United States did not ratify the Kyoto Protocol, the possibilities of meeting its standards in time for the 2012 deadline became more remote.

With the deadline quickly approaching, the chance that the United States will ratify the Protocol and meet its commitment is basically nil.

Did You Know?

The United States' refusal to ratify the Kyoto Protocol has angered environmentalists the world over. But how successful has the Kyoto Protocol actually been?

If current data is to be believed, the answer is: not very. As of 2007, only 6 of the 23 "first-world" countries had seen drops in carbon dioxide emissions. (The former-Soviet bloc also saw reductions, but only because they were being measured against emissions levels from before the fall of communism.) Many others have seen increases, including a 27% increase in Canada to a 61% increase in Spain. As a developing nation, China was not required to reduce their emissions when they signed the Kyoto Protocol; since then, the country's emissions have risen by a whopping 138%.

The Tipping Point

After almost 30 years of stops and starts on environmental policy, two events are widely seen as bringing about a tipping point on climate change. The first was the 2005 Hurricane Katrina disaster. It is difficult to prove a direct link between the hurricane and global warming; hurricanes of Katrina's intensity (Category 3) are relatively common, and it is impossible to pinpoint a single cause for storms of Katrina's complexity. However, psychologically, the sight of a major U.S. city being toppled by a single storm became a wake-up call for many Americans about the destructive power of nature. The question of whether climate change was a contributing factor became a major topic of discussion in the media's analysis of what went wrong.

The second event was the 2006 release of former Vice President Al Gore's documentary *An Inconvenient Truth*. The movie, which simply follows Gore as he gives a PowerPoint presentation discussing human's contribution to global climate change, was an instant phenomenon, reaching a mass audience and inspiring a national discussion on America's role in curbing greenhouse gas emissions.

By the time of the next election, Gore's "inconvenient truth" had been accepted as fact by all of the major presidential candidates. For the first time since the environmental movement began, the candidates agreed that global climate change was a real phenomenon for which humans were at least partly responsible. No one used the stock political response that the effects of climate change would "have to be studied more closely" before we could begin to address the issue. Instead, all the candidates attempted to portray themselves as the candidates who would do the most to fix the environment. It had been a long time coming, but the environmental movement had finally entered the mainstream of U.S. politics.

Eco-Quiz

Which U.S. president do historians consider to be the "first conservation president?"

    a. *Andrew Jackson*

    b. *Theodore Roosevelt*

    c. *John F. Kennedy*

    d. *Richard Nixon*

Answer: b. Theodore Roosevelt. *An avid nature lover, President Roosevelt entered office with a mission of protecting our natural lands for future generations. Some of Roosevelt's accomplishments included the establishment of the U.S. Forest Service, the creation of five national parks, and the establishment of the first federal bird reserve.*

Section 3: What Are Green Jobs?

During the 2008 presidential election, one could hardly turn around without hearing someone talking about "green" or "green-collar" jobs. It had taken years for politicians to agree that global climate change was a real phenomenon. Now, as the need to fix our environmental woes finally began to take hold, it felt like everyone was trying to make up for lost time. Be they Democrat or Republican, each candidate highlighted his or her environmental bona fides as proof that he or she was the person who could best create the green jobs that would save our environment and our economy in one fell swoop. Senators Hillary Clinton and Barack Obama each pledged to create "five million green-collar jobs." Senator John McCain agreed that "green jobs and green technology will be vital to our economic future."

During the election, the candidates and the press often used the terms *green jobs* and *green-collar jobs* interchangeably. But do they really mean the same thing? And how does someone decide what industries fall under the umbrella of these jobs?

The Origin of Green–Collar Jobs

Although the term *green-collar jobs* has only recently moved into the public lexicon, you might be surprised to learn that the term was actually coined in the 1970s. In 1976, university professor Patrick Heffernan delivered a paper at a congressional hearing entitled "Jobs for the Environment—the Coming Green Collar Revolution." Heffernan's declaration of *revolution* was about 30 years premature; had he presented his paper in the year 1999, he may have gotten a lot more credit.

Green Quotes

Green-collar jobs are the jobs that surround this new, green economy. When we talk about production of wind turbines, for example, someone has to design those wind turbines, someone has to build those wind turbines, someone has to install the wind turbine, someone has to maintain it. [Those are] jobs. And those are jobs that are going to contribute to a clean environment, but at the same time create a whole new economy for America.

—Jerome Ringo, President of the Apollo Alliance in an interview with
   NPR's All Things Considered, *February 15, 2008*

Or perhaps not, if the story of Northwest Environment Watch is any indication. In 1999, Northwest Environment Watch, a not-for-profit research and communication center, published a small book entitled *Green-Collar Jobs* about the growth of environmentally conscious industries in the Pacific Northwest. Writer Alan Durning had not heard of Heffernan's paper when he was working on the book; their mutual coinage of the term was simply one of those coincidences that happen to the best of writers. Although the book was well-received, the term met with little fanfare, and Northwest Environment Watch went about their noble business of promoting sustainability in their part of the country.

Seven years later, in 2006, San Francisco State University professor Raquel Pinderhughes published an article called "Race, Poverty, and the Environment." In the article, Pinderhughes used a term she had found in a small book about sustainability in, you guessed it, the Pacific Northwest. Pinderhughes liked the term, but felt that it could apply to a much broader range of careers than those to which Durning had originally applied it. As Pinderhughes wrote in her 2007 paper "Green Collar Jobs: An Analysis of the Capacity of Green

Businesses to Provide High Quality Jobs for Men and Women with Barriers to Employment,"

Green collar jobs are blue collar jobs in green businesses—that is, manual labor jobs in businesses whose products and services directly improve environmental quality.

Later in the paper, she provides a list of 22 different sectors of the economy that she considered green-collar (see below).

22 Sectors of the Economy that Provide Green-Collar Jobs
(Pinderhughes, 2006)

1. bicycle repair and bike delivery services
2. car and truck mechanic jobs, production jobs, and gas station jobs related to biodiesel, vegetable oil, and other alternative fuels
3. energy retrofits to increase energy efficiency and conservation
4. food production using organic and sustainably grown agricultural products
5. furniture making from environmentally certified and recycled wood
6. green building
7. green waste composting on a large scale
8. hauling and reuse of construction and demolition materials and debris (C&D)
9. hazardous materials cleanup
10. green (sustainable) landscaping
11. manufacturing jobs related to large-scale production of a wide range of appropriate technologies (i.e., solar panels, bike cargo systems, green waste bins, etc.)
12. materials reuse/producing products made from recycled, nontoxic materials
13. nontoxic household cleaning in residential and commercial buildings
14. parks and open space maintenance and expansion
15. printing with nontoxic inks and dyes and recycled papers

16. public transit jobs related to driving

17. recycling

18. solar installation and maintenance

19. tree cutting and pruning

20. peri-urban and urban agriculture

21. water retrofits to increase water efficiency and conservation

22. whole home performance

Not long after that, a colleague of Pinderhughes's named Van Jones began using the term in his speeches. Van Jones first came to national prominence for his work as a community activist in Oakland, California. As the founder of an Oakland-based non-governmental organization (NGO) called the Ella Baker Center for Human Rights, Jones spearheaded a Green-Collar Jobs initiative that trained workers in economically impoverished areas for careers in environmentally conscious fields. After seeing his program meet with great success in Oakland, Jones created Green for All, an NGO that took the work he was doing on a local level to the national stage. There was little to not admire about Van Jones's mission of saving the environment and lifting the poor out of poverty all at once, and the three major candidates in the 2008 presidential campaign took notice. After 30 years of fits and starts, the idea of green-collar jobs suddenly exploded into the national consciousness.

Green Quotes

The possibility of an economic recovery based on clean energy (to increase supply) and on wasting less energy (to cut demand) is not a daydream. There is already a huge green economy developing. It is growing despite inadequate and inconsistent support from a public sector that is still easily cowed by the big polluters. In 2006, renewable energy and energy-efficiency technologies generated 8.5 million jobs, nearly $970 billion in revenue and more than $100 billion in industry profits. This is happening while the government is still giving billions of dollars in subsidies to the oil and coal companies. Imagine what would happen if the public sector fully and passionately supported the shift to clean, renewable power—and gave those supports to the next generation of power producers.

—Van Jones, in the introduction to his influential 2008 book
   The Green-Collar Economy: How One Solution Can Fix Our Two Biggest Problems

Green Jobs versus Green-Collar Jobs

There was only one problem with the sudden fascination with "green-collar jobs": no one could really agree upon what they are. According to Pinderhughes's definition, **green-collar jobs** are essentially environmentally friendly versions of blue-collar, or manual labor jobs. Her 22 categories of green-collar jobs include such preexisting careers as "car and truck mechanic" and "furniture-making," retrofitted to include environmentally friendly materials and processes. For example, a car and truck mechanic would be considered a green-collar position if the mechanic worked on cars that ran on alternative fuels.

As the term moved into greater use, many began to drop the *-collar* part of the term and simply to use the term *green jobs* to refer to any job in an environmentally friendly industry. This broader term could now incorporate traditionally white-collar positions as well, such as environmental lawyers, policy experts, and scientists.

There are those who advocate for use of the term *green-collar* as a way of breaking down the traditional barriers between blue- and white-collar jobs. In the opinion of Phil Angelides, a venture capitalist and chair of the green employment advocacy group Apollo Alliance, a green-collar job is not simply a job that fuses new technologies with old work habits. According to Angelides, in order for a job to truly be considered "green," it must meet three criteria:

1. It must pay decent wages and offer benefits that can support a family.

2. It must be part of a career path, with potential for advancement.

3. It needs to reduce waste and pollution and to benefit the environment.

In a 2008 interview with National Public Radio, Angelides said that green-collar jobs can "also include white-collar jobs that are turning with a green tint." In the same interview, *Columbia Journalism Review* reporter Russ Juskalian acknowledged that the definition of the term was still up for debate.

Bob Garfield: We just got finished talking to Phil Angelides of the Apollo Alliance about green-collar jobs. And he defined it, but is there a universally accepted definition of what constitutes green-collar anything?

Russ Juskalian: I don't think there is really agreement at all on this. It's all over the place. Is the guy who works for the construction company who is putting out concrete and building foundations for big buildings who, you know, one [of his] job[s] happens to be putting up a foundation for a windmill—now, is that person's job a green-collar job?

*In the campaigning in the Rust Belt, Hillary [Clinton] at one point said,
"You've heard white-collar jobs and blue-collar jobs—we're going to create
green-collar jobs." And what that means, in reality, [laughs] is something that
never really got answered.*

Later in the interview, Juskalian brings up another term that got a lot of
attention during the 2008 campaign: *greenwashing*. **Greenwashing** refers to
the process whereby companies or politicians attempt to portray themselves
as environmentally friendly when they, in fact, are doing nothing to help the
environment. With the vast majority of the American public having a favorable view of companies that work to improve the environment, perpetuating an
environmentally friendly image has become a smart business decision, regardless of its basis in reality. One major concern of green activists as we seek to
define this new kind of workforce is that the idea of green and green-collar
jobs will become diluted to the point where it will no longer have a meaning.

Did You Know?

*The Apollo Alliance is an organization of business and environmental leaders who are
working on practical solutions for making U.S. energy independent. In its 2008 report,
The New Apollo Program: An Economic Strategy for American Prosperity, the Apollo
Alliance gave five key recommendations for how the United States can establish a
clean energy economy, including investments in training for green jobs and producing
25% of our power from renewable energy sources by 2025. If implemented properly,
the Alliance claims The New Apollo Program will create 5 million new jobs with
an investment of $500 billion—about half the amount that was lent to American
Insurance Group (AIG) during their 2008 government bailout.*

Just to add an extra layer of confusion to the green/green-collar jobs definition dilemma, some people have suggested that the word *green* itself should be
replaced. These critics argue that so many companies have adopted the word
green that the word has already been rendered meaningless. Because of this,
one will often see phrases like *clean energy* and *clean tech jobs* in place of *green
energy* and *green-collar jobs*.

How Does This Book Define Green Jobs?

For the purpose of this book, I use the term **green jobs**, which I define as: *any
career-oriented job in an industry that will benefit the long-term health of the planet.*
In some cases, this has led to some tough decisions. Unfortunately, no matter

how hard a company like British Petroleum works to clean up their act, oil is inherently unsustainable; therefore, any job in the oil industry will automatically be excluded. On the other hand, even though buses run on oil, driving a bus *is* considered a green job, because a good public transit system is a key to lowering air pollution.

Although I personally agree with Phil Angelides' position that all employers should offer "benefits and wages that can support a family" and "opportunities for advancement," it is somewhat difficult to gauge how well any individual employer lives up to these criteria, particularly during the economic climate in which this book is being written. Therefore, although I believe any job that benefits the environment has a longer shelf life than jobs that do not, I can't guarantee that every job listed in this book will continue to be in demand in 25 years. However, one thing is certain: Fixing the planet is going to take an awful lot of work . . . and an awful lot of work means an awful lot of new jobs.

Sidenote: A Word on Clean Coal

When I was deciding which industries to include in this book, one particular industry caused more trouble than others: clean coal. *Clean coal* is a buzz phrase for coal-fired power plants that use a complex technology called *carbon capture and storage* (CCS). Instead of sending carbon dioxide into the atmosphere, clean coal power plants capture the carbon dioxide and compress it into a liquid form. This liquid can then be either sold to companies that use carbon dioxide (such as makers of carbonated beverages) or pumped into underground rock formations.

The idea of clean coal is extremely controversial. Proponents of clean coal contend that half of our country's electricity is powered by coal, and we can reduce carbon dioxide emissions more quickly if we outfit power plants with CCS technology than if we try to change the system completely. Opponents argue that the technology is prohibitively expensive right now, that CCS has never been successfully implemented on a mass scale, and that there have been no long-term studies on the effects of pumping CO_2 back into the earth. Reactions are even split in the environmental community: The Natural Resources Defense Council (NRDC) and the Environmental Defense Fund (EDF) both support clean coal, while the Sierra Club and Greenpeace are against it.

In the end, I decided to side with the Sierra Club and Greenpeace on this issue, for one major reason: Although we may be able to make the process of burning coal cleaner, the process of extracting coal will never be clean. Coal extraction techniques like strip-mining and mountaintop removal create waste that poisons rivers and streams and causes lung disease in coal workers. CCS technology may be a great way to reduce greenhouse gas emissions, but at the end of the day, it is a quick fix for a problem that needs longer-term solutions. By investing in an ultimately unsustainable fuel source like coal, we are simply pushing our hard decisions off to be dealt with by subsequent generations.

Section 4: Rethinking the Way We Work

As one of the leading voices in the green jobs movement, Van Jones is not without his share of controversy. In 2009, he resigned his post as the special advisor for Green Jobs, Enterprise, and Innovation for the White House Council on Environmental Quality upon charges that his activist background made him too radical to serve in the White House. Still, even his critics recognize that Van Jones's book *The Green-Collar Economy* presents an intriguing new way of looking at work that is worthy of debate. As Jones sees it, the conversion to a green economy will affect much more than just the environment; it will change our communities, our politics, and the very way we think about work. In *The Green-Collar Economy*, Jones writes:

> *The green economy should not just be about reclaiming thrown-away stuff. It should be about reclaiming thrown-away communities. It should not just be about recycling materials to give things a second life. We should also be gathering up people and giving them a second chance.*
>
> *We have the chance now to create new markets, new technology, new industries, and a new workforce. Let's do it right—with good wages, equal opportunity, and pathways to success for those whom the pollution-based economy left behind.*

Jones believes that, in order for a job to be considered green, it must be sustainable not just for the earth, but for the worker. "We should never consider a job that does something for the planet and little to nothing for the people or the economy as fitting the definition of a green-collar job," he writes. "A worthwhile, viable, and sustainable green economy cannot be built with solar sweatshops."

The very idea of *industrialized* countries comes from the Industrial Revolution, which was made possible by unsustainable energy sources: fossil fuels.

In the ideal green economy, *none* of our energy will come from unsustainable sources. Our cars, our airplanes, our factories, our appliances: *Everything* will be powered by fuel sources that could be replaced in perpetuity. The energy grid would be modernized in such a way that when vehicles and machinery are not being used, any excess energy they had stored up would flow back into the grid for use elsewhere. Under this system, energy will become so inexpensive that it will no longer be a commodity, but a basic human right, like air or water.

Once we move to a world that is fueled by sustainable energy, Jones argues, this transformation will have a profound effect on corporate culture. As we move away from a culture of waste, corporations will begin to recognize that nothing is disposable . . . especially workers. Instead of the "win at all costs" corporate culture that we have right now, companies that are most successful in the new economy will be those that are most committed to fairness, equality, and employee and customer satisfaction.

This transformation won't just come naturally, however. If we truly want to create a workplace of sustainability, we must model the green jobs of today on our hopes for the future. To date, the environmental movement has largely been seen as the province of the upper-middle to upper classes. The wealthy are the ones who can afford to make their homes energy-efficient, to buy organic food, or to drive hybrid cars. Meanwhile, the environmental problems caused by global climate change disproportionately affect lower-income Americans . . . to which anyone who remembers Hurricane Katrina can attest.

Jones believes that our economy and environment will not be fixed until the classes can work together in pursuit of a shared vision of the future. If we hope to remake our economy, we will need the wealthy to continue buying hybrid cars and supporting sustainable agriculture. However, we will also need plenty of laborers to build the wind turbines, to install the solar panels, and to raise the food that will put our country back on the path to economic and ecological strength. We'll need policy activists to fight for smart policy changes, lawyers to uphold environmental legislation, and entrepreneurs to invent more efficient products and services. If we hope to save the planet, we must make energy independence an issue of concern to every segment of society. And the best way to get everyone working together is to make green jobs at all levels the best, most coveted jobs in the country, with good benefits, living wages, and plenty of opportunity for advancement.

Eco-Quiz

Match each set of words with the vocabulary word that connects them.

Sets

1. {oil, coal, natural gas}
2. {the wind, the sun, wood}
3. {carbon dioxide, methane}
4. {corn husks, newspaper, plants}
5. {soda cans, water bottles, candy wrappers}

Answer Choices

a. post-consumer waste
b. renewable resources
c. biodegradable
d. greenhouse gases
e. fossil fuels

Answers: 1-e, 2-b, 3-d, 4-c, 5-a

CHAPTER TWO

THE GREEN HORIZON

Chapter Overview

If you're thinking about going into a green job, make sure you're making a smart career choice. What does the future look like for green jobs? This chapter examines how green jobs are becoming integrated into the economy, and why now is a smart time to start learning about this growing field of opportunity.

Section 1: Why Green, Why Now?
You may be hesitant to pursue a green career because it feels like green industries are still in their infancy. However, in this section, you'll discover why this makes it a perfect time to switch to a green career.

Section 2: Government Resources
The Obama administration has stated its commitment to making the United States the world leader in green technology. In this section, we take a look at how government policy is shaping the jobs of the future . . . and how the government's commitment can benefit you.

Section 3: Location, Location, Location

For many green jobs, location is crucial. There aren't many wind farms being built in the center of New York City, and the desert is probably not the smartest place to move for those who are looking to get involved in green architecture. In this section, we discuss location-specific jobs, and you'll learn which states are contributing the most to the green economy.

Section 4: Green Industry Overview

Some industries, like recycling and wind turbine manufacturing, are a direct outgrowth of environmental policy. Other industries are working hard to change their processes and policies to a more environmentally friendly model. In this section, you'll learn about the job sectors that are included under the *green job* umbrella, and how we decided what types of jobs to include in this book.

In Their Own Words: Sefton Hirsch, Rob Hoyt, and Adam Quinn from Seventh Generation

Established in 1989, the Burlington, Vermont-based company Seventh Generation develops and manufactures environmentally friendly household products. I spoke with three employees at Seventh Generation to find out how the company's commitment to social responsibility translates to the workplace.

Sefton Hirsch, Consumer Insights

How did you end up working at Seventh Generation?

I was basically working a job that didn't seem like it was feeding my soul at all. I felt like there was a gap between my morals and my ethics and what I did during the day. For the longest time I felt like work is work, and your personal life is your personal life. But I always had a hard time separating the negative environmental impact my company was having from the things I believed in. So I went looking for a company that was going to be responsible in all aspects. And I came across Seventh Generation and felt like it was really right in line with my moral beliefs.

How did you go about getting a job there once you figured out that was where you wanted to be?

I was just waiting for the right position to come up, as far as what my qualifications made me suitable for. It was a long, extensive process. . . . I guess they had about 150 applicants for my position. It's interesting, the interview process here is really more like a date. You're looking for someone you want to hang out with, whom you want to be with throughout the day, and you're on the same page. Of course, you also have to have the skills, but it's just as important that you fit into our family.

And how does your environmental agenda play out on a daily basis in the workplace? What do you guys do that's different from other businesses in how you function as a company?

If you walk into our office, it's going to look different from any other office you've been in. It's extremely open and bright with natural light everywhere. Every employee can see outside from their desk. Things like that might be small things, but they really help with the quality of your day. Of course, you're going to see recycling bins everywhere.

Seventh Generation is also really adamant about quality of life. We have a gym right across the street from us where we can all go during our lunch break, and the company picks up the tab. You'll see a lot of employee support here. The benefits are really good, and it's because they, first, want to retain the employees, and second, to give you a good quality of life so you can do your best work.

Rob Hoyt, Shopper Marketing Manager
When did you know you wanted to work at Seventh Generation?

I always felt like a part of my job was missing. I was working for a brand marketing firm before this, and I couldn't get that passionate about convincing people to buy more spaghetti sauce, or buy more peanut butter. It just wasn't something I felt was connected to a cause. I liked being connected to sales; I just wanted something a bit more altruistic.

So I quit, and I went back to school full-time. I got my MBA at Boston University, and while there, I sort of got really involved in this idea of corporate responsibility, corporate social responsibility, sustainable business practices.

Was that a new field that was just emerging when you were going to school?

Well, I just graduated last year. So I would say it's still emerging. I think Europeans are much further along than the United States is in viewing business in terms of its social impact. Here, corporate responsibility is just getting going. I think 20 years from now we're going to have much different business models that are helping the world in much better ways.

Do you like working there?

I love it for several reasons. For one, because I feel like I'm working toward something that's a positive change in the world. Two, I like the size of the organization. I get to touch and feel lots of different pieces of the business, rather than being in a silo focused strictly on the sales and marketing efforts. You end up getting involved in operations and sourcing and all these different components, just by the mere size of the organization. You know who's doing what. And the people, the city and the things to do around here are great as well. So I think I have been able to strike a pretty good work/life balance, although the work has been a lot lately . . . [laughs]. But even when it's busy, I really like it here.

Adam Quinn, IT Support Analyst

Was Seventh Generation's environmental reputation a factor in your getting a job there?

Oh yeah, definitely. My job was really secure at my previous company. . . . I work in information technology . . . and at this manufacturing company I was the only IT person there. I knew the systems inside and out, and I got along really well with my coworkers. But I kind of kept an eye out for opportunities in the green-collar type of industries. I saw a job was available at Seventh Generation, so I sent out my resume, and they responded. I came in, we had a great discussion, and I ended up working there. I'm much happier working for a company that's doing something that's good for the planet and trying to create a better environment out there.

Are you working with mostly network stuff?

Yep, networks, e-mail . . . we have all laptops here, so there's a lot of laptop repairs, hardware troubleshooting, stuff like that. One thing that's really cool about this IT department is that last, I guess it was about six months ago or so, we got an award from Computerworld for being number 8 in the top 12 green IT departments in the nation. So as far as green IT goes, I've learned a lot of things about, for example, virtualization, where you take a rack of servers and you condense them into one box, so it's using a lot less power and a lot less heat. It's just a win-win; you're saving money, you're not burning as much power, you're not using as much air-conditioning. With everyone using laptops, too, it really cuts down on power usage. It's important to me to be an example to some companies on what they can do to better their network systems and become more green.

Does it make for a nicer work environment, as well?

Yeah, and that kind of makes me think about our printing. We only have one copier per floor, and those copiers are in a specially environmentally controlled room, so the air-conditioner isn't competing with the heat that's being expelled from those copiers. Also, copiers expel a little bit of toner whenever they're being used, which could be a hazard to our coworkers. That specially air-conditioned room also has an intake, so that air from that room is being sucked through the heating and ventilation system; it gets filtered so the small particulates aren't being expelled into the workplace. Even some of that behind-the-scenes stuff is creating a better workplace for us.

What would you say to someone who wanted to follow in your footsteps and get a job at a green company?

Right now the green industry is very high in demand. People want to have a job at a company that's doing their part for the planet. So with that being said, the green companies are probably going to have the pick of the litter. You might not be able to get that green job that you've been envisioning right out of college. For instance, what I had to do was get experience. It wasn't a bad thing for me; I worked for a company where I wasn't completely behind the product, but I liked my job, and I liked what I did for the company. But I just couldn't take a genuine interest in what that company did. However, I feel like that experience at that company gave me the opportunity to work for this company where I'm now very happy. So my advice to people going to college is that you might not get that green job right off the bat, but be patient. You may need to get that experience under your belt, first.

Section 1: Why Green, Why Now?

We all want to ensure that our planet will be around for future generations. I'm sure no one reading this book is interested in watching humanity suffer while the planet slowly burns to a crisp. If this *is* one of your interests, then perhaps a green career is not the right choice for you. Consider picking up a guide to Best Careers for Supervillains instead.

Those of us who are not planning to pursue a career in supervillainry have our work cut out for us. In its latest climate change assessment, the Intergovernmental Panel on Climate Change (IPCC) projects that if we continue to emit greenhouse gases at the same rate, worldwide temperatures could increase by 10.6°F by the end of this century. Although this may not seem like a huge increase on its surface, the IPCC projects that temperature increases of this magnitude would cause

> major changes in ecosystem structure and function, species' ecological interactions and shifts in species' geographical ranges, with predominantly negative consequences for biodiversity and ecosystem goods and services (e.g., water and food supply).

So the easiest answer to the question posed by this chapter is that we really have no other choice if we would like Earth to remain habitable by humans.

But that answer probably doesn't mean a lot to you. Unless you're a head of state or the CEO of an oil company, there isn't much you can do by yourself that will make a significant dent in greenhouse gas emissions or water safety. Certainly, everyone should do his or her best to cut down on waste and to conserve energy, but the most valuable changes we can make will be systemic changes that are beyond the control of most individuals.

The good news for all of us is that the people who *are* in control are rapidly waking up to the necessity of change. During the 2008 campaign, President Obama pledged to invest $150 billion in clean technology projects over 10 years, creating more than 5 million new jobs. So far, the administration appears to be surpassing its pledge. According to staterecovery.org, once all federal, state, and local environmental spending through the 2009 American Recovery and Reinvestment Act is tallied, the final figure from that act alone could go as high as $280 billion.

Even better news is that many of these jobs are either brand new or just in the early stages of existence. If you're looking for a green career, chances are strong that you won't be competing with veterans of the industry—because for many of these jobs, there *are* no veterans of the industry. In fact, one of the things that has prevented the green industry from expanding more rapidly is that there aren't enough qualified workers to fill the jobs that are available. Why Green, Why Now? Simple: because that's where the jobs are!

Green and Growing

By all accounts, green industries are growing at a faster rate than just about any other segment of the workforce. (See Figure 2.1) In a 2009 report entitled

FIGURE 2.1 Actual and Projected Growth of Environmental-Related Occupations versus All Other Occupations, 2000–2016

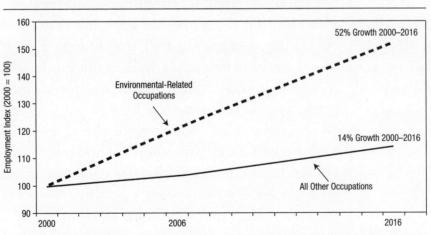

Sources: "Occupational Employment Projections to 2010." Bureau of Labor Statistics.

Monthly Labor Review. November 2001. "Occupational Employment Projections

to 2016." Bureau of Labor Statistics. *Monthly Labor Review.* November 2007.

"The Clean Energy Economy: Repowering Jobs, Businesses, and Investments across America," researchers from the Pew Charitable Trusts wrote:

> *Despite a lack of sustained policy attention and investment, the emerging clean energy economy has grown considerably . . . between 1998 and 2007, clean energy economy jobs—a mix of white- and blue-collar positions, from scientists and engineers to electricians, machinists, and teachers—grew by 9.1 percent, while total jobs grew by only 3.7 percent.*

Government support for environmental projects promises to provide major assistance in getting many of these industries off the ground. For instance, $85 billion of the 2009 American Recovery and Reinvestment Act (ARRA) is devoted to spending and tax-incentives for clean energy and public transportation. (See Figure 2.2)

As our country begins to move in a greener direction, the types of jobs that will offer the most opportunity will change. According to the Pew study, 65% of today's green jobs are in the fields of Conservation and Pollution Mitigation, that is, jobs that control the harm we've already done to the planet and that look to limit the amount of harm we continue to do. (See Figure 2.3) However, the sectors of the economy that are experiencing the most growth are Clean Energy, Energy Efficiency, and Environmentally Friendly Production, that is, jobs that create viable alternatives for unsustainable processes. In addition, "about 80% of venture capital investments in 2008 were in the sectors of Clean Energy and Energy Efficiency." In other words, the jobs are moving from sectors that are dedicated to cleaning up the messes we've already made to sectors that will ensure we don't make the same kinds of messes in the future. The reasons for this switch are clear: As the amount of waste we produce decreases, so, too, will the number of people needed to control that waste.

Did You Know? According to the American Solar Energy Society (ASES), there are currently more than 9 million jobs available in the renewable energy and energy-efficiency industries, with some sectors expected to grow by more than 25% each year. The ASES predicts the renewable energy industry will grow three times as quickly as the U.S. economy.

FIGURE 2.2   Environmental Spending through the ARRA (billions of dollars)

Type of Funding	Direct Public Speaking	Grants	Tax Incentives	Loan Guarantees	Bonds	Total
Federal Spending						
Renewable energy	$2.5	$2.3	$16.0	$4.0	$0.6	$25.3
Energy efficiency	7.2	14.4	2.0	0	0.8	24.4
Transporatation	0.6	20.1	2.1	0	0.3	23.0
Grid	6.6	4.4	0	2.0	0	13.0
Nuclear decontamination	6.0	0	0	0	0	6.0
Fossil		3.4	0	0	0	3.4
Science	1.6	0	0	0	0	1.6
Other	2.3	0.7	0	0	0	3.0
Government administration	0.75		0	0	0	0.8
Total	$27.6	$45.3	$20.1	$6.0	$1.7	$100.5
State/local government and private investment						
State/local government and private spending induced by federal funds: *as proportion of federal funds*	0	Ranges by program between 0–3 times federal spending	Up to 2.3 times federal spending	Up to 10 times federal spending	Up to 3 times federal spending	—
State/local government and private spending induced by federal funds: *as dollar amounts*	0	$68 estimated (= 1.5 *times federal spending average*)	Up to $46	Up to $60	Up to $5.1	Up to $179.1
Total, all sources	$27.6 billion	Up to $113.3	Up to $66	Up to $66	Up to 6.8	Up to $280.0

Note: Total amounts may not add up due to rounding

Sources: ARRA; grants.gov; irs.gov; www.staterecovery.org; dot.gov/recovery; edocket

.access.gpo.gov; epa.gov; www.recovery.gov; bo.gov; dsire.org.

FIGURE 2.3   The U.S. Clean Energy Economy: Jobs of Today and Jobs of Tomorrow

65 percent of today's clean energy economy jobs are in the category of Conservation and Pollution Mitigation. Growing recognition among the public, policy makers, and business leaders of the need to recycle waste, conserve water, and work to mitigate emissions of greenhouse gases and other pollitants has led to growth in this category. But growth trends paint a different picture for the future of the clean energy economy. Jobs in Environmentally Friendly Production, Clean Energy, and Energy Efficiency are growing much faster in response to new market demands.

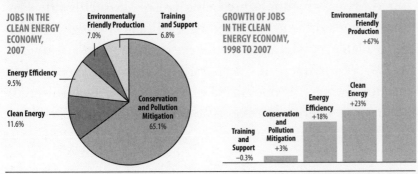

Source: Clean Economy Report.

Once one begins investigating the green job opportunities available today, the possibilities start to seem limitless. In a single day during the writing of this book, the following articles appeared in newspapers and websites:

- The *Hartford Courant* ran an article detailing how Connecticut has already created 4,500 jobs that are directly related to sustainability and energy conservation . . . and 7,200 jobs that are indirectly linked to these sectors of the economy.

- The *Seattle Post-Intelligencer* reported that Maine had reached an agreement with the Federal Energy Regulatory Commission to construct underwater turbines off the coast of Maine that produce electricity using tidal power.

- *The Oregonian* discussed a new program called Clean Energy Works Portland, which offers loans to help homeowners pay for energy-efficient remodeling. The loans can be paid back over the course of time through small monthly charges on the homeowners' utility bills.

- The Sierra Club released a report detailing efforts to rebuild New Orleans using sustainable building methods.

- The governor of Iowa signed an executive order creating a task force to find ways of bringing green-collar jobs to the state.

And that's just a random selection from one day's worth of media. Start paying attention to the media landscape, and you'll be amazed by how many new initiatives, companies, and projects are being announced in the green sector every day.

Perhaps the most remarkable thing I've discovered while researching this book is this: *Almost all of these articles are positive.* In a world in which we're constantly being pummeled by bad news, the green economy provides a ray of hope. New companies are being started and expanding rapidly. Laid-off workers are getting retrained to fill immediate job openings.

All over the United States, green jobs are being created at such a rate that many companies are having a difficult time finding qualified workers to fill the positions they have available. At the time of this writing, the national unemployment rate is 9.7%. With Americans desperate for jobs and green-collar employers desperate for workers, it doesn't take a (sustainable fuel-powered) rocket scientist to figure out where job seekers should focus their searches.

Eco-Quiz

According to a 2009 Newsweek *study, which company is the greenest major corporation in America?*

a. *Hewlett-Packard*

b. *Nike*

c. *Starbucks*

d. *McDonald's*

Answer: a. *Hewlett-Packard. Bet you guessed Starbucks, didn't you? Surprisingly, all four of these companies made it to the top 25. McDonald's was the lowest at #22. Starbucks came in at #10, and Nike came in at an impressive #7. Hewlett-Packard topped the list for its strong effort to reduce greenhouse gas emissions and its commitment to making its products free of toxic substances.*

Today's Best Opportunities

According to the Pew report, there are currently more than 750,000 jobs connected to the clean energy economy in the United States, which represents .5% of all jobs. Annual incomes for green workers range from $21,000 to upwards of $100,000, with the majority of these jobs paying as well or better than similar jobs in non-clean sectors.

As mentioned previously, the bulk of green jobs today are centered in the Conservation and Pollution Mitigation sector. The jobs that are experiencing the most investment right now, and will be likely to grow quickly over the coming years, are jobs in creating new types of energy (such as wind turbine and solar cell manufacturing) and installing this technology to increase the energy efficiency of factories, buildings, and homes. Of the energy generation jobs, 62.5% of the 2007 jobs were in solar, with the next highest sector being wind power, at 9.7%.

Another sector that is seeing a lot of growth is *smart grid* technology. The electricity grid as it exists today is a patchwork series of independently operated power stations. In a smart grid, the country's power plants will be connected in a single network, much as the Internet connects computer users to one another. Once the power plants are connected, electric companies will be able to deliver power more efficiently from one part of the country to the other. So, for instance, if there is a heat wave in New York and usage of air-conditioners increases, the city will be able to siphon electricity from a part of the country in which usage is lower. As homes become equipped to generate their own electricity from solar and wind power, consumers will sell their unused energy back into the grid, lowering electricity costs and dramatically reducing the amount of power generated from the burning of fossil fuels. With 42% of America's carbon dioxide emissions being generated by the outmoded energy grid—two times the amount that is released by all the vehicles in the country—smart grid technology is a crucial step in our move toward reduction of greenhouse gas emissions, and one that is attracting a huge amount of investment from venture capitalists and federal grants.

Then there are jobs connected to the green economy, like environmental law, advocacy, and education. We need lawyers and accountants to work with the new green corporations, lobbyists to fight in Washington for policy change, and teachers to teach people how to do their new jobs. For anyone just going into or returning to college, all of these jobs are viable career choices that will most certainly be in demand for years to come.

So which sector provides the most opportunities today? The best answer to that question is: Which sector interests you the most? Right now, there is no such thing as a green job that's on its last legs. If you pursue a job in which you have little interest just because they're hiring, you're going to be miserable, no matter how smart a career move it may seem at the time.

Green Quotes

In a 2009 article for San Diego News Network, writer Kim Brauer spoke with Jacques Chirazi, a specialist on Clean Tech for the city of San Diego:

> *Many green jobs are jobs that never existed before. In the IT market in the late 1970s and into the 1980s, no one knew that jobs for webmasters would exist. Sometimes technology gets ahead of the skill sets we need, so we have the technology, but we don't yet have the application for it, or we don't have the skills and job title to match it yet.*

No matter what your interests are, chances are strong that there are challenging and rewarding career opportunities available for someone with your skills and interests right now. The sooner you get started, the better your chances will be to get in on the ground floor at industries that are poised to remake the world as we know it.

Keeping an Eye on the Future

Before you begin your job search, a word of warning about career longevity is necessary. Wherever you land, it's doubtful that you will spend the rest of your life working at the same place. There was a time in the United States when a young adult could graduate from high school and get a well-paying job in a factory where he or she would work until retirement. Thanks in part to the internationalization of the manufacturing process, that kind of job security is rare.

Today, workers need to stay ahead of the curve. Whatever job you do, it is important that you always keep learning about your field. This is especially true for green jobs, which are, in many cases, still being actively developed. Continued innovation is one of the keys to the growth of the green economy. As new technology is developed and companies continue to innovate and refine their processes, job duties will most certainly change as well.

Green Quotes

Nobody's going to have a career that lasts their whole life anymore," says Gabriel Metcalf, executive director of San Francisco Planning and Urban Development, an urban planning think tank. "You're going to have lots of different jobs, and you need to prepare to learn new things and switch gears for your entire life. You need to view what you do as a portfolio of projects and jobs. If you only have one thing going on, that's unstable and insecure. There are always exceptions, but any young worker should try to keep that concept in their minds.

I am not saying that the idea of job security is gone forever. As discussed in the previous chapter, green jobs activist Van Jones believes a job should not even be considered green unless it is sustainable for its employees. A growing number of studies show that companies that report the highest employee satisfaction also have higher retention rates, lower rates of illnesses, and higher productivity. (Of course, as the Dot Com boom showed us, employee satisfaction cannot sustain a business all by itself; it's also crucial to be providing a product or service that people actually need!)

Fortunately for job seekers, many green companies are making employee satisfaction a top priority right out of the gate. For example, Gamesa Corporation, a Spanish wind turbine manufacturing company with facilities in Pennsylvania, makes a 10 point pledge to its workers, including promises to:

- foster a work environment that is appealing, motivating, and stimulating, and that allows people to align their personal and professional goals

- develop a compensation strategy that ensures attractive remuneration that is also a market reference, recognizing the individual and collective contribution to the creation of value

- promote equality and balance of professional and family life

Gamesa's pledges are not just empty rhetoric; in 2008, the company won the prestigious Eleanor Roosevelt Human Rights Award from American Rights at Work (ARAW), a labor rights advocacy group, for its commitment to its workers.

Another company that has seen excellent results from enhanced employee satisfaction is NetApp, a data storage company based in Sunnyvale, California. Although NetApp's services are only indirectly related to the green economy, the company is a recognized innovator in finding ways to reduce its power usage. NetApp's environmental commitments extend beyond the workplace; the company built its headquarters across from a Caltrain station to allow its employees easy access to public transportation, it provides free bike lockers for its employees on campus, and it awards reserved parking spots to carpool groups. Perks for employees include an onsite gym and golf course and a yearly five-day volunteer vacation in which employees are paid to volunteer at a charity of their choice. NetApp's commitment to the welfare of its employees earned it the #1 spot in *Fortune* magazine's 2009 list of 100 Best Companies to Work For. This commitment paid off in spades, too; NetApp entered the economic recession with more than $2 billion of cash on hand, while other companies were struggling to avoid bankruptcy.

Interestingly, according to a 2008 study by customer research group Brockmann and Company, being green in itself has been determined to be an important factor in employee satisfaction. According to Peter Brockmann, president of Brockmann and Company, "Companies that focus on recycling in the office, reducing energy consumption in the office, and use video conferencing or telepresence technologies intensively, also have higher customer satisfaction, higher employee satisfaction, and higher revenues per employee."

Leading the Charge

We've seen why going green now is a smart idea for workers: Green jobs are a growing part of the economy at a time when few other industries are expanding. But it is also a smart idea for the United States of America to go green. Converting to a clean energy economy is a crucial move to save the environment for future generations, but it also gives America the opportunity to once again lead the world in industrial innovation. As our country converts to clean energy, the developing world will most likely follow suit, upgrading their fossil fuel-burning plants to technology to greener, more efficient technology that will, with any luck, be made in America. If we play our cards right, instead of importing our products from China and India, we'll be exporting our technology to them—which will go a long way toward reclaiming America's place as the economic world leader.

Green Quotes

Since 1999, a total of 4.6 million U.S. manufacturing jobs have disappeared, many of them sent overseas. More than one million manufacturing jobs have been lost since the start of the current recession in December 2007, including 200,000 in January 2009 alone. These are some of the country's best middle-class jobs, paying an average of $25,000 more per year than service sector jobs and often providing benefits such as health care and pensions. For workers without four-year college degrees, these jobs have long been the ticket to the American middle class. As manufacturing and associated jobs disappear, the only option for many of these workers is a low-paid service sector job without clear career advancement opportunities. The result: growing inequality and a dramatically shrinking middle class.

—Make It in America: The Apollo Green Manufacturing Action Plan. March 2009

The switch to a clean energy economy will not just enhance our reputation abroad, however. For years, the gap between America's lowest paid workers and its highest paid workers has been growing. A recent report by University of California, Berkeley professor Emmanuel Saez found that, in 2007, the nation's wealthiest .01%—that is, one hundredth of 1%—earned 1,080 times as much as the average of the bottom 90%. The wealthiest 1% takes in 23.5% of all the nation's income. So 1% of the country makes nearly $\frac{1}{4}$ of the money. This is the largest income disparity ever reported in U.S. history.

Most economists agree that it is economically beneficial for a country to have a strong middle class. The loss of manufacturing jobs, the decline of the family farm, and skyrocketing amounts of personal debt have combined to help the rich get richer and the poor get poorer, leaving the middle class out in the cold. Green jobs offer the opportunity for us to bring jobs back to the people who need them the most, strengthening our entire country in the process. "In short," write the editors of "Green-Collar Jobs in America's Cities," a joint report created by the Apollo Alliance and Green for All, "green jobs are the kind of family-supporting jobs that once anchored the American middle class, but in the industries of the future: industries like wind turbine manufacturing, solar panel installation, energy-efficiency retrofits, and green building."

In addition to the economic and environmental benefits, switching to alternative energy will have an important effect on our national security. Our dependence on foreign oil forces us to make alliances with countries that do not often share our views on human and civil rights. It also often places the United States in the center of conflicts that are detrimental to our reputation at home and abroad. As fossil fuels become scarcer and more expensive, it could lead to our involvement in ever-greater conflicts. The sooner we are able to generate our own energy, the easier it will be for us to embrace our democratic principles, and to set a positive example for the rest of the world.

Green Quotes

The economic crisis, the security crisis, and the climate crisis are all intertwined, and the common thread running through them is our absurd and dangerous overdependence on carbon-based fuels. If you grab hold of that thread and pull on it, all three of these crises will unravel, and we'll hold in our hand the solution to all three of them—that is, to make a transition to a low-carbon economy and to put people to work doing it.
—Al Gore, speaking at the second National
   Green Energy Summit in August 2009

Section 2: Government Policy and Incentives

How Government Policy Is Shaping the Jobs of the Future

In June 2009, the Political Economy Research Institute (PERI) and the Center for American Progress collaborated on a paper entitled "The Economic Benefits of Investing in Clean Energy." The authors of this paper examined how two government initiatives would affect the green jobs landscape—the clean-energy funding included in the American Recovery and Reinvestment Act (ARRA) (known popularly as the *economic stimulus*), and the American Clean Energy and Security Act (ACESA), which is making its way through the Senate at the time of this writing. The authors found that "these two measures operating together can generate roughly $150 billion per year in new clean-energy investments in the United States over the next decade." (See Figure 2.4.) This is great news for employment seekers: That $150 billion is expected to generate 1.7 million new jobs every year.

The clean-energy funding in ARRA and the ACESA bill are both directed at a massive undertaking: remaking the way our energy is produced, delivered, and used. The reason why the authors of the PERI/Center for American Progress include only a rough estimate of how much money the bills will generate is because it is impossible to tell how quickly the initial spending and incentives will create a domino effect of private spending. If ACESA is passed, corpora-

FIGURE 2.4 Breakdown of $150 Billion in Potential Annual U.S. Clean-Energy Investment. (Includes only clean-energy investment areas that expand job opportunities)

Clean-Energy Investment Area	Potential Annual Investment Level
Energy efficiency	
Building retrofits	$80 billion
Smart grid	$20 billion
Public transporatation	$5 billion
Cogeneration	$5 billion
Renewable Energy	
On grid renewable electricity	$30 billion
Off grid renewable electricity	$3 billion
Off grid renewable—nonelectrical	$3 billion
Alternative motor fuels	$5 billion
Total	**$151 billion**

tions all over the United States will have to reevaluate their methods of doing business and upgrade everything from the equipment they use to the buildings in which they are located. If ACESA is not passed, then we'll have to rely on the marketplace to convince businesses and homeowners that clean energy is worth the investment.

As the example of Ray Anderson shows in the introduction to this book, moving to clean energy has been shown to have a positive impact on a company's bottom line; however, the upfront costs can sometimes be prohibitive. Despite the positive public relations opportunities created by going green, it is unlikely that the bulk of U.S. businesses will voluntarily spend money that they don't have to. Therefore, as much as ARRA clean-energy funds are helping to spur innovation and investment, the effect would potentially be multiplied greatly if going green became something businesses and homeowners had to do, rather than something they wanted to do.

The part of ACESA that has received the most attention is the idea of *cap-and-trade* legislation. Cap-and-trade creates a system whereby the government sets limits on allowed levels of greenhouse carbon dioxide emissions (the "cap"). Companies are given a certain number of pollution credits that they can use. Companies that emit less than their credits allow can then resell their credits to heavier polluters (the "trade"). Every year, allowed emission levels will tighten, with the eventual goal of banning carbon dioxide emissions entirely.

In addition to cap-and-trade, ACESA includes several other measures designed to clean up U.S. energy, including:

- funding for a study on carbon emission capture-and-storage technology
- standards for lower-carbon fuel
- energy-efficient building standards
- increased fuel-efficiency standards for motor vehicles
- new energy-efficiency standards for factories and industrial plants

Did You Know?

As can be expected of any idea the government comes up with, cap-and-trade has generated its share of controversy. Critics in the environmental movement argue that cap-and-trade gives the market too much power over the fate of our planet. On the other side, some conservative economists worry that the costs associated with cap-and-trade would be passed directly on to consumers, weakening an already fragile economy. Cap-and-trade legislation isn't unprecedented; a similar system has been in place in the European Union since 2005. So far, the EU cap-and-trade has met with mixed results; during the first phase of the program, many complained that the caps were not strict enough, leading to little difference in the overall amount of carbon dioxide emissions.

Interestingly, the United States has already proven that the cap-and-trade model can work. The 1990 Clean Air Act established an emission trading system for sulfur dioxide, a gas that is a major cause of acid rain. Since the sulfur dioxide emission trading system has been in place, sulfur dioxide emissions have been reduced by over 50%. Whether the carbon dioxide cap-and-trade program included in ACESA will meet with the same success remains to be seen.

Although ACESA has not yet been passed, many states have already instituted standards and programs to encourage greater efficiency. For example:

- 46 states have tax incentives to help businesses and residents upgrade to an energy-efficient system and equipment, such as more effective insulation methods or environmentally friendly heating and cooling systems.

- 29 states, plus the District of Columbia, have instituted requirements for state utilities to generate between 10%–25% of their power from renewable energy sources by a target date.

- 22 states, plus the District of Columbia, offer incentives for installing solar panels or switching to solar water heat.

Increased regulations and financial incentives are the key to the new jobs creation. For instance, the PERI/Center for American Progress report estimates that there are 110 million units of housing in the United States. With simple changes to those homes and apartments, such as plugging leaks, installing new windows, and installing energy-efficient appliances, families could save about 30% per year on their energy bills. The one obstacle to making those changes, for many families, is the high upfront cost of the work. However, if the government helped subsidize these retrofits, energy demand would go down, families would save money, and millions of people would be put to work.

Training for Green-Collar Workers

The PERI/Center for American Progress report has hopeful news for workers looking to enter the green job market. For starters, the authors estimate that the two stimulus packages examined in their report will lead to the creation of 2.5 million new green jobs. These jobs did come at a price—assuming that fossil fuel spending was to decrease by the same amount as green job spending increased, the authors estimate this will lead to 800,000 jobs lost in the fossil fuel industry. These workers could potentially be retrained to work new green-collar jobs, however—jobs that would for the most part be safer, healthier, and more sustainable than the workers' previous occupations. And if every last one of these workers moved into green jobs, there will still be 1.7 million brand-new jobs available. According to the authors of the study, these jobs alone will be enough to lower the unemployment rate an entire percentage point.

The American Reinvestment and Recovery Act included a total of almost $4 billion for job training programs. One-eighth of that $4 billion ($500 million) was allocated to train workers in sustainable energy jobs. That $500 million will be split between five different types of grants, to be allocated to nonprofit organizations, national labor–management organizations, and state workforce investment boards. These five types of grants are:

1. **Pathways Out of Poverty Grants** ($150 million): to create green job training programs for impoverished and disadvantaged workers, including "unemployed individuals, high school dropouts, individuals with a criminal record, and disadvantaged individuals living in areas of high poverty."

2. **State Energy Sector Partnership and Training Grants** ($190 million): to be awarded to state workforce investment boards. Of this $190 million, $25 million is to be awarded to communities impacted by changes in the automotive industry.

3. **Energy Training Partnership Grants** ($100 million): to create job training programs for workers "impacted by national energy and environmental policy," including current energy industry workers who need retraining.

4. **Green Capacity Building Grants** ($5 million): to be awarded to pro-labor organizations that are currently receiving Department of Labor grants.

5. **State Labor Market Information Improvement Grants** ($50 million): for state labor agencies to create methods of collecting, analyzing, and disseminating information about careers in renewable energy and energy-efficient industries.

ARRA isn't the only source of funding for green job training, however. Several states have taken the initiative in creating green energy training programs for job seekers.

- In California, Governor Arnold Schwarzenegger announced plans for a $75 million "clean energy workforce training program"—the nation's largest state-sponsored green job training program. The program would train more than 20,000 young and unemployed workers to install solar panels, design energy-efficient buildings, and weatherize them.

- New Jersey implemented a Green Job Training Partnership Program, an 8 to 10 week course of training that is expected to train more than 300 workers per year for upwardly mobile green workers.

- With a grant from the EPA, New York's East Harlem Employment Services, Inc., created a training program to instruct workers in the reclamation and cleanup of potentially reusable areas that have been contaminated by hazardous wastes (aka *brownfields*).

- In Austin, Texas, a job training organization called American Youthworks is using a $750,000 grant from the U.S. Department of Commerce to train teens and young adults in renewable energy jobs.

- Massachusetts received $500,000 from the U.S. Department of Labor to create green job training programs for veterans.

These are just a few examples of the training programs being implemented; across the country, labor organizations and nonprofits are developing green job-training programs for job seekers of all ages and experience levels. Many of these programs offer low-cost, subsidized, or free training. In Chapter 9, I provide a list of websites you can visit to find out more information about green job-training programs available in your state.

Section 3: Location, Location, Location

One of the greatest things about green jobs is that many of them can never be outsourced. A building owner can't send his building to India to be brought up to energy-efficiency standards, for instance. Other green industries, such as waste management and transportation solutions, are just as site-specific. Although manufacturing can happen anywhere, transportation of manufactured goods is something that will likely meet with stricter regulations in the near future, giving U.S. industries an economic incentive to keep manufacturing jobs in the country. All of this is great news for workers looking for long-term opportunities in their communities.

Without a doubt, the United States could use a new source of economic stability. The manufacturing sector, which has historically been a major source of employment for the American middle class, has been on the decline for years. According to the U.S. Bureau of Labor Statistics, manufacturing industry jobs declined by more than 20% from 1998–2008, from 17.6 million

FIGURE 2.5   Decline in U.S. Manufacturing

The manufacturing industry has decreased its percentage of the GDP by 3.7 percent in the past decade and it currently employs around 4.5 million fewer workers than it did at the beginning of 1998.

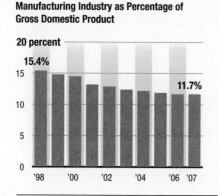

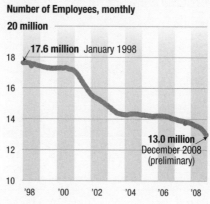

Sources: Bureau of Labor Statistics; Bureau of Economic Analysis.

jobs to 13.0 million. (See Figure 2.5.) When the housing bubble burst in 2008, states that had been losing manufacturing jobs to Mexico and China for years became even more strapped for cash, with budget shortfalls projected to total $165 billion nationwide. Many states are putting their hopes in the green sector to create much needed jobs for their residents and to help boost their flagging economies.

The current leader in clean-energy jobs is California. As of 2007, 10,209 clean-energy businesses operated in the state, providing 125,390 jobs. Other states with strong and growing green economies include Colorado (17,008 jobs, 18.2% growth in clean-energy jobs between 1998–2007), Indiana (17,298 jobs, 17.9% growth), Massachusetts (26,678 jobs, 4.3% growth), and Oregon (19,340 jobs, 50.7% growth). As Figure 2.6 shows, however, every state has a piece of America's clean-energy economy. Texas, for instance, generates more electricity from wind than any other state, had more than 55,000 clean-energy

FIGURE 2.6 The U.S. Clean-Energy Economy by the Numbers

By 2007, 68,203 businesses in the United States had generated more than 770,000 jobs in the clean-energy economy. And between 2006 and 2008, about $12.6 billion of venture capital investments was directed toward clean technology businesses in 40 states and the District of Columbia. The U.S. clean-energy economy is an emerging source of jobs that achieve the double bottom line of economic growth and environmental sustainability. Every state has a piece of America's clean-energy economy.

	Clean Businesses 2007	Clean Jobs 2007	Clean Job Growth 1998–2007	Overall Job Growth 1998–2007	Venture Capital 2006–2008 (thousands)		Clean Businesses 2007	Clean Jobs 2007	Clean Job Growth 1998–2007	Overall Job Growth 1998–2007	Venture Capital 2006–2008 (thousands)
Alabama	799	7,849	2.2%	1.6%	$0	Montana	408	2,155	0.2%	12.7%	$0
Alaska	350	2,140	9.4	15.7	0	Nebraska	368	5,292	108.6	−4.9	0
Arizona	1,123	11,578	21.3	16.2	31,106	Nevada	511	3,641	28.8	26.5	19,804
Arkansas	448	4,597	7.8	3.5	22,845	New Hampshire	465	4,029	2.0	6.8	66,917
California	10,209	125,390	7.7	6.7	6,580,427	New Jersey	2,031	25,397	−9.6	−2.7	282,568
Colorado	1,778	17,008	18.2	8.2	622,401	New Mexico	577	4,815	50.1	1.9	147,913
Connecticut	857	10,147	7.0	−2.7	30,050	New York	3,323	34,363	−1.9	−2.6	209,590
Delaware	211	2,368	−2.3	−8.9	3,342	North Carolina	1,783	16,997	15.3	6.4	82,571
District of Columbia	280	5,325	18.8	−7.1	89,877	North Dakota	137	2,112	30.9	9.4	0
Florida	3,831	31,122	7.9	22.4	116,980	Ohio	2,513	35,267	7.3	−2.2	74,224
Georgia	1,827	16,222	10.8	15.7	179,686	Oklahoma	693	5,465	6.8	2.4	5,192
Hawaii	356	2,732	43.6	7.3	12,304	Oregon	1,613	19,340	50.7	7.5	70,002
Idaho	428	4,517	126.1	13.8	27,890	Pennsylvania	2,934	38,763	−6.2	−3.1	232,897
Illinois	2,176	28,395	−2.5	−2.5	108,519	Rhode Island	237	2,328	0.7	0.6	22,845
Indiana	1,268	17,298	17.9	−1.0	26,000	South Carolina	884	11,255	36.2	2.2	0
Iowa	729	7,702	26.1	3.6	149,237	South Dakota	169	1,636	93.4	4.9	0
Kansas	591	8,017	51.0	−0.3	13,275	Tennessee	1,090	15,507	18.2	2.5	16,329
Kentucky	778	9,308	10.0	3.6	0	Texas	4,802	55,646	15.5	6.7	716,894
Louisiana	995	10,641	19.5	3.0	0	Utah	579	5,199	−12.4	10.8	26,957
Maine	725	6,000	22.7	3.3	0	Vermont	311	2,161	15.3	7.4	53,747
Maryland	1,145	12,908	−2.4	1.3	323,996	Virginia	1,446	16,907	6.0	6.6	70,828
Massachusetts	1,912	26,678	4.3	−4.4	1,278,462	Washington	2,008	17,013	0.5	1.3	635,109
Michigan	1,932	22,674	10.7	−3.6	55,099	West Virginia	332	3,065	−4.1	0.7	5,741
Minnesota	1,206	19,994	11.9	1.9	49,938	Wisconsin	1,294	15,089	−5.2	3.4	46,743
Mississippi	454	3,200	24.8	3.6	30,384	Wyoming	225	1,419	56.4	14.0	6,942
Missouri	1,062	11,714	5.4	2.1	24,480	U.S. Total	68,203	770,385	9.1	3.7	12,570,110

Note: Venture capital values are adjusted for inflation and reported in 2008 dollars. See appendices for the complete data sets.

Source: Pew Charitable Trusts, 2009 based on the National Establishment Time Series Database and data from the Cleantech Group LLC; analysis by the Pew Center on the States and Collaborative Economics.

economy jobs in 2007, and attracted more than $716 million in venture capital funds for clean technology between 2006–2008. Michigan, which saw overall jobs decrease by 3.6% between 1998–2007, saw clean-energy jobs increase by 10.7% during the same period.

So which state provides the most opportunities for people seeking jobs in the green economy? At this point, it's difficult to say. In Wisconsin, for example, clean-energy jobs decreased by 5.2% between 1998–2007; however, in 2008, the state launched a $150 million grant program to encourage innovation in renewable energy. No one can say for sure if any city will become as dominant in clean energy as Detroit once was in the automotive industry, but even states whose economy relies on fossil fuels are vying to become a part of the clean-energy economy. In Wyoming, the biggest coal producer in the Union, clean-energy jobs grew by an astounding 56.4% between 1998–2007—due to healthy investment and a proactive government, the state is on track to supplant its domination of the coal industry by becoming the leading provider of wind energy in the country.

Section 4: Green Industry Overview

Over the past two chapters, I've attempted to explain why it's a wise career decision to pursue a green job. Hopefully, you're now fully convinced and eager to get the job search underway. Only one important question remains . . . what *are* these jobs?

In a 2009 report entitled "The Clean Energy Economy: Repowering Jobs, Businesses, and Investments across America," researchers from the Pew Charitable Trusts identified five different sectors of green jobs that they believe will continue to be a necessary part of the new economy. These sectors are: (1) Clean Energy; (2) Energy Efficiency; (3) Environmentally Friendly Production; (4) Conservation and Pollution Mitigation; and (5) Training and Support. These five sectors are broken down into 16 segments, including "Energy Generation," "Business Services," and "Finance/Investment," which are in turn broken down into concrete positions, such as "Solar," "Energy Conservation Software," and "Advanced Packaging." In total, the Pew Charitable Trusts identified 82 different jobs that they consider to be part of the Clean Economy. (See Figure 2.7.)

FIGURE 2.7   Clean Economy Report

	Subsegment	Examples of Occupations
CLEAN ENERGY		
Energy Generation	Energy consulting	Electrical engineering technicians
	Energy management (software, services, devices)	Computer systems analysts
	Biomass (hydrogen, other, waste-to-energy)	Power plant operations technicians, process engineers
	Geothermal (geothermal drilling, generation, development, hardware)	Operating engineers and other construction equipment operators, drilling engineers (geothermal)
	Hydro	Plumbers, power plant operators
	Marine and tidal	Mechanical engineering technicians
	Hydrogen	Mechanical engineering technicians, chemists
	Multiple	Solar and wind system installers
	Other (combined heat/power, hydrogen production, natural gas, onsite systems, waste heat, renewable energy providers)	Plumbers, electrical engineers
	Research and testing	Electrical engineers
	Solar (material feedstock supplier, PV: thin film, PV: polysilicon, concentrated PV, BIPV, solar thermal, solar installers and contractors, equipment sales and distribution)	Photonics engineers, solar power plant technicians
	Co-generation	Mechanical engineering technicians, boiler process engineers
	Accessory equipment and controls (solar, wind)	Electricians
	Other generation equipment	Mechanical engineering technicians
	Wind (consulting, water pumping systems, wind plant operators and developers, turbine and tower manufacturing, equipment sales and distribution)	Electricians, wind turbine service technicians
Energy Transmission	Cable and equipment	Electrical power-line installers and repairers
	Services (power monitoring and metering, power quality and testing)	Electricians, power distributors and dispatchers
	Transmission (sensors and controls, smart grid)	Electrical and electronic equipment assemblers
Energy Storage	Advanced batteries (Li-Ion, NiMH, advanced PB-acid, charging and management, nickel zinc, other technologies, thin film, ultra capacitors, multiple)	Electrical and electronic engineering technicians
	Battery components and accessories	Electrical and electronic equipment assemblers, tool and die makers
	Fuel cells (methanol, PEM, solid oxide, systems Integrators, zinc air)	Electro-mechanical technicians
	Hybrid systems (flywheels, heat storage, hydrogen storage)	Mechanical engineers
	Uninterruptible power supply	Electrical engineers
ENERGY EFFICIENCY		
Energy Efficiency	Machinery (geothermal heating and cooling, HVAC-R, boilers, water heating, efficient motors)	Heating and air-conditioning mechanics and installers, thermal engineers
	Energy conservation consultant	Energy auditors
	Energy conservation software	Network systems and data communications analysts
	Energy conservation products	Electrical drafters, weatherization technicians/installers
	Glass	Press operators
	Lighting (CFL, solid state lighting, smart lighting systems, ballasts and controls)	Electricians; lighting design engineer; mixing and blending machine setters, operators, tenders (e.g., CFL/LED manufacturing)
	Meters and measuring devices (wireless)	Electrical engineering technicians
	Energy research	Electrical engineers
	Solar appliances and devices (solar cooker, solar heating, lighting)	Electrical and electronic equipment assemblers
ENVIRONMENTALLY FRIENDLY PRODUCTION		
Transportation	Alternative fuels (fueling Infrastructure, biodiesel, ethanol, hydrogen)	Fuel system specialists
	Logistics (fleet tracking, traffic monitoring software)	Operations managers, logistic engineers
	Motor vehicles and equipment (electric bicycles and scooters, electric and hybrid vehicles, logistics/public transit vehicles, natural gas vehicles, diesel technology, vehicle components/engines, water transport, catalytic converters)	Electromechanical equipment assemblers, engine and chassis test engineers, engine and other machine assemblers
Manufacturing/ Industrial	Advanced packaging (containers, packing)	Materials scientists
	Industrial surface cleaning	Lab technicians
	Process management (construction/fabrication, process efficiency, resource utilization, toxin/waste minimization)	Mechanical engineering technicians, robotics technicians
	Monitoring and control (sensors, software, systems)	Systems analysts
Construction	Building materials (e.g., alternative cement)	Operating engineers and other construction equipment operators
	Design and construction (nonresidential architectural and engineering services, nonresidential building construction, residential architectural and engineering services, residential building construction, software)	Architect, roofer, construction and building inspectors (e.g., LEED certification)
	Site management (deconstruction)	Environmental protection technicians
	Real estate and development	Construction and building inspectors

FIGURE 2.7 *(continued)*

Subsegment	Examples of Occupations
ENVIRONMENTALLY FRIENDLY PRODUCTION	
Agriculture	
Aquaculture (farms, health and yield)	Environmental science technicians
Land management (crop yield, precision agriculture, smart irrigation, sustainable forestry)	Irrigation system installers, precision agriculture technicians
Supplies and materials (alternative pest control, fertilizer)	Environmental science technicians
Agribusiness consultant	Agricultural sustainability consultants
Energy Production	
Biofuel (distillation and distribution)	Installers of industrial equipment, fuel distillers and distributors
Coal gasification and pyrolysis	Geologists to assess basins for CO2 storage, chemists creating catalysts/enzymes to remove CO2 from coal power generation, power plant operators that operate equipment that transports CO2
Materials	
Bio (bioplastics, advanced processes, biodegradable products, catalysts)	Mixing and blending machine setters, operators and tenders
Chemical (coatings, composites, polymer)	Coating, painting, and spraying machine setters, operators and tenders
Nano (catalysts and additives, detectors and sensors, gels and coatings, lubricants and films, powders)	Laboratory technicians
Other (adhesives, ceramics, electro textiles)	Laboratory technicians
CONSERVATION AND POLLUTION MITIGATION	
Air and Environment	
Emissions monitoring and control (air quality, chemical sensors, carbon dioxide sensors, wireless sensors, sorbents, measurement and testing, software/systems)	Environmental science technicians
Environmental consulting (environmental engineering, management and public relations, permitting, regulation and documentation, testing and certification, sustainable business/development consultant)	Environmental sustainability consultants, environmental compliance coordinators
Environmental remediation (remediation equipment, ocean restoration)	Environmental engineering technicians
Cleanup/safety (EHS and ERM, hazardous waste/toxins control, leak detection)	Hazardous materials removal workers, industrial hygienists
Recycling and Waste	
Consulting	Materials scientists
Recycling (waste paper, paperboard and cloth materials, waste materials, metal, plastics and rubber scrap, bottles, automotive wrecking and recovery, oil and lubricants, electronic waste, recycling machinery manufacturing)	Refuse and recyclable material collectors, solids control technicians
Waste treatment (environmental disposal, hazmat and plasma destruction)	Water and liquid waste treatment plant and system operators
Water and Wastewater	
Consulting	Environmental science and protection technicians, including health; wetlands environmental biologists
Pumps	Mechanical engineering technicians
Research and testing	Geological science technicians
Water conservation (recycling and management, metering and control)	Soil and water conservationists
Water and wastewater treatment (contaminate detection, desalination, filtration and purification, plant and equipment, biological)	Chemical laboratory technicians, groundwater engineers
TRAINING AND SUPPORT	
Business Services	
Legal services	Lawyers, paralegals and legal assistants
Marketing/public relations	Public relations specialists
Green firm business portal	Marketing analysts
Staffing services	Human resources assistants
Finance/ Investment	
Project financing (e.g., solar)	Financial accountants
Project insurance	Credit risk analysts
Venture capital/private equity	Investment bankers
Emissions trading and offsets (carbon/emissions)	Statistical assistants, carbon credit traders
Research and Advocacy	
Alternative fuels (hydrogen)	Biological technicians
Geothermal	Geological sample test technicians
Public education, job training	Vocational education teachers in postsecondary institutions, grant writers, environmental education specialists
Solar	Heating and air-conditioning mechanics and installers
Wind	Mechanical engineering technicians
Energy generation	Electrical engineering technicians
Energy storage	Chemical laboratory technicians, fuel cell engineers
Green building	Cost estimators
Transportation	Mechanical engineering technicians

In this book, I've included a list of jobs that draws from and expands upon the Pew Charitable Trust's definition. Most of the literature produced to date about green jobs concentrates on green variations of blue-collar jobs, such as energy-efficient construction and installing smart grid electrical equipment. Without a doubt, these are important segments of the green economy in which jobs are readily available, and this book provides helpful information for anyone looking to get involved in these fields. If your interest isn't in construction or electrical work, however, there are many excellent, ecologically friendly jobs available; jobs that are often overlooked in discussions of green careers. I've tried to include descriptions of jobs for people of all interests, as well as resources you can use to explore beyond the jobs listed in this book.

Eco-Quiz

In October 2009, President Obama signed an executive order requiring all agencies of the federal government to measure their greenhouse gas emissions for the first time. Where does the federal government rank in the list of top U.S. energy consumers?

a. *first*

b. *second*

c. *third*

d. *fourth*

Answer: a. First. *With 500,000 buildings, 600,000 vehicles, and more than 1.8 million workers, the federal government is the #1 biggest energy consumer in the United States.*

The careers covered in the next chapter have been divided into eight different categories. These categories are:

1. **Renewable Energy.** Types of jobs covered: Solar Energy System Installer, Solar Operations Engineer, Wind Turbine Machinist, Hydro-Electric Electrical Engineer, Hydrogeologist, Battery Design Engineer

2. **Building.** Types of jobs covered: Field Energy Consultant, Civil Engineer, Landscape Architect, Electrical System Installer

3. **Transportation.** Types of jobs covered: Hybrid Powertrain Development Engineer, Train System Operator, Biofuel Plant Field and Operations Engineer, Diesel Retrofit Designer

4. **Food and Agriculture.** Types of jobs covered: Organic Farmer, Soil Scientist, Environmental Horticulturist, Agroecologist

5. **Recycling and Waste Management.** Types of jobs covered: Recycling Center Operator, Hazardous Waste Management Specialist, Associate Engineer—Wastewater Treatment

6. **Conservation.** Types of jobs covered: Arborist, Botanical Technician, Air Pollution Specialist, Climatologist, Land Steward

7. **Nonprofits, Policy, and Advocacy.** Types of jobs covered: Conservation Policy Analyst and Advocate, Environmental Law, Water Resource Policy Specialist and Advocate

8. **Entrepreneurial.** Includes information about industries that are growing rapidly and attract investment from venture capitalists.

CHAPTER THREE

GREEN INDUSTRIES

Chapter Overview

In this chapter, we take a closer look at specific jobs from eight different segments of the green economy: Renewable Energy; Building; Transportation; Food and Agriculture; Recycling and Waste Management; Advocacy; Conservation; Nonprofits, Policy, and Research; and Entrepreneurial. Aside from the Entrepreneurial section, the jobs in each section are divided according to required education level. No matter what your educational experience, this chapter presents you with a range of interesting, career-minded jobs that are available today. In addition, each section contains profiles of companies that are on the cutting edge of the new economy.

As you look through the job listings in this chapter, please keep in mind that no list of careers can ever be complete. All of the following industries listed also employ workers that can be found in any other industry, from human resources managers to accountants. I've chosen to concentrate on job descriptions that are either specific to these industries or that are a major part of green development; for instance, mechanical engineers can find work in a variety of non-green industries, but they are such a crucial part of sustainable energy development that I have included several types of mechanical engineers in the lists of sustainable energy careers.

Much of the job description and salary information for this chapter comes from the *Green Jobs Guidebook*, an informative report compiled by the Environmental Defense Fund. The link to this report can be found in Chapter 9. The websites *greencareersguide.com* and *greenjobs.com* also supplied valuable information. In many cases, the salary figures vary significantly between sources; as with any job, salary is commensurate with experience. If you are interested in any of the jobs listed in this chapter, you should do additional research to determine current salary standards.

Section 1: Renewable Energy
Renewable energy is the most rapidly expanding segment of the green economy. In this section, I describe jobs in the five major segments of renewable energy that currently show the most promise: solar, wind, hydropower, geothermal, and bioenergy.

Section 2: Building Design, Construction, and Efficiency
Residential and commercial buildings are by far the biggest consumers of energy in the United States, accounting for 40% of all power usage and carbon emissions. One of the quickest ways to cut down on the country's energy consumption and emissions is to retrofit buildings for energy efficiency. Architects are needed to design energy-efficient new buildings, construction workers are sought to erect these buildings, and inspectors are needed to make sure the buildings are up to code. This section reveals the wide variety of jobs available in green building.

Section 3: Transportation
With oil prices on the rise and fossil fuels on the way out, Americans are beginning to take a hard look at the environmental impact of our methods of transportation. From electric cars to bullet trains, a new generation of vehicles is poised to change the way we travel from place to place. In this section, we examine some of the opportunities available in the transportation segment of the economy.

Section 4: Food and Agriculture

The organic food movement has exploded in recent years as Americans have become more concerned about the effects of processed food on our weight and health. Large factory farms, which provide the bulk of food to national supermarket chains, are facing increased scrutiny for unsustainable farming practices that harm the environment and produce unhealthy, sometimes dangerous food. In this section, we explore some of the opportunities available for those interested in how our food is produced, sold, and used.

Section 5: Recycling and Waste Management

Although recycling programs have been in place throughout the country for decades, it is only in the past 10–15 years that recycling has become as easy and common for Americans as taking out the trash. As long as humans continue to consume, waste management will always be a necessary part of the economy; in this section, we explore jobs that are being created by innovations in recycling and waste management.

Section 6: Conservation

The environmental movement began life as the *conservation* movement. Before we knew anything about global warming or greenhouse gas emissions, conservationists were fighting to protect natural lands from development, leaving segments of America's wilderness intact. Today, the conservation movement is still alive and well, working to preserve and clean up our land, water, and air for future generations. In this section, we focus on some of the opportunities available for people who are interested in conservation of our most precious natural resources.

Section 7: Nonprofits, Advocacy, and Policy

The environmental movement would be nowhere today if it weren't for the passionate advocacy groups, lawyers, and nonprofits that kept the issue of the environment alive even during hostile political climates. This section examines some of the jobs available at nonprofits and environmental advocacy groups, as well as environmental research organizations.

Section 8: Entrepreneurial

The amount of money being invested in green technology today is truly staggering. For anyone with an entrepreneurial streak, the field is wide open for people with innovative ideas and the drive to make them a reality. In this section, we take a look at some of the areas that are attracting investment from venture capitalists. This section also provides a list of trade shows where aspiring green entrepreneurs can meet with other business owners in their field.

In Their Own Words: Eric Heineman, Sustainability Policy Advisor for the Office of the Governor of Illinois

Eric Heineman became active in campus environmental issues while an undergrad at the University of Vermont, where he majored in Environmental Studies. After working as a middle school computer teacher for two years, his environmental interests led him to work as the Project Manager for Campus Sustainability at the University of Chicago, and then finally to his current position in the governor's office.

Is Illinois committing a lot of resources to green projects?
We're trying to. A lot of the money coming down the pipeline is capital bill funding. That's a state program that provides money to make improvements on things like state buildings getting retrofitted to become more energy-efficient. And then there's all this recovery funding that's coming from the federal government. We're getting money for things like renewable energy programs, energy-efficiency programs, thermal efficiency programs, and biofuel production, and these are grants that will go to nonprofit organizations, businesses, governmental agencies, public or private schools, and universities. There's actually a ton of money coming in.

Do you think, as far as the promises that have been made by the government about funding go—have they been coming true?
Yeah, I think it's just sort of slow. The recovery funding is the first funding that gets right out the door. So those are going to be the immediate jobs you will see.

How do you ensure that jobs will be created by these projects?
When the schools, universities, or nonprofits propose one of these projects, they have to show how many people they will employ. The idea is that they're all supposed to be *shovel ready*, meaning the project will start within the next two years. And so as part of the application proposal they have to say, "We're going to create x amount of jobs."

Are any training programs being started?
Community colleges throughout Illinois are jumping on it. There are different kinds of certificates you can get—wind technician, or water conservation, for example—those sorts of programs are being offered by a bunch of community colleges around the state.

When people get this training, are jobs available right now?
Yes, it just depends on what type of job you're looking for. If a school applies for funding to hire a teacher or a sustainability person for the school, the ARRA recovery funding won't cover those kinds of positions. They do cover the labor costs for building the green roof that's going on your school.

Are there any specific fields you think are moving faster than others?
I always see a lot of jobs for engineers that can do energy audits. Anything related to energy efficiency seems to be the hot ticket. Industrial hygienists are in demand, who are environmental health people working for businesses or organizations.

If someone was interested in doing what you do, what kind of experience do you think they should get?
It can be hard to break into the green field, but once you get some experience, you become really marketable—especially if you have "sustainability" in your title. I had that as part of my university position, and I think that helped me get my job here.

When I got hired for the university, I think they were interested in me because I had experience talking and working with a lot of different groups of people about greening initiatives—administration, parents, students, staff. Really, you can start greening your office or school, wherever you are. You can become that person in that office who's sort of the green nerd or green leader, and all of that helps.

And anyone can do that. You don't need any special skills to start calling people and starting a recycling program.
Right. And I think a lot of times people are interested and excited about starting these things; they just don't want to put in the work. But if you're willing to go through the purchasing catalog and say, "Okay, here are the things that we should be buying," if you can show that economic argument, people will work with you. So if you're trying to get a green job, you should look at the low-hanging fruit around you and just start working to fix that stuff.

Section 1: Renewable Energy

At the center of the green economy is renewable energy. The key to reversing the tide of global climate change is developing trustworthy, practical energy sources that will be viable alternatives to oil and coal. With the Obama administration's stated goal of generating at least 25% of the country's energy from sustainable sources by 2025, the market for renewable energy workers is all but guaranteed to continue growing at a phenomenal clip over the next several years.

Which renewable energy source is the most promising? It is doubtful that one particular renewable energy source will dominate all the others; rather, our energy will come from a combination of sources that take advantage of the different types of terrain and ecological conditions in the country. For instance, middle-American states like Kansas and Montana make ideal spots for wind farms because they have large areas of open land, while California is the best state for solar energy plants due to its abundance of sunny days.

Over the next few pages, we examine the five main renewable energy sources that are currently producing energy: solar, wind, hydroelectric, geothermal, and biogas/biomass.

Green Quotes

One of the most promising new ventures for American manufacturing is clean energy. Despite its recession-induced woes, the clean energy sector is on the rise. The domestic market for solar panels, wind turbines, fuel cells, combined heat and power (CHP) systems, and biomass engines is projected to reach $226 billion annually by 2016. Demand for solar and wind power will continue to expand over the next 20 years, and between 70 and 80 percent of the new jobs created in those industries will be in the manufacturing sector.

—Make It in America: The Apollo Green Manufacturing Action Plan. March 2009

Solar Energy

Although solar power currently generates less than 1% of energy in the United States, solar technology has been growing by leaps and bounds, and as manufacturing prices decrease, solar is destined to become a major player in the renewable energy economy.

There are two methods for turning sunlight into energy that are currently in use: photovoltaic panels, which convert sunlight into electricity, and steam generation (otherwise known as *concentrating thermal*), which uses fields of mirrors to create steam that drives a turbine. The major hurdle that solar power has to overcome is efficiency. While photovoltaic cells have shrunk considerably in recent years, they are still not efficient enough to independently power an entire house or building. The steam generation method beats photovoltaic cells for efficiency, but it requires large expanses of land and long power lines. To this end, a slew of companies, including Google, are working to create thinner, more efficient photovoltaic panels and new mirrors for inexpensive steam generation. One promising technology comes from the California firm Nanosolar, which has developed a conductive ink that can be printed onto inexpensive materials to dramatically lower the cost of photovoltaic cells.

Green Quotes

The total power needs of the humans on Earth is approximately 16 terawatts. In the year 2020 it is expected to grow to 20 terawatts. The sunshine on the solid part of the Earth is 120,000 terawatts. From this perspective, energy from the sun is virtually unlimited.

—Eicke Weber, director of the Franhofer Institute for Solar Energy Systems,

   as quoted in the National Geographic

One thing's for certain: From research and development to solar panel installation, the field of solar power offers a slew of great opportunities for job seekers of all education levels. The following tables list some of these excellent, high-demand green jobs.

Entry Level Jobs for Workers with High School Diplomas or GEDs

Job Title	Salary	Helpful Experience	Duties
Solar and Photovoltaic Installer: Roofer	$15–$20/hour	knowledge of electrical engineering, construction background	install solar panels on roofs of commercial and residential sites
Solar Energy System Installer Helper	$10–$15/hour	NABCEP Entry Level Certification	assist in installation and repair of solar energy systems for use in residential, commercial, or industrial buildings
Solar Fabrication Technician	$10–$15/hour	construction background, experience with machine tools and common construction equipment	fabricate and assemble arrays of solar panels for power companies
Solar Hot Water Heater Installer	$13–$20/hour	knowledge of solar power technology	design, install, and maintain solar hot water systems
Solar Installation Electrician	$17–$31/hour	NABCEP Solar PV Installer Certification	install solar power systems at commercial and residential sites
Solar Sales	$43,000–$85,000/year	sales experience, strong knowledge of solar power technology	sell solar equipment to residents and businesses

Jobs for Workers with Associate Degrees, Trade School, or On-the-Job Training

Job Title	Salary	Education Experience	Helpful Experience	Duties
Photovoltaic Fabrication Technician	$22–$27/hour	Associate Degree in Electronics, Electrical Engineering, Material Science, Physics, or Chemistry; or electrician certification	knowledge of photovoltaic construction and technology	test and assemble solar cells into solar panels
Solar Energy Systems Designer	$22–$29/hour	trade school or apprenticeship	knowledge of equipment controls, plumbing, and electrician training	design solar hot water and space heating systems for residential and commercial properties that conform to local weather conditions
Solar Energy Systems Installer	$14–$20/hour	trade school or apprenticeship	NABCEP Solar Thermal Installer Certification	install and repair solar energy systems for use in residential, commercial, and industrial buildings
Solar Lab Technician	$19–$27/hour	Associate Degree in Engineering	previous experience working with solar technologies, strong analytical abilities	research and develop solar energy equipment
Solar Thermo-electric Plant Manager	$74,000–$88,000/year	trade school or apprenticeship, Professional Engineering Certification	Electrical, Electronic, or Energy Engineering classes	oversee all operations of a solar thermoelectric plant

Did You Know?

In 2007, a massive tornado tore through the farming community of Greensidebarurg, Kansas, destroying homes and killing 11 people. Residents of Greensidebarurg turned their tragedy into triumph, incorporating renewable resources and energy-efficient technology into their new buildings. Today, the 900-person community has two LEED platinum-certified buildings with six other LEED certified buildings on the way. City planners have incorporated green technology as well; streetlamps were replaced with light-emitting diode (LED) lamps which save approximately 70% energy and maintenance costs, and the city is in the process of building a wind farm that will eventually generate 100% of Greensidebarurg's electricity. According to former Governor (and current secretary of Health and Human Services) Kathleen Sibelius, Greensidebarurg is on track to become "the greenest town in rural America."

Jobs for Workers with Higher Education

Job Title	Salary	Education Experience	Helpful Experience	Duties
PV Power Systems Engineer	$76,000–$88,000/year	Master's Degree in Electric Power Engineering or Energy Efficiency	experience working with energy grids	design and implement power grids for photovoltaic cells
PV Solar Cell Designer	$77,000–$91,000/year	Bachelor's Degree in Electrical Engineering, Materials Science, Chemistry, or Physics	strong knowledge of photovoltaic technology	design photovoltaic cells to be manufactured
Solary Energy Engineer	$75,000–$80,000/year	Bachelor's Degree in Engineering	Certified Energy Manager certification, Professional Engineering Certification	design and implement solar systems
Solar Operations Engineer	$52,000–$62,000/year	Bachelor's Degree in Engineering	NABCEP certification, electrical contractor's license, construction experience	design solar power plants and oversee their construction

Spotlight On: Evergreen Solar

Location: *Marlboro, MA*

Typical job openings: *Electro/Mechanical Technician, Operations Manager, PLC and Instrumentation Technician*

What they do: *Evergreen Solar created a new design for the* silicon wafers *that make up the bulk of solar panels. Their* String Ribbon *technology blows the silicon wafers up like soap bubbles, which can be used to create lightweight, efficient, and inexpensive solar cells for commercial or residential use. Evergreen Solar has manufacturing plants in Devens, MA, and Midland, MI, with sales and customer service offices located in Marlboro, MA; Oakland, CA; and Berlin, Germany.*

Interesting fact: *In a study by the TUV Rheinland Group, a German testing institute, Evergreen Solar's* String Ribbon *panels were found to deliver more kilowatt hours of electricity than any other leading brand of solar panels.*

Wind

Wind power is the fastest growing renewable energy source in the world, with an average growth of 29% every year between 1999–2009. According to the American Wind Energy Association, in 2008, wind power created 35,000 new jobs in the United States and accounted for 42% of new energy generating capacity. In addition to power stations, more than 55 new manufacturing facilities opened in 2008. The United States currently generates more of its power from wind than any other country in the world.

Wind power suffered a setback in 2009 when the construction of a major wind farm development in Texas was put on hold. The wind farm, which was to be the largest facility of its kind ever built, had attracted major media attention due to its primary financial backer, oil billionaire T. Boone Pickens. The project was put on hold when Pickens's BP Capital Management was unable to raise the $2 billion needed to connect the wind farm to the electric grid. Nonetheless, Pickens remained committed to wind energy, with plans to utilize his wind turbines on smaller farms across the United States and Canada.

Despite Pickens's setback, the outlook for wind turbines remains strong. Listed on the next few pages are a variety of opportunities for workers in the expanding field of wind turbine manufacturing, installation, and power generation.

Eco-Quiz

What type of renewable energy currently contributes the most electricity to America's power grid?

a. *solar*

b. *wind*

c. *hydropower*

d. *geothermal*

Answer: **c.** *hydropower. According to the Hydro Research Foundation, more than 90% of all renewable energy produced in the United States comes from hydropower. Overall, hydropower accounts for 10% of all electricity generation in the United States and 20% of all electricity generated worldwide.*

Entry Level Jobs for Workers with High School Diplomas or GEDs

Job Title	Salary	Helpful Experience	Duties
Wind Energy Technician	$15–$22/hour	mechanical and electrical experience, some trade school or apprenticeship	maintain turbines on wind farms
Wind Generating Installer	$14–$20/hour	experience working with wind turbine parts	assemble and install electrical and mechanical parts that are used to power wind turbines
Wind Power Field Salesperson	$43,000–$73,000/year	sales, customer relations, knowledge of turbine technology	sell wind turbines to consumers and businesses
Wind Turbine Installer	$15–$20/hour	construction experience, knowledge of zoning laws	assemble and install wind turbines in residential areas

Jobs for Workers with Associate Degrees, Trade School, or On-the-Job Training

Job Title	Salary	Education Experience	Helpful Experience	Duties
Electro-Mechanical Wind Turbine Technician	$17–$21/ hour	Associate Degree or trade school	knowledge of wind turbine functioning	install and maintain wind turbines
Wind Farm Electrical Systems Designer	$30,000– $80,000/ year	Associate Degree in Engineering	knowledge of wind turbine functioning	design, develop, test, and maintain the electrical system at a wind farm
Wind Field Service Technician	$22–$26/ hour	trade school or apprenticeship	experience working in metal shops, knowledge of wind turbine functioning	perform status checks on turbines and repair problems
Wind Turbine Machinist	$12–$21/ hour	apprenticeship or trade school	background working with machine tools	manufacture metal or plastic parts for wind turbines

Jobs for Workers with Higher Education

Job Title	Salary	Education Experience	Helpful Experience	Duties
Wind Development Director	$54,000– $75,000/ year	Bachelor's Degree in Engineering or Business	meteorology, experience managing construction work, at least 5 years' experience in the wind power industry	select sites for wind farms, oversee building of wind farms
Wind Farm Construction Manager	$60,000– $80,000/ year	Bachelor's Degree in Management or extensive experience managing construction sites	managerial experience, knowledge of power plant construction	oversee construction of wind farms

Jobs for Workers with Higher Education (continued)

Job Title	Salary	Education Experience	Helpful Experience	Duties
Wind Field Operations Manager	$24–$28/ hour	Bachelor's Degree	courses in renewable energies, engineering, industrial operations, technical experience on wind farms	manage all operations on wind farms, lead in the installation and commission of wind turbines in a wind field
Wind Power Plant Project Engineer	$60,000–$90,000/ year	Bachelor's Degree in Mechanical or Electrical Engineering, PE license	5–10 years high-level experience at power plants	oversee all technical details at a wind power plant, manage workers and budgets
Wind Turbine Drivetrain Engineer	$52,000–$62,000/ year	Bachelor's or Master's Degree in Mechanical Engineering, PE license	field experience working with wind turbine drivetrains	design, develop, and test wind turbine drivetrains
Wind Turbine Electrical Engineer	$90,000/ year and up	Bachelor's Degree in Electrical Engineering, PE license	knowledge of wind turbine electrical components	design, develop, and test wind turbine electrical components
Wind Turbine Mechanical Engineer	$90,000/ year and up	Bachelor's Degree in Mechanical Engineering, PE license	knowledge of wind turbine mechanical components	design, develop, and test wind turbine mechanical components

Green Quotes

In states such as Michigan and Ohio, whose manufacturing industries have been crippled by the economic crisis, there is potential to benefit from the growth of the wind power industry. The Michigan Economic Development Corporation estimates that approximately 700 companies in Michigan are emerging wind power manufacturing industry participants. According to Ohio's Department of Economic Development, 532 companies in the state are involved, or have plans to become involved in the wind supply chain.

—The Center on Globalization Governance and Competitiveness report "Wind Power: Generating Electricity and Employment"

Location: *Wilton, CT*

Typical job listings: *Renewable Energy Consultant, Solar Installer, Solar Project Manager*

What they do: *Alteris Renewables was formed in 2008 as a merger of two smaller companies with more than 30 years of experience installing renewable energy systems. Alteris is a full-service renewable energy company, guiding photovoltaic, solar thermal, and wind energy projects from design to installation. Although they are headquartered in Connecticut, they also have offices in Massachusetts, New Hampshire, New York, Rhode Island, and Vermont.*

Interesting fact: *In 2009, Alteris Renewables was ranked the 10th fastest growing energy company in the United States.*

Hydropower

Hydropower, or hydroelectric power, is energy created from the flow of bodies of water using water turbines. There's nothing futuristic about the technology behind hydroelectric power; in fact, the United States has been generating electricity using water since 1882. However, the benefits of hydropower have long been mired in controversy. Large scale hydroelectric plants require massive dams that disrupt the natural flow of water and can cause damage to aquatic ecosystems.

Despite the potential for disruption of water sources, hydropower is among the most sustainable and efficient methods of energy generation, producing no carbon dioxide emissions. Recently, there has been a push to move to "low impact hydro." The Low Impact Hydropower Institute, a Maine-based non-profit organization, has developed a certification system to encourage hydroelectric plants to build in environmentally friendly ways that do not disrupt the local ecology. In addition, micro hydropower generators that rely on the natural flow of streams and rivers are a viable alternative power source for residences and businesses located near sources of water.

Eco-Quiz

What percentage of U.S. water usage goes toward producing electricity at thermoelectric plants?

a. *4%*

b. *16%*

c. *23%*

d. *49%*

Answer: d. 49%. A 2009 report found that overall water usage by Americans decreased from 1980–2005, in spite of a 30% population increase. The report found that the biggest consumers of water in the United States are hydroelectric plants, accounting for almost half of all water usage. The second highest consumers were farms, which used 31% of the water supply for irrigation. Consumers accounted for only 11% of total water usage.

Entry Level Jobs for Workers with High School Diplomas or GEDs

Job Title	Salary	Helpful Experience	Duties
Hydroelectric Operations Maintenance Worker	$17–$29/ hour	construction work, knowledge of hydroelectric generators	inspect, maintain, and repair hydroelectric generators
Hydroelectric Plant Efficiency Operator	$23–$26/ hour	HAZMAT certification	maintain and monitor hydroelectric plant equipment, dispose of hazardous materials

Jobs for Workers with Associate Degrees, Trade School, or On-the-Job Training

Job Title	Salary	Education Experience	Helpful Experience	Duties
Hydroelectric Component Machinist	$12–$21/ hour	apprenticeship or trade school	background working with machine tools	manufacture metal or plastic parts for hydroelectric generators
Hydroelectric Plant Installation Technician	$35,000–$50,000/ year	apprenticeship or trade school, journeyman level technician status	experience working with internal systems, such as plumbing or pipefitting	install and maintain equipment at hydroelectric plant
Hydroelectric Plant Electrical Operations Supervisor	$78,000–$92,000/ year	Associate Degree in Business or technical field, Journeyman level technician status	managerial experience, experience working with systems at a hydroelectric plant	oversee maintenance operations at a hydroelectric power plant
Micro Hydropower System Installer	$40,000–$50,000/ year	apprenticeship or trade school	knowledge of water sources, construction experience	design, construct, and maintain small scale water turbines

Jobs for Workers with Higher Education

Job Title	Salary	Education Experience	Helpful Experience	Duties
Hydroelectric Electrical Engineer	$90,000/year and up	Bachelor's Degree in Electrical Engineering, PE license	knowledge of water turbine electrical components	design, develop, and test water turbine electrical components
Hydroelectric Mechanical Engineer	$90,000/year and up	Bachelor's Degree in Mechanical Engineering, PE license	knowledge of water turbine mechanical components	design, develop, and test water turbine mechanical components
Hydroelectric Power Generation Engineer	$90,000–$140,000/year	Bachelor's Degree in Mechanical Engineering, PE license	experience working with mechanical equipment at a power plant	design and plan systems at a hydroelectric power plant
Hydrologist	$55,000–$65,000/year	Bachelor's Degree in Hydrology	experience with on-site groundwater studies and monitoring	monitor groundwater, study the movement of water for use in generation of hydroelectric power

Spotlight On: Verdant Power

Location: *New York, New York*

Typical job listings: *Project Manager, Mechanical Engineer, Electrical Engineer*

What they do: *Verdant Power designs custom-made hydropower systems using their proprietary* Free Flow *technology. The systems, which do not require dams, can be scaled to fit into a diverse range of locations as standalone turbines or as part of a larger energy system. The company, which has locations in New York City and Lynwood, Washington, estimates that its technology produces "approximately double" the amount of energy of wind and solar power systems.*

Interesting fact: *Verdant Power was named by* BusinessWeek *as one of the 25 Companies to Watch in Energy Tech.*

Geothermal

Geothermal energy is power created from the Earth's natural heat. The most well-known example of the geothermal heating effect can be seen in *hot springs*, which are areas where water that has been heated geothermally escapes through fissures into small bodies of water at the surface of the earth. Geothermal heat has been in use since ancient times. The Romans used geothermally heated water for bathing and warming homes.

Like wind or water power, geothermal power uses turbines to create electricity. Unlike these two technologies, geothermal energy isn't quite "plug and play;" geothermal power plants must drill deep beneath the earth's surface to utilize geothermal heat—and even then, the plants must be located near areas that have the proper conditions. Geothermal energy is not without its drawbacks, either. Drilling for a planned power plant in California was put on hold in 2009 upon fears that the drilling would generate earthquakes.

Still, geothermal power has a lot of potential. Reykjavik, Iceland, heats more than 95% of its buildings using geothermal energy; as a result, Reykjavik has become one of the greenest cities on Earth. Most of the geothermal power plants in the United States are located in California, but as the technology improves, expect to see geothermal power becoming a larger part of the sustainable energy economy.

Entry Level Jobs for Workers with High School Diplomas or GEDs

Job Title	Salary	Helpful Experience	Duties
Geothermal Operations Maintenance Worker	$17–$29/ hour	construction work, knowledge of geothermal generators	inspect, maintain, and repair geothermal generators
Geothermal Plant Efficiency Operator	$26–$30/ hour	HAZMAT certification	maintain and monitor geothermal plant equipment, dispose of hazardous materials

Jobs for Workers with Associate Degrees, Trade School, or On-the-Job Training

Job Title	Salary	Education Experience	Helpful Experience	Duties
Geothermal Drilling Engineer	$75,000/year	Associate Degree, on-the-job training	experience in well design, program development, and drilling operation management, PE certification	develop business proposals for drilling geothermal wells, oversee drilling, monitor well conditions
Geothermal Heat Pump Machinist	$12–$21/hour	apprenticeship or trade school	background working with machine tools	manufacture metal or plastic parts for geothermal heat pumps
Geothermal Installer	$15–$20/hour	HVAC certification (see Chapter 4)	construction experience	install home geothermal systems
Geothermal Plant Installation Technician	$35,000–$50,000/year	apprenticeship or trade school, Journeyman level technician status	experience working with internal systems, such as plumbing or pipefitting	install and maintain equipment at geothermal plant

Jobs for Workers with Higher Education

Job Title	Salary	Education Experience	Helpful Experience	Duties
Geologist	$38,000–$48,000/year	Bachelor's Degree in Geology	field work on geological studies	study groundwater sources, monitor geothermal wells
Geothermal Electrical Engineer	$90,000/year and up	Bachelor's Degree in Electrical Engineering, PE license	knowledge of geothermal heat pump electrical components	design, develop, and test geothermal heat pump electrical components
Geothermal Mechanical Engineer	$90,000/year and up	Bachelor's Degree in Mechanical Engineering, PE license	knowledge of geothermal heat pump mechanical components	design, develop, and test geothermal heat pump mechanical components
Geothermal Operations Engineer	$70,000–$80,000/year	Bachelor's Degree in Engineering, PE license	experience working with geothermal wells	study performance of geothermal wells, diagnose and fix problems

Spotlight On: Ormat Technologies, Inc.

Location: *Reno, Nevada*

Typical job listings: *Ormat does not provide online job listings; if you are interested in working for Ormat Technologies, Inc., you can find an online application at www.ormat.com/about.php?did=154.*

What they do: *Ormat has been working in the field of geothermal energy for more than 40 years. They develop, build, own, and operate geothermal and recovered energy generation (REG), a process of capturing waste heat from industrial processes power plants. They currently operate 12 geothermal power plants worldwide and four REG plants in the United States.*

Interesting fact: *Ormat's Mammoth Pacific geothermal plant has twice been awarded the California Department of Conservation's Outstanding Lease Maintenance Award, an award given to businesses that operate in an environmentally sound manner. In the second quarter of 2009, Ormat's revenues increased by 24.9%.*

Website: *www.ormat.com*

Bioenergy

One of the most interesting technologies that has come from the green energy revolution is bioenergy generation. Bioenergy is fuel created using biologically derived materials, such as plants or animal waste. Bioenergy consists of two different methods of energy generation: *biogas* and *biomass*. Biogas is renewable energy created from food-processing waste and animal manure. It is created using a biochemical process known as "anaerobic digestion," in which bacteria are used to digest manure and food waste, breaking the materials down into their gas components. The gas is then collected and used for a wide variety of applications, including electricity production, heating, and vehicle fuel.

Biomass utilizes crops, trees, and other renewable resources to create fuel. One of the most prominent examples of biomass fuel is ethanol. Because most ethanol is currently derived from corn, it has come under some scrutiny in recent years. Critics charge that corn ethanol uses more energy to produce than it creates, and that using a food source to create energy negatively impacts food supplies. To that end, scientists are actively working to increase the efficiency of ethanol production and to create new types of ethanol using waste products, such as corn husks and switchgrass.

Entry Level Jobs for Workers with High School Diplomas or GEDs

Job Title	Salary	Helpful Experience	Duties
Biomass Collector, Separator, and Sorter	$28,000–$45,000/year	factory experience	separate usable from unusable materials at a biomass plant
Landfill Gas Technician	$10–$15/hour	knowledge of earth sciences	perform checks for landfill gas leaks, assist landfill operator in daily operations

Jobs for Workers with Associate's Degrees, Trade School, or On-the-Job Training

Job Title	Salary	Education Experience	Helpful Experience	Duties
Biofuel Plant Field Technician	$16–$22/hour	trade school or considerable on-the-job training	knowledge of power plant operations	maintain pumps at a biofuel plant, repairs and maintenance, perform measurements for lab tests
Biomethane Gas Collection System Technician	$28,000–$45,000/year	trade school, apprenticeship, or associate's degree	knowledge of power generation operations, chemistry	operate and maintain equipment that processes animal waste and methane gas
Landfill Gas Collection System Operator	$20–$24/hour	trade school, apprenticeship, or associate degree	knowledge of power generation operations, chemistry	capture and extract landfill gas, maintain and repair machinery

Jobs for Workers with Higher Education

Job Title	Salary	Education Experience	Helpful Experience	Duties
Alternative Fuels Policy Analyst and Business Sales	$60,000/year	Bachelor's Degree	marketing and sales experience, knowledge of alternative fuels	market alternative fuels to consumers and businesses, research new types of fuels and fuel-production technology

Jobs for Workers with Higher Education (continued)

Job Title	Salary	Education Experience	Helpful Experience	Duties
Biofuel Plant Operations Engineer	$70,000–$80,000/year	Bachelor's Degree in Engineering	experience working with biofuel production, PE certification	collect and research biofuel well-field and plant performance, maintain and repair well irregularities
Biofuel Technology and Product Development Manager	Varies	Bachelor's Degree in Chemistry, Engineering, or Biology	experience working in power plants, knowledge of alternative fuels	research and implement new types of biofuels and biofuel production
Biomass Plant Operations, Engineering and Management	$70,000–$80,000/year	Bachelor's Degree in Engineering	knowledge of resource engineering, PE certification	design, operate, manage and/or maintain biomass plants
LGE Plant Operations, Engineering and Management	$70,000–$80,000/year	Bachelor's Degree in Engineering	knowledge of resource engineering, PE certification	design, operate, manage and/or maintain delivery systems at LGE (landfill gas to energy) plants

Spotlight On: Sapphire Energy

Location: *San Diego, CA*

Typical job listings: *Biochemist, Research Associate*

What they do: *Started by a team of scientists, Sapphire Energy was formed to develop types of biofuels that would provide an alternative to ethanol. The product they created uses algae to convert sunlight, CO_2, and water into "renewable gasoline." According to Sapphire Energy, their fuel is 100% carbon neutral and chemically identical to fossil fuels.*

Interesting fact: *In 2009, Sapphire converted a Toyota Prius into the Algeus, the world's first algae powered plug-in electric hybrid vehicle.*

Website: *www.sapphireenergy.com*

General Energy and Plant Operations

Renewable energy power plants are in need of the same kinds of workers as any other type of power plant, usually with some degree of specialized knowledge in that particular field. Following are some of the most promising career paths that are available today in renewable energy power plants.

Entry Level Jobs for Workers with High School Diplomas or GEDs

Job Title	Salary	Helpful Experience	Duties
Instrument, Control, and Electrical (ICE) Technician	$16–$22/hour	experience working with instruments at power plants	install, monitor, and repair the instruments, controls, and electrical systems at a power plant
Power System Operator	$25–$30/hour	computer programming	monitor and operate equipment at an electrical power plant
Program Logic Controller (PLC) Technician	$16–$22/hour	experience working with instruments at a power plant	work with electrical control components at a power plant, troubleshoot problems

Jobs for Workers with Higher Education

Job Title	Salary	Education Experience	Helpful Experience	Duties
Energy Commission Specialist	$70,000–$83,000/year	Bachelor's Degree	knowledge of public policy	develop public policy for sustainable energy
Environmental, Health and Safety Engineering Manager	$113,000–$138,000/year	Bachelor's Degree in Environmental Science, Health & Safety Management, or Environmental Engineering	previous work with environmental health and safety in an industrial setting	manage environmental health and safety issues at manufacturing plants and at businesses; ensures compliance with state and federal regulations
Plant Maintenance Supervising Technical Operator	$27–$30/hour	Bachelor's Degree in Engineering	experience working with technical equipment in a power plant setting	manage daily technical operations at sustainable energy power plants

Jobs for Workers with Higher Education				
Job Title	*Salary*	*Education Experience*	*Helpful Experience*	*Duties*
Plant Safety Engineer	$90,000– $107,000/ year	Bachelor's Degree	knowledge of safety regulations and safe workplace practices	inspect sustainable energy power to ensure compliance with safety measures
Safety Investigator/ Cause Analyst	$88,000– $104,000/ year	Bachelor's Degree in Business or Engineering	knowledge of safety regulations and safe workplace practices	investigates employee claims regarding workplace safety issues
Smart Grid Engineer	$91,000– $107,000/ year	Bachelor's Degree in Engineering	experience working with power grids	develop the smart electricity grid

Did You Know?

According to Laurence Bender's 2009 book 200 Best Jobs for Renewing America, *the top 10 fastest-growing green jobs are:*

1. Environmental Engineers. *Growth: 25.4%; average annual earnings: $72,350*

2. Environmental Scientists and Specialists. *Growth: 25.1%; average annual earnings: $58,380*

3. Geoscientists. *Growth: 21.9%; average annual earnings: $75,800*

4. Industrial Engineers. *Growth: 20.3%; average annual earnings: $71,430*

5. Construction and Building Instructors. *Growth: 18.2%; average annual earnings: $48,330*

6. Construction Managers. *Growth: 15.7%; average annual earnings: $76,230*

7. Plumbers, Pipefitters and Steamfitters. *Growth: 10.6%; average annual earnings: $44,090*

8. Carpenters. *Growth: 10.3%; average annual earnings: $37,660*

9. First-Line Supervisors/Managers of Construction Trades and Extraction Workers. *Growth: 9.1%; average annual earnings: $55,950*

10. Electricians. *Growth: 7.4%; average annual earnings: $44,780*

Section 2: Building Design, Construction, and Efficiency

The most immediate opportunities in green building are in the world of retrofitting, that is, upgrading preexisting buildings with energy-efficient technology and materials. Many of these jobs are only minimally different from construction jobs that have existed for years; the technology used to build an energy-efficient window pane may be innovative, but the installation process is, for the most part, no different from installation of an ordinary window.

I tried to limit this section to jobs that are unique to green building and conservation. There are many more jobs in green building than I'm able to describe here; basically, any construction job you can think of has its place in the world of green building. If you're interested in learning more about the opportunities in green building that are available today, there are many great online resources where you can find job listings and descriptions. A listing of some of these resources is included in Chapter 9 of this book.

Eco-Quiz

How much of a household's typical energy usage comes from electronic products that are plugged in but not in use?

a. *5%*
b. *10%*
c. *15%*
d. *20%*

Answer: c. *15%. According to the International Energy Agency, consumer electronics account for 15% of energy usage in households. Many consumer devices like cable boxes, DVD players, televisions, and microwaves consume energy even when they're turned off, resulting in massive amounts of wasted electricity. To reduce the effect of these "vampire power" suckers on your electric bill, invest in a Smart Strip— a power strip that monitors power usage and automatically blocks power to devices that are not in use.*

Entry Level Jobs for Workers with High School Diplomas or GEDs

Job Title	Salary	Helpful Experience	Duties
Construction Worker	varies	construction experience, knowledge of green building materials	roofing, carpentry, welding, electrical work, plumbing, etc.
Energy Conservation Representative	$20–$32/hour	construction knowledge, knowledge of energy-efficient technology	inspect homes for utility companies in search of energy-efficient solutions
Insulation Installer	$10–$12/hour	construction experience	install insulation in residential, commercial, and industrial buildings
Residential Air Sealing Technician	$15–$30/hour	construction experience	seal windows, doors, and cracks in homes to increase energy efficiency
Water Purification Systems Service Technician	$20–$23/hour	chemistry knowledge	install and service water purification systems in residential, commercial, and industrial buildings
Window or Door Retrofit Technician	$15–$30/hour	construction experience	retrofit parts of windows or doors to make them more energy efficient

Spotlight On: Gerding Edlen Development

Location: *Portland, Oregon*

Typical job listings: *Gerding Edlen does not list job opportunities on their website. If you are interested in working at Gerding Edlen, visit their website at www.gerdingedlen.com/contact.php for further information.*

What they do: *Gerding Edlen retrofits commercial and residential buildings to increase energy efficiency and sustainability. They take a holistic approach to their work, assessing buildings for areas of improvement and creating innovative building solutions that promote energy efficiency without sacrificing the user experience.*

Interesting fact: *Gerding Edlen Development was ranked the #1 Best Green Company in Oregon by* Oregon Business Magazine.

Jobs for Workers with Associate Degrees, Trade School, or On-the-Job Training

Job Title	Salary	Education Experience	Helpful Experience	Duties
Electrical System Installer	$21–$27/ hour	trade school or apprenticeship	experience with energy-efficient wiring techniques, knowledge of smart grid technology	install electrical systems in residential, commercial, and industrial buildings
Energy Field Auditor	$12–$14/ hour	Associate Degree in Building Materials, Environmental Studies, Energy Management	construction knowledge, knowledge of HVAC systems and energy-efficient building techniques	assess energy efficiency possibilities for residential, commercial, and industrial buildings
HVAC Engineer	$34–$50/ hour	trade school, apprenticeship, or Associate Degree, Journeyman status	work with heating, ventilation, and air-conditioning systems	design and install energy-efficient heating, ventilation, and air-conditioning systems for buildings
Land Survey Technician	$29,230/ year	Associate's Degree in Geomatics or Land Surveying	strong math skills, observation skills	survey land to determine best building practices for different topographic features
Water Systems Designers and Engineers	$15–$30/ hour	trade school or apprenticeships, PE license	experience with water systems, knowledge of plumbing, pipefitting	design and install energy-efficient water systems for buildings

Jobs for Workers with Higher Education

Job Title	Salary	Education Experience	Helpful Experience	Duties
Civil Engineer	$73,000–$84,000/year	Bachelor's Degree in Civil Engineering, PE license	knowledge of land use, green building techniques and technology	oversee the overall design and construction of green buildings
Electrical and Lighting Consultant	$80,000–$100,000/year	Bachelor's Degree in Electrical Engineering	experience working with electrical and lighting systems	consult companies on energy-efficient electricity and lighting solutions
Energy Consultant	$30–$35/hour	Bachelor's Degree in Engineering or Management	strong knowledge of energy alternatives and building retrofitting	work with companies to develop energy-saving solutions
Energy Engineer	$75,000–$80,000/year	Bachelor's Degree in Engineering, LEED Certification, PE license	managerial experience, knowledge of energy-efficient technology	analyze energy-efficiency of systems in industrial, commercial, and residential buildings
Energy Procurement Manager and Analyst	$80,000–$100,000/year	Bachelor's Degree in Energy Analysis, Sciences, or Business Administration	knowledge of federal and state environmental regulations and energy efficient technology	audit industrial and commercial facilities for energy efficiency
Environmental Compliance Specialist	$20–$30/hour	Bachelor's Degree in Science or Engineering	knowledge of federal and state environmental regulations	assess buildings for compliance with federal and state regulations
Green Building and Retrofit Architect	$90,000–$107,000/year	Bachelor's Degree in Architecture, LEED certification	knowledge of LEED standards	draft and design buildings that meet LEED standards for energy efficiency

Job Title	Salary	Education Experience	Helpful Experience	Duties
Jobs for Workers with Higher Education (continued)				
Industrial Green Systems and Retrofit Designer	$32,000–$52,000/year	Bachelor's Degree in Architecture, LEED certification	knowledge of energy-efficient technology	redesign industrial or commercial building technology to increase energy efficiency
Land Surveyor	$39,970	Bachelor's Degree in Surveying, Engineering, or Survey Science	strong analytical abilities	survey land to determine boundaries and building regulations; write reports
Landscape Architect	$65,000–$83,000/year	Bachelor's Degree in Landscape Architecture, LEED certification	knowledge of urban planning and green building techniques	design indoor and outdoor landscape spaces using energy-efficient design techniques
Structural Design Engineer	$75,000–$88,000/year	Bachelor's Degree in Engineering, LEED certification, PE license	managerial experience, knowledge of structural analysis techniques	design structural elements of buildings according to building codes using sustainable technologies
Weatherization Operations Manager	$30,000–$60,000/year	Bachelor's Degree	knowledge of local weather patterns, construction	manage weatherization efforts for residential, commercial, and industrial buildings

Spotlight On: IBC Engineering Services, Inc.
Location: *Waukesha, WI*

Typical job listings: *IBC Engineering Services does not list job openings on their website. If you are interested in job opportunities at IBC, visit their website at www.ibcengineering.com/contact/.*

What they do: *IBC Engineering Services design and commission energy-efficient mechanical, electrical, plumbing, and fire protection systems for commercial and residential properties. In addition to the home office in Waukesha, WI, they also have offices in Florida and Washington, DC*

Interesting fact: *IBC Engineering Services was chosen by* Inc. Magazine *as one of The Green 50, the 50 most promising green companies in the United States*

Website: *www.ibcengineering.com*

Did You Know?

Innovalight, a solar tech company based in Sunnyvale, CA, has developed a proprietary silicon ink that can be used to print solar panels. Innovalight's unique solar powered ink can produce solar panels with record-high efficiency at half the price of previously used methods. If Innovalight's technology takes off, there may come a day when we'll be able to paint our cars with silicon ink to create instant solar-powered cars!

Section 3: Transportation

A 2009 report by The Pew Center on Global Climate Change estimated that almost 28% of all greenhouse gas emissions in the United States come from transportation, second only to electricity generation. This number is derived from all forms of transportation in use in the United States, from aircraft to trains. Passenger vehicles are by far the biggest offender, generating 61% of emissions. Second are medium- and heavy-duty trucks, responsible for 19%. The transportation sector is also the largest consumer of oil. As we work to curb greenhouse gas emissions, look to the transportation sector to be a major source of new, green jobs.

Consumer Vehicles

Before 2000, many Americans who were concerned about the environmental impact of driving had one alternative: Buy a bike. That all changed with the release of the Honda Insight, the first consumer hybrid automobile available in the United States. Later that year, the Toyota Prius was released, and the battle for fuel economy/low emissions supremacy was on. The original hybrids didn't fly off the shelves, but due to rising gas costs and increased fuel efficiency standards, subsequent models met with brisk sales. In 2009, Toyota announced that it had sold over 1,000,000 Priuses in the United States since the car's initial release, and American car companies were scrambling to catch up with consumer demand for energy-efficient vehicles.

Entry-Level Jobs for Workers with High School Diplomas or GEDs

Job Title	Salary	Helpful Experience	Duties
Diesel Retrofit Installer	varies	knowledge of engine design	install filters on diesel-powered vehicles
Electric Vehicle Electrician	$22–$26/ hour	knowledge of engine design	implement electric systems on electric vehicles, install dedicated circuits for high-current charging systems

Jobs for Workers with Associate Degrees, Trade School, or On-the-Job Training

Job Title	Salary	Education Experience	Helpful Experience	Duties
Diesel Retrofit Manufacturer	varies	trade school or apprenticeship	knowledge of engines, air quality standards	manufacture diesel filters and other retrofitting technology for diesel vehicles

Jobs for Workers with Higher Education

Job Title	Salary	Education Experience	Helpful Experience	Duties
Automotive Power Electronics Engineer	$75,000–$80,000/year	Bachelor's Degree in Engineering	knowledge of alternative fuels, experience as an automotive engineer and with motor and power electronics controls	develop controls for electric traction motors and power electronics for hybrid and electric vehicles
Diesel Retrofit Designer	$90,000–$150,000/year	Master's Degree in Engineering	several years of experience working with diesel engine technology	design and develop retrofitting technology for diesel engines
Hybrid Powertrain Development Engineer	$75,000–$80,000/year	Bachelor's Degree in Electrical or Mechanical Engineering	knowledge of powertrain technology and hybrid powertrain development	develop powertrain designs for hybrid vehicles
Powertrain Control Systems and Software Engineer	$75,000–$80,000/year	Bachelor's Degree in Electrical or Mechanical Engineering	excellent computer skills, experience working with embedded control software	design powertrain control systems software

Spotlight On: Tesla Motors

Location: *San Carlos, CA*

Typical job listings: *Mechanical Engineer, Director of Chassis Engineering, Electro-Mechanical Assembler*

What they do: *Tesla Motors designs, manufactures, and sells high-performance, 100% electric vehicles. They were founded in 2003 and assisted by an investment from Google founders Sergey Brin and Larry Page. With the help of a $465 million loan from the U.S. Department of Energy, Tesla is poised to become a major player in the world of energy-efficient passenger vehicles.*

Interesting fact: *The Tesla Roadster, Tesla's first-produced vehicle, can go 220 miles on a single charge, with a top speed of 220 mph.*

Website: *www.teslamotors.com/*

Public Transportation

Outside major urban areas, there is a decided lack of good, reliable transportation in the United States. With the coming of the green revolution, this might finally change. In addition to the significant role public transportation plays in lowering greenhouse gas emissions, the American Public Transportation Association concluded in a 2009 study that individuals using public transportation can save an average of $9,167 every year over the cost of driving.

Congress included $8.4 billion for public transportation in ARRA, assuring that public transportation will become a transportation priority in the coming years. Across the United States, cities are putting this money to work by building new subway lines, increasing their fleets of busses, and creating new modes of public transportation. Also included in the funding was an additional $8 billion to construct a new high-speed rail system that would connect 10 different corridors throughout the United States, with eventual plans to expand the network across the country.

Green Quotes

Investments in public transportation put people to work, but they also get people to work in a way that moves us toward our long-term goals of energy security and a better quality of life. That is why transit funding was included in the ARRA and why we think it is a key part of America's transportation future.
—U.S. Transportation Secretary Ray LaHood

Entry Level Jobs for Workers with High School Diplomas or GEDs

Job Title	Salary	Helpful Experience	Duties
Bus Driver	$11–$17/hour	Class B driver's license	drive a bus
Train System Operator	$20–$24/hour	on-the-job training	drive a subway train

Did You Know?

A 2009 report by Environment America, a federation of environmental advocacy organizations, found that public transit ridership increased by 4% in 2008. The report estimated that the 4% increase reduced global warming pollution by 37 million tons and saved an equivalent of 7.2 million cars worth of fuel.

Jobs for Workers with Associate Degrees, Trade School, or On-the-Job Training

Job Title	Salary	Education Experience	Helpful Experience	Duties
Rail Traffic Controller	$43,534	Associate Degree, on-the-job training	interest in rail systems, good communication skills	coordinate movement of passenger and freight trains
Railcar Repair Technician	$18/ hour	apprenticeship, on-the-job training	certification	service, maintain, and repair railroad equipment, including locomotives, subway cars, and streetcars
Railway Conductor	$44,491	Associate Degree, on-the-job training	good communication skills	ensure adherence to schedules, communicate with train crew members and passengers

Jobs for Workers with Higher Education

Job Title	Salary	Education Experience	Helpful Experience	Duties
Civil Engineer	$73,000–$84,000/ year	Bachelor's Degree in Civil Engineering	knowledge of land use and green building developments, PE certification	design, construct, and maintain public works projects, including bridges, roads, and train systems
Environmental Engineer	$21–$31/ hour	Bachelor's Degree in Environmental Engineering	experience in science, chemistry, and engineering, PE certification	plan and design a variety of construction projects, including roads, railroads, power plants, and public works projects
Environmental Engineering Manager	$62,400–$82,900/ year	Bachelor's Degree in Engineering	management experience	develop and coordinate environmental control activities, evaluate potential environmental hazards of environmental engineering projects

Jobs for Workers with Higher Education (continued)

Job Title	Salary	Education Experience	Helpful Experience	Duties
Energy Infrastructure Engineer	$77,000–$91,000/year	Bachelor's Degree in Mechanical Engineering	engineering experience, Certified Energy Manager (CEM) certification, PE certification	engineer transit/rail and other infrastructure construction projects
Environmental Planner	$30–$37/hour	Bachelor's Degree in Environmental Science or Environmental Studies	knowledge of social sciences, land use	assess and develop in a wide range of ecologically beneficial projects
Program Manager Environmental Construction	$72,000–$85,000/year	Bachelor's Degree in Engineering	management experience	hire and manage subcontractors for environmental construction projects
Rail Engineer		Bachelor's Degree in Engineering	knowledge of railroads, PE license	design and implement all aspects of mechanical and electrical structures of a rail system
Urban Planner	$25–$35/hour	Bachelor's Degree in Urban Planning	experience in planning and development, interest in environmental impact of development projects	develop and assess plans for community development projects in urban and rural cities

Spotlight On: Siemens Mobility

Location: *New York, New York*

Typical job listings: *Environmental Engineer, Rail Engineer*

What they do: *Siemens Mobility is a division of Siemens AG, one of the biggest electronics and electrical engineering firms in the world. Siemens Mobility plans public transportation projects and currently produces one out of every three light rail vehicles in North America.*

Interesting fact: *Siemens has developed a variety of light rail cars that increase the energy efficiency of public transportation systems, including the Valaro, a multiple unit train that was designed to create significantly smaller CO_2 emissions during production and in the field.*

Website: *www.mobility.siemens.com*

Section 4: Food and Agriculture

Since the early days of our country, the business of agriculture has changed dramatically. Today, the bulk of the food sold in supermarkets is grown and raised on massive factory farms that specialize in specific types of crops or animals. As we've become more aware of how these farming practices impact the quality of our food and our environment, however, there has been a growing movement of Americans who want to return to a smaller, more local way of producing and distributing our food. One needs only to visit the local supermarket for evidence that Americans are becoming more aware of what goes into the food we eat; the organic products that were once confined to a shelf or two in the back of the store are now mixed in with the rest of the food, their labels proudly trumpeting their organic status. As Americans continue to demand higher-quality food, expect to see environmentally friendly farms expanding and creating more opportunities.

Entry Level Jobs for Workers with High School Diplomas or GEDs

Job Title	Salary	Helpful Experience	Duties
Farmhand	$25,000–$35,000	general farming background	operate farm equipment, maintain crops

Jobs for Workers with Associate Degrees, Trade School, or On-the-Job Training

Job Title	Salary	Education Experience	Helpful Experience	Duties
Agricultural Technologist	$28,579	Associate Degree in Agriculture, Biology, Microbiology, Wildlife, or Resource Management	chemistry and science background	study farming practices, investigate soils, help develop and implement sustainable farming practices
Plant Breeding Technologist	not available	Associate Degree in Botanical Technology or Plant Breeding Technology	interest in plants, ability to work outdoors	research methods to improve plant breeding

Jobs for Workers with Higher Education

Job Title	Salary	Education Experience	Helpful Experience	Duties
Agronomist	$48,670	Master's Degree in Agriculture, Forestry, Biology, Environmental, or Earth Sciences	chemistry background	study soil and food production, develop sustainable soil management practices
Agriculturist	$48,670	Bachelor's Degree in Agriculture	background in agriculture, science	assess farms for sustainability, research new farming technologies and practices
Animal Scientist	not listed	Bachelor's Degree in Agriculture	background in agriculture, zoology studies, experience working with animals	work with farmers and farm animals to create healthy, sustainable animal farming practices
Crop Scientist	$48,670	Bachelor's Degree in Agriculture	background in agriculture, knowledge of insects, soil, weather, and plants	work with crops and soil to ensure maximum harvests and quality of food

Spotlight On: New Belgium Brewery

Location: *Fort Collins, Colorado*

Typical job listings: *Technical Brewer, Marketing Manager*

What they do: *New Belgium Brewery creates and produces Belgian-style beers, including the popular Fat Tire amber. They are committed to building a fully sustainable operation, producing all of their electricity by wind power and wastewater.*

Interesting fact: *In 2008, they were named by the* Wall Street Journal *as one of the 25 best small workplaces in America.*

Website: *www.newbelgium.com*

Section 5: Recycling and Waste Management

According to the EPA, without factoring in industrial, mining and oil, or agricultural waste, Americans throw away an average of 4.6 pounds of waste per person, *per day*. If we're serious about cleaning up our planet, tackling our waste problem is a good place to start.

Fortunately, many communities around the country are taking great steps to reduce their garbage and increase recycling programs. In Oregon, garbage generation fell by 9% in 2008, and recycling rose by about 3%. California has already met its goal of recycling 50% of consumer waste statewide. Many states and cities are also creating composting programs to cut down on food waste. Waste is a fact of life that won't just go away, and as recycling programs expand, expect recycling and waste management to provide plenty of opportunities for job seekers.

Entry Level Jobs for Workers with High School Diplomas or GEDs

Job Title	Salary	Helpful Experience	Duties
Hazardous Waste Materials Removal Worker	$20–$25/ hour	on-the-job training	identify, remove, transport, and dispose of hazardous waste materials
Recycling Center Operator	$11–$18/ hour	experience working as a general laborer	sort and separate recyclable materials, perform other operations at a recycling center
Recycling Collections Driver	$9–$12/ hour	driver's license	drive a recycling truck

Jobs for Workers with Associate Degrees, Trade School, or On-the-Job Training

Job Title	Salary	Education Experience	Helpful Experience	Duties
Hazardous Waste Management Specialist	$25–$35/ hour	Associate Degree in Chemistry or other science	training in a health and safety program	study hazardous waste management projects, determine environmental impact of waste and support cleanup projects

Jobs for Workers with Higher Education

Job Title	Salary	Education Experience	Helpful Experience	Duties
Nuclear Waste Management Engineer	$89,000–$106,000/ year	Bachelor's Degree in Nuclear Engineering	knowledge of nuclear waste containment and disposal procedures	design procedures for safe disposal of nuclear waste
Waste Management Engineer	$76,000–$84,000/ year	Bachelor's Degree in Engineering or Environmental studies	Engineer-in-Training certification	design and implement solid waste projects, including composting and recycling
Waste Reduction Consultant	$60,000–$80,000/ year	Bachelor's Degree in Waste Management	experience working within the waste management industry	consult with municipalities and businesses to create waste reduction programs
Wastewater Engineer	$75,000–$100,000/ year	Bachelor's Degree in Engineering	knowledge of air emissions and water regulations	design and implement wastewater programs for industrial facilities and municipalities

Spotlight On: EnerTech Environmental, Inc.

Location: *Atlanta, GA*

Typical job listings: *Waste Management Engineer*

What they do: *EnerTech Environmental holds the patent to a unique technology called SlurryCarb that processes biosolids (the organic material that remains after sewage treatment) into a fuel source known as E-Fuel. In addition to their home office in Atlanta, EnerTech owns and operates a processing facility in Rialto, CA.*

Interesting fact: *SlurryCarb was a runner-up in the* Wall Street Journal's *2007 Technology Innovation Awards.*

Website: *www.enertech.com*

Section 6: Conservation

Long before there were municipal recycling programs (or even such a thing as recycling technology), the conservation movement recognized the importance of protecting our natural resources. During the Great Depression, the United States built a popular job relief program around conservation work. Called the Civilian Conservation Corps (CCC), the program trained and put almost 3 million people to work in conservation jobs. Although the CCC was disbanded in the 1940s, today there are approximately 113 similar corps programs in the United States. If you're interested in a career in conservation, volunteering for one of these corps programs would be a great place to gain valuable experience.

There is not necessarily a conservationist industry, but conservationists play an important role in many different fields, from the national park system to farming. New conservation studies and projects are initiated every day, and with the funding coming in from ARRA, expect there to be more new projects in need of workers with a conservation background.

Entry Level Jobs for Workers with High School Diplomas or GEDs

Job Title	Salary	Helpful Experience	Duties
Environmental Sampling Technician	$16–$22/ hour	interest in science, environmental studies	manage and test air samples for levels of contaminants

Jobs for Workers with Associate's Degrees, Trade School, or On-the-Job Training

Job Title	Salary	Education Experience	Helpful Experience	Duties
Arborist	$33,000	Associate Degree, ISA (International Society of Arboriculture) certification	knowledge of horticulture and arboreal plants	inspect, maintain, and care for trees in parks, forests, rangelands, and protected wild lands
Botanical Technician	$35,318	Associate Degree in Botany	laboratory experience, knowledge of plants	study and maintain plant life in parks, forests, rangelands, and protected wild lands
Environmental Technician	$40,000–$53,000/year	Associate Degree in Engineering	experience working in scientific research	perform labor and collection duties for environmental studies

Jobs for Workers with Higher Education

Job Title	Salary	Education Experience	Helpful Experience	Duties
Air Permit Engineer	$30–$40/hour	Bachelor's Degree in Engineering, Science, or related field	knowledge of engineering practices, analytic ability	review permit applications to ensure compliance with greenhouse gas emissions standards
Air Pollution Specialist	$64,000–$74,000/year	Bachelor's Degree in Chemistry, Chemical Engineering, or Physical Science	strong knowledge of climate change science	investigate land use activities, estimate and analyze greenhouse gas emissions for buildings and businesses
Air Quality Control Engineer	$80,000–$120,000/year	Bachelor's Degree in Chemical Engineering or related field	knowledge of federal and state environmental programs	analyze air quality, implement environmental compliance policies and systems

Jobs for Workers with Higher Education (continued)

Job Title	Salary	Education Experience	Helpful Experience	Duties
Air Quality Specialist and Enforcement Officer	$30–$37/ hour	Bachelor's Degree in Engineering, Science, or related field	experience working in air quality and environmental issues	consults on air quality and pollution issues
Air Resource Engineer	$72,000–$85,000/ year	Bachelor's Degree in Engineering	knowledge of greenhouse gas emission standards	develop strategies for reducing greenhouse gas emissions
Climato-logist	$65,000–$85,000/ year	Bachelor's Degree in Engineering or scientific field	interest in weather patterns	research and analyze data about air, soil, and water pollution and how it relates to global climate change
Conserva-tion of Resources Commis-sioner	$82,900–$113,500	Master's Degree in Environ-mental Studies or related fields	experience working within government	direct conservation programs and help establish standards for resource usage
Conserva-tion Scientist	$54,970	Bachelor's Degree in Forestry, Biology, Natural Resource Management, or Environmental Sciences	interest in working outdoors, a strong interest in nature	work with landowners, farms, and government agencies to manage, improve, and protect natural resources
Engineer-ing Geologist	$31–$37/ hour	Bachelor's Degree in Engineering Geology	interest in working outdoors	study soil, rock, and water conditions for a variety of public and private construction projects

Jobs for Workers with Higher Education (continued)

Job Title	Salary	Education Experience	Helpful Experience	Duties
Environmental Research Manager	$40/hour	Master's Degree in Chemical Engineering, Chemistry, Environmental Science, or Atmospheric Science	experience leading teams of researchers	perform research and analyze data related to property development and environmental hazards
Environmental Scientist	$65,000–$85,000/year	Bachelor's Degree in Engineering or scientific field	background in environmental work	perform a variety of research and data analysis centered around environmental issues
Geographic Information Systems (GIS) Specialist	$46,000-$57,000/year	Bachelor's Degree in Geography	computer knowledge, GIS training	use Geographic Information Systems methodologies to study geographic changes
Land Steward	$47,000/year	Bachelor's Degree in Biology, Ecology, Forestry, or related field	ability to perform physically demanding tasks, management skills	plan and manage land conservation programs, oversee contractors
Water Quality Consultant	$72,000–$92,000/year	Bachelor's Degree in scientific field	experience working with water quality issues	consult about issues of water quality
Water Resource Consultant	$72,000–$92,000/year	Bachelor's Degree in scientific field	experience working with water quality issues	study issues of water management and discharge
Water Resource Engineer	$65,000–$74,000/year	Bachelor's Degree in Environmental Science, Engineering, or related fields	experience in water quality compliance, knowledge of environmental standards	research and analyze data related to health and efficiency of water resources

Spotlight On: The Nature Conservancy

Location: *All 50 states, 30 foreign countries*

Typical job listings: *Land Steward, Project Manager*

What they do: *The Nature Conservancy's stated mission is "to preserve the plants, animals and natural communities that represent the diversity of life on Earth by protecting the lands and waters they need to survive." Over the next 10 years, they have a goal to double the rate of conservation around the planet.*

Interesting fact: *Since its founding in 1951, the Nature Conservancy has protected more than 119 million acres of land and 5,000 miles of rivers.*

Website: *www.npca.org*

Section 7: Nonprofits, Advocacy, and Policy

When many people hear the term *nonprofit*, they assume that means volunteer work. Not necessarily. Although people don't tend to get rich working in the nonprofit world, the nonprofit sector provides many great jobs with competitive wages. In addition, nonprofits are often more committed to providing excellent benefits to their workers than for-profit companies, including generous vacation policies and quality health insurance.

I've also included policy and advocacy jobs in this section. Policy jobs are generally government-based jobs that deal with researching and suggesting environmental policy, while advocacy jobs are legal careers related to environmental law.

This section is somewhat shorter than the others, because many jobs in the nonprofit, policy, and advocacy fields aren't green specific. For example, while these types of companies often employ grant writers, there is no special class of worker known as "green grant writers." Also, although no jobs are listed for workers without four-year degrees, there are often opportunities at nonprofits, governmental offices, and legal firms for workers without advanced degrees, from assistant work to maintenance. And remember: If you're interested in working for a nonprofit, a great way to get your foot in the door is to volunteer for them—most nonprofits could use the help!

Eco-Quiz

What percentage of worldwide greenhouse gas emissions are produced by the United States?

a. *10%*

b. *20%*

c. *25%*

d. *50%*

Answer: c. *25%. Although the United States has only 4% of the world's population, we produce 25% of the world's greenhouse gas emissions.*

Jobs for Workers with Higher Education

Job Title	Salary	Education Experience	Helpful Experience	Duties
Climate Change Policy Specialist and Advocate	$30,000 and up	Master's Degree in Environmental Studies or related field	interest in climate change policy	study climate change science and develop programs to help combat climate change
Conservation Policy Analyst and Advocate	$30,000 and up	Master's Degree in Environmental Studies or related field	interest in wildlife conservation	plan and manage conservation programs
Environmental Lawyer	$60,000–$103,000/year	accredited law degree	interest in environmental issues	work on individual litigation or class action lawsuits involving environmental issues; advise individuals and companies on legal issues connected to the environment
Greenhouse Gas Emissions Permitting Consultant	$50,000 and up	Bachelor's Degree in Engineering or Science	knowledge of greenhouse gas emissions standards	consult companies on greenhouse gas emission compliance, gather and analyze data

Jobs for Workers with Higher Education (continued)

Job Title	Salary	Education Experience	Helpful Experience	Duties
Greenhouse Gas Emissions Report Verifier	$50,000 and up	Bachelor's Degree in Engineering or Science	experience in energy management and efficiency and knowledge of greenhouse gas emissions standards	conduct audits of reported greenhouse gas emissions
Urban Renewal Manager	$73,200– $89,200/ year	Master's Degree in Urban Planning or related field	interest in land use issues	study and make recommendations to cities regarding land use, housing, transportation, and other issues affecting urban planning
Water Resource Policy Specialist and Advocate	$30,000 and up	Master's Degree in Environmental Studies or related field	interest in water resource issues	study water resources in the field and in simulations, and create programs for conserving water resources

Spotlight On: GreenOrder

Location: *New York, NY*

Typical job listings: *Energy Consultant, Marketing Manager*

What they do: *GreenOrder is a consulting firm that helps major companies like DuPont, Ralph Lauren, and General Motors increase the energy efficiency of their manufacturing processes and business practices. They also consult on marketing and communication strategies to help companies get the word out about their sustainability efforts.*

Interesting fact: *GreenOrder was named one of the Foremost World-Changing Agencies by* Fast Company *magazine.*

Website: *www.greenorder.com*

Section 8: Entrepreneurial

Green Quotes

The timing couldn't be better for those contemplating a leap into green business. The $787 billion federal stimulus bill will make funding available for everything from green construction to alternative fuels, and consumer demand for green products continues to rise. But keeping an eye on the (triple) bottom-line: people, the planet, and profits, is a necessary step to success.
—Lydia Dishman, "Turning a Green Business Into Gold,"
Entrepreneur Magazine, *August 13, 2009*

In every state in the union, green businesses are cropping up to meet the demand for alternative energy and energy-efficient products. The $80 billion in the ARRA stimulus package targeted toward renewable energy projects is a nice incentive for anyone thinking of starting a green business; that kind of investment from the government says the country is serious about building our sustainable infrastructure. And it's not just government that's getting in on the act. Venture capitalist firms are throwing money hand-over-fist into what they predict will be highly profitable clean tech investments. If you can find the right product or service to provide, the chances of getting your company off the ground have never been better.

Businesses in Demand

The biggest recipient of the federal windfall and venture capital dollars is likely to be clean tech firms, notably solar, wind, smart grid technology, and biofuels. In the third quarter of 2009, investments in clean tech rose to $1.9 billion, an incredible amount of activity during an otherwise slow period of business investment. Other industries that saw a large amount of investment in 2009 included transportation and green building materials.

On a local level, companies that retrofit buildings for energy efficiency are guaranteed to be in high demand for the foreseeable future. All you need to start a retrofitting business is construction experience, certification, and knowledge of the latest energy-efficient building techniques. As one of the biggest bang for your buck opportunities, retrofitting is attractive to building owners and investors alike. At the 2009 Clinton Global Initiative meeting, organizations like Pegasus Sustainable Century and the Jack D. Hidary Foundation pledged millions of dollars to retrofitting projects.

The great thing about starting a green business right now is that ideas don't necessarily need to be revolutionary to increase our energy efficiency and make money. The move to sustainable energy will require a million little tweaks to everything in our lives. It's up to you as a green entrepreneur to find the tweak that can launch a lucrative business.

Green Quotes

We're calling on small businesses to lead the recovery and do it with green jobs and clean energy innovation. Targeting the recovery with green businesses is the most practical way to get the economy going.

—Byron Kennard, executive director of the
  Center for Small Business and the Environment

Getting Started

The most important thing to do before you start your green business is to research, research, research. Read up on other companies that are working on green products and services. Talk to people who work in environmental businesses and find out what kinds of tools they feel would help them do their jobs. Pay attention to the latest trends in sustainable energy and green products and try to figure out if there's something you could do just a little bit better than everyone else.

Once you've figured out what your business will do, start working on a business plan. Be practical about your goals; although your idea may be brilliant enough to secure a multimillion dollar investment from a venture capital firm, you won't get your foot in the door without a solid foundation. Find a mentor in your business who can help guide you through the stages of starting a business. You'd be surprised at how many people are willing to share their knowledge if you respectfully ask for their help.

No matter what business you choose to start, remember that it's important to "walk the walk." You probably wouldn't go to a dentist who had rotten teeth; likewise, it's doubtful your green business will get many repeat customers if you run it in a wasteful manner. Lead by example, and keep your practices efficient.

Conferences and Trade Shows

Conferences and trade shows are a great way to see what kinds of products and services are available and to talk to other business owners. Seeing what kinds of companies are in the market can spur creative thinking and introduce you to excellent resources for green business information. New green conferences and trade shows are being announced every day; following are listed a few of the most popular.

Building Energy Conference

Who it's for: Architects, engineers, planners, scientists, or anyone interested in green building

Website: www.buildingenergy.nesea.org/

Fortune Magazine's Brainstorm: GREEN

Who it's for: Business leaders, environmentalists

Website: www.timeinc.net/fortune/conferences/brainstormgreen/green_home.html

Green Business Conference

Who it's for: Green business owners or anyone interested in starting a green business

Website: www.greenamericatoday.org/cabn/conference/

Green Jobs Conference

Who it's for: Community and business leaders, union members, environmentalists

Website: www.greenjobsconference.org/

Green Manufacturing Expo

Who it's for: Energy consultants, energy software developers, green manufacturers

Website: www.devicelink.com/expo/gmx10

Greenbuild Expo

Who it's for: Architects, contractors, developers, engineers, builders, students, urban planners

Website: www.greenbuildexpo.org

NAHB National Green Building Conference

Who it's for: Architects, builders, land planners, energy efficient product manufacturers

Website: www.nahb.org/conference_details.aspx?conferenceID=59

Opportunity Green

Who it's for: Business owners and anyone interested in starting a green business

Website: www.opportunitygreen.com

West Coast Green

Who it's for: Green innovators, business leaders, and entrepreneurs

Website: www.westcoastgreen.com/

CHAPTER FOUR

LEARNING THE ROPES: GETTING A GREEN EDUCATION

Chapter Overview

Before we can march bravely into our green energy future, there's a lot we will have to learn. From high schools to community colleges to trade schools to universities, America's centers of education are stepping up to equip students and workers with the skills they'll need to make it in the new economy. In this chapter, we look at some of the information green workers are expected to know in various fields. We also examine some of the learning opportunities available around the United States, including the best free training opportunities, community college programs, and four-year programs.

Section 1: Building and Skilled Trades

As we saw in the previous chapter, many of the most immediate green opportunities are in traditional blue-collar areas like roofing, plumbing, and energy auditing. Workers who are interested in a career in these green-collar fields can increase their opportunities exponentially with job-specific training, such as apprenticeships and certification. In this section, we look at how to get started in an apprenticeship and examine the new certifications that are becoming requirements for the next generation of builders and skilled tradespeople.

Section 2: College Programs

Colleges have always been early adopters of societal change. America's universities and colleges have been leading the charge to green up their campuses for many years. However, until recently, there were only a handful of dedicated schools around the country that put as much energy into their environmental studies programs as they put into their campus policies. With the sudden influx of green opportunities, however, education providers everywhere are getting in on the green act, offering classes with names like Introduction to Sustainable Development, Environmental Writing, and Environmental Racism and Justice. In this section, we examine 12 public and private colleges that are training today's students to become tomorrow's leaders in renewable energy and sustainability.

Section 3: Other Educational Opportunities

There are other ways to learn green jobs skills than entering an extended apprenticeship or a four-year college. From community colleges to the year-long Greencorps training program, there are classes and training programs available to suit any schedule. You just have to know where to look. Section 3 examines alternative ways to start learning about and preparing for a green career.

Section 1: Building and Skilled Trades

The United States would not have a strong middle class if it weren't for blue-collar workers, but with traditional blue-collar jobs being shipped overseas in record numbers, the middle class is struggling to keep its head above water. Many green job advocates believe that the building and skilled trade jobs created by the green economy may be the thing that saves the U.S. middle class from extinction. The workplace has changed considerably since the middle class's post–World War II heyday, however, and the modern job seeker needs to adapt to an environment in which jobs are more competitive. As of this writing, U.S. unemployment rates are still hovering around an astronomical 10%. Today, it isn't enough to just show up at an employer's doorstep and sign in; if you really want to get your foot in the door of the green economy right now, you'll need to get some training.

Eco-Quiz

Which type of investment produces the most bang for your buck in terms of job creation?

a. *Transit/rail*

b. *Building retrofits*

c. *Biomass*

d. *Solar*

Answer: a. *Transit/rail. According to a study by the University of Massachusetts Amherst and the Center for American Progress, every $1 million investment in mass transit and rail creates 22 jobs. That same investment will create 17 jobs in building retrofits and biomass, and 14 jobs in solar.*

In Their Own Words: Jon Brophy, Environmental Management and Sustainability Master's Degree student at the Illinois Institute of Technology's Stuart School of Business

So you're following a green career path in school right now?

Yeah, I'm actually connected to the field in a few ways. I'm working for I-GO car sharing, which prides itself on being a low-cost, retail friendly model of car shared ownership. I'm also an intern for the City of Chicago's Department of the Environment in their energy and air quality division, where I'm mostly working on building out the different businesses and government fleets with electric vehicles. And then for school, I'm going to the Illinois Institute of Technology's Stuart School of Business, for an Environmental Management and Sustainability Master's Degree.

How did you get started on this path?

Well, I was a lifeguard when I was 16, until about 21, over the summers. And I was noticing more and more that the beaches would have closings over the summer because of increasing amounts of *e. coli* in the water. Also that the water level was dropping from year to year. And we're talking about Lake Michigan, you know—it's not a small lake. So I took an environmental law class at Boston College, and I figured out that whenever it rains heavily, they open up the locks from the Chicago River, and all the raw sewage gets dumped into the lake. They don't have to account for it because it's not a point source of pollution. It's a nice little legislative loophole that's been created and upheld by the Supreme Court of the United States. So I started looking into this, and the more I learned about it, the more interesting it became. And then I found this program through IIT and it included information about wind, solar, environmental management—everything. It was exactly what I wanted to learn.

How has the experience been?

It's been insane. The classes are amazing. I've been working my ass off, but the door will just be opened wide after this. We did a business project for an electric vehicle company. We got to go to Pittsburgh Carnegie Mellon to present for a competition over there. Out of that came a bunch of opportunities, including working as an intern for the city, which I think is going to be really helpful when I graduate.

So you're working two jobs and going to school full time at the same time?

Yeah. And I've got a girlfriend. She's very understanding. [*Laughs*] But you know, now's the time to go after the degree. It's going to be worth it at some point, and it's actually worth it now, 'cause I'm having fun. No time like the present.

As someone who's in school right now, what do you say the climate's like with your classmates? Are people worried about getting jobs out of school?

Well, we want climate change legislation to be passed, 'cause that would basically guarantee everything, and we'd be gold when we graduate. That would be nice. But really the biggest problem people have is that some of the classes focus a little bit on the gloom and doom scenarios. You know, like the oceans are going to become too acidic for fish to live in them, or that the polar ice caps are going to melt and not regenerate. But I believe there's a lot of opportunity to stop the world from screwing itself up. Mine is a very entrepreneurial group. So I think everybody's a little upbeat. There are not a lot of people who are too worried about what's going to happen after they graduate. The practicality of it is that it's going to take awhile to get the high salary job, but hopefully it will happen.

So do you feel you're being prepared more to go out and start your own thing, than to fit into a mold at some company?

A little bit of both. IIT is great, 'cause we have an engineering school, a business school, and a design school, and we're actually in the same building at Kent Law School. So really, education is whatever you want to do with it. You can talk to any professor in any department, so if you want to get into the law aspect, you can; if you want to get involved in the corporate world, to be a Sustainability Coordinator for Coca-Cola, you could do that. It's not just the hippie stuff. You can also do practical health and safety studies.

Your degree is flexible enough that if you got out of school and started looking around, you'd have a good background for a number of different jobs.

Right, yeah, almost any. It's almost like how engineers get out of school and now they think like an engineer. You kind of think, "How do we increase the energy of sunlight? How do we make the environment cleaner?" And it can be applied to any business, any government, any neighborhood, any system in general. So hopefully, I'm just beginning to look at things differently.

There are some concrete skills that people in my degree program are going to be missing, but I'm sure there's going to be on-the-job training wherever you head. And once people get loans for things, there will be a lot of people working for themselves. The people in the classes come from every background. There are engineers, lawyers, educators. It's a lot of money to dump on a degree, but it's good to have something that's relatively concrete in terms of training.

Do you have any advice for someone who wants to get involved in green jobs or clean-tech jobs? Is there anything you'd recommend that they think about?

Well, I know there are colleges that are starting to offer green careers as a major. A lot of junior colleges, too, are doing specific training like wind turbine technician, solar installer. And those guys are going to have a more guaranteed job than I will. 'Cause you can always cut a manager loose, but the installers will still be needed.

I guess I would say don't necessarily just put your head down and drop into a four-year void of whatever they tell you 'cause you're going to learn almost as much from the Sustainability Coordinator at your school as you would in your classes. Or go to a junior college for two years and become a wind turbine technician. If you want to go into a four-year program after that, you can go that route, but as a starting point, it'll be cheaper, and you'll be qualified for a job for the rest of your life.

Apprenticeships

As long as there have been trades in America, there have been apprentices. (In fact, apprentices have been around since the Middle Ages, although back then, apprenticeship was a younger man's game: seven to 10 years old, to be exact!). Notable Americans who have spent time as apprentices include Benjamin Franklin (printing), George Washington (surveying), and Henry Ford (machining). The modern apprenticeship era dates to 1937, when Congress passed the National Apprenticeship Act, which establishes regulations for apprenticeships and on-the-job training programs.

So what exactly is an apprentice? A Registered Apprentice is a worker-in-training under the supervision of a trade professional in any career that requires specialized knowledge. A wide range of careers incorporate apprenticeship programs, from electricians to chefs to dental assistants to carpenters. Apprentices receive valuable on-the-job experience, certification, a paycheck, and, in many cases, college credit. In addition, many Registered Apprenticeship programs require apprentices to spend time working for the employer who trained them, guaranteeing an immediate job after certification.

Aspiring apprentices can begin training as early as 16, although certain hazardous occupations set the minimum age at 18. Registered Apprenticeship programs are sponsored by employers, employer associations, and labor–management organizations. Qualifications vary by employer, but most apprenticeship programs require applicants to have a high school diploma or GED.

For more information about apprenticeship programs, visit the Department of Labor's Office of Apprenticeship at www.doleta.gov/oa/. A list of occupations that incorporate Registered Apprenticeship programs can be found at www.iowaworkforce.org/apprenticeship/apprenticeableoccupations.pdf. If you would like to apply for a Registered Apprenticeship program, you should start by looking through the list of occupations and find the jobs that interest you. Then, do some research on those occupations to find out which employers in your area sponsor Registered Apprenticeship programs in your fields of choice, and get in touch with those employers to find out how to apply. If you're specifically interested in a green career, be sure to find out whether your employer offers training in sustainable and energy-efficient practices and technology.

Sustainable Energy and Building Certifications

The movement toward green building has brought with it a number of new types of certification for builders and sustainable energy workers. Because codes and regulations are not standardized across the country, it can be difficult for workers to determine what credentials will make them the most attractive to potential employers. Over the next few pages, I discuss the most common new certifications and how you can get certified.

LEED

The godfather of all sustainable building standards is the U.S. Green Building Council's (USGBC) Leadership in Energy and Environmental Design (LEED) standard. The USGBC is a nonprofit organization that

Did You Know? In 2007, Sheikh Mohammed bin Rashid Al Maktoum, the prime minister of the United Arab Emirates, mandated that all new buildings in the UAE must meet LEED standards. Dubai, one of the seven United Arab Emirates, has the largest construction growth in the world, making the UAE the world leader in green building.

was formed "to transform the way buildings and communities are designed, built, and operated, enabling an environmentally and socially responsible, healthy, and prosperous environment that improves the quality of life." The first LEED set of standards, known as LEED Version 1.0, was launched in 1998. Since then, LEED has become the most well-recognized worldwide standard for environmentally sustainable construction, with over 35,000 participating projects in 91 countries. In April 2009, LEED launched its latest set of standards: LEED V3. The new version of LEED incorporates the latest technologies and construction techniques to create the most sustainable set of building standards to date.

LEED for Buildings   LEED V3 certification for buildings concentrates on seven key areas.

1. *Sustainable Sites:* ensuring that the building is being built on land that does not negatively impact local resources or create environmental pollution.

2. *Water Efficiency:* ensuring that toilets, faucets, showerheads, and so on use water in an efficient manner.

3. *Energy and Atmosphere:* ensuring that electrical systems are efficient and do not have a negative impact on the climate or ozone layer.

4. *Materials and Resources:* ensuring that waste is collected and recycled or disposed of properly; using recycled, reused, or sustainable materials in building.

5. *Indoor Environmental Quality:* ensuring high air quality for building residents, workers, and visitors through the use of proper ventilation and efficient HVAC design.

6. *Innovation in Design:* going above and beyond LEED standards through creative design.

7. *Regional Priority:* being designated an environmentally important building for a specific region.

Projects that are aiming for LEED certification are inspected and given points according to these criteria. Buildings that receive less than 40 points are not considered up to LEED standards. Buildings receiving 40–49 points are designated LEED Certified, 50–59 points are designated LEED Silver, 60–79 points are designated LEED Gold, and 80 points and above are designated LEED Platinum, the highest level of building efficiency possible. Although the program is strictly voluntary, the number of projects being built according to LEED standards is rising every day, in the assumption that what is voluntary today will become mandatory tomorrow.

LEED for Workers What does this mean for job seekers? In addition to the LEED building certification, LEED also has an accreditation program for builders and architects. There are currently two different types of accreditation.

1. *LEED Green Associate:* LEED Green Associate accreditation is for "professionals who want to demonstrate green building expertise in non-technical fields of practice." In order to become an accredited LEED Green Associate, candidates must pass a 100-question multiple-choice test featuring questions about sustainable building practices and LEED standards. Any type of worker can take the LEED Green Associate test, as long as he or she has worked on a LEED-registered project, been previously employed in a sustainable field of work, or is enrolled in a green-building educational program.

2. *LEED Accredited Professional:* LEED AP certification "signifies an advanced depth of knowledge in green building practices." In order to become a LEED Accredited Professional, candidates must pass both the LEED Green Associate exam and one of five job-specific exams, such as Operations and Maintenance, or Interior Design and Construction. To take the LEED Accredited Professional, the worker should have a history of leadership roles on LEED certified projects.

For workers interested in taking the LEED Green Associate exam, the green-building educational requirement can be satisfied by taking one of the many LEED workshops offered by the USGBC. These workshops are offered in cities across the country; visit the USGBC website for more information.

Although it is not imperative that builders get LEED accredited, anyone looking to have an advantage in a competitive marketplace would be wise to get his or her accreditation. It's not cheap; the exam costs $200 to take, plus another $200 for the study guide, but by all indications, LEED standards are here to stay, and getting accredited will show employers that you could be a serious asset for their company.

Further information can be found at www.usgbc.org and www.gbci.org.

RESNET

RESNET, or the Residential Energy Services Network, is an organization that rates homes according to their energy efficiency. The agency analyzes residential buildings according to its HERS (Home Energy Rating System) index, which measures homes from 0 (using no purchased energy) to 100 (Standard American Building). Older homes can go over 100, but for the most part, new buildings fall within the 0–100 range. The HERS index is based on the Energy Star guidelines, a set of energy-efficiency guidelines established by the EPA and the U.S. Department of Energy.

RESNET currently offers four different kinds of certification.

1. *Certified Rater:* Certified Home Energy Raters are accredited to "inspect and evaluate a home's energy features, prepare a home energy rating and make recommendations for improvements that will save the homeowner energy and money." In order to become an accredited Rater, workers must take a RESNET training class from a registered Rater Training Provider and pass a 50-question true/false and multiple-choice test. After passing the test, candidates must perform three probationary ratings; assuming those go well, Raters will enlist with a local Rater Provider and receive their certification.

2. *Rating Field Inspector:* Field Inspectors work directly underneath Certified Raters to inspect homes for energy ratings. The Field Inspector level is considered the entry level to becoming a Certified Rater. Accredited Field Inspectors are required to pass a 50-question true/false and multiple-choice test.

3. *Home Energy Survey Professional:* Home Energy Survey Professionals ensure the quality of home energy surveys performed by Certified Raters. Accredited Home Energy Survey Professionals are required to pass a 50-question online test.

4. *Quality Assurance Designee/Trainer:* QA Designee/Trainers are allowed to administer the RESNET tests to potential RESNET providers. Accredited QA Designee/Trainers are required to pass a 100-question open-book test.

RESNET certification can be attained in a fairly short period of time, from training to the probationary ratings. Although the training courses and equipment require an initial investment of a few thousand dollars, RESNET is intent on preparing its workers for the future, including training them to conduct emissions audits for the cap and trade system. Unlike LEED, RESNET certification requires no educational or construction background, making it a great place to start for people looking to get involved in energy auditing.

Further information can be found at www.natresnet.org.

BPI

The Building Performance Institute accredits contractors to "diagnose the critical performance factors of a building that can impact health, safety, comfort, energy efficiency, and durability." BPI training focuses on the interrelationship between the systems in a house and how problems in one system affect the efficiency of the other systems in the network.

BPI certifications are broken down into two different models: Residential Homes and Multifamily Buildings.

1. *Residential Homes:* There are five different types of certifications for residential home energy analysts: Building Analyst Professional, Envelope (the area between the interior and exterior of a building) Professional, Manufactured Housing Professional, Heating Professional, and A/C or Heat Pump Professional. Candidates for certification are required to complete a field examination and a 100-question multiple-choice exam.

2. *Multifamily Buildings:* There are four additional certifications for multifamily homes: Building Analyst, Energy Efficient Building Operations, Hydronic Heating System Design, and Advanced Heating Plant Technician. To qualify for multifamily certification, candidates must have certification in one of the Residential Homes areas.

BPI training and certification focuses on the *house-as-a-system* concept, teaching analysts to look at the relationship between systems in a house to determine how these systems can function together in the most energy-efficient manner. Because of the holistic nature of the BPI approach, BPI certification is advantageous to workers looking to get involved in retrofitting houses.

For further information, visit www.bpi.org.

AEE

The Association of Energy Engineers' mission is "to promote the scientific and educational interests of those engaged in the energy industry and to foster action for sustainable development." They offer an exhaustive list of 14 different types of certifications for energy workers: Certified Energy Manager, Energy Manager in Training, Certified Sustainable Development Professional, Certified Carbon Reduction Manager, Certified Energy Auditor, Certified Building Commissioning Professional, Certified Business Energy Professional, Certified Measurement and Verification Professional, Certified Energy Procurement Professional, Certified Lighting Efficiency Professional, Distributed Generation

Certified Professional, Certified Green Building Engineer, Certified GeoExchange Designer, and Certified Power Quality Professional. Some of these certifications, like Energy Manager in Training and Certified Business Energy Professional, can be attained through a combination of tests and training courses, while other certifications are reserved for candidates with higher degrees or years of experience.

For further information on AEE certifications and training, visit www.aeecenter.org.

NABCEP

The North American Board of Certified Energy Practitioners (NABCEP) is an organization for members of the solar energy industry. It certifies workers to install solar energy systems. NABCEP currently offers three different types of certification.

1. *Entry-Level Certificate:* The Entry Level Certificate program is the lowest level of certification. It demonstrates basic knowledge of solar system operations. Applicants for Entry-Level Certificates are required to complete an approved course on solar power systems.

2. *PV Installer Certification:* PV (photovoltaic) Installers are responsible for supervising installation of photovoltaic systems. To attain PV Installer certification, workers must have at least two years of experience working in the field of electrical construction, or at least 40 hours of training. Candidates are then required to pass a multiple-choice test of approximately 60 questions.

3. *Solar Thermal Installer Certification:* Solar Thermal Installers are responsible for supervising installation of solar thermal systems. To attain Solar Thermal Installer certification, workers must have at least two years of experience working in the field of electrical construction, or at least 40 hours of training. Candi-

Green Quotes
Achievable gains in energy efficiency, renewable energy, forest conservation, and sustainable land use worldwide could achieve up to 75 percent of needed global emissions reductions in 2020 at a net savings of $14 billion.
—From "Meeting the Climate Challenge," an October 2009 joint report by the Center for American Progress and the United Nations Foundation

dates are then required to pass a multiple-choice test of approximately 60 questions.

For workers who would like to get into solar energy installation, NABCEP certification is essential. NABCEP certifications are the industrywide standard, and as the solar industry grows, NABCEP is certain to grow with it.

Further information can be found at www.nabcep.org.

Green Quotes

A 2009 survey by the Association of Energy Engineers found that 72% of respondents "indicate a heightened shortage of qualified professionals in the energy-efficiency and renewable energy fields in the next five years," while 70% of respondents "indicate a need for national and state training for 'Green Jobs' to address job shortages that are impairing growth in green industries."

—"Green Jobs: Survey of the Energy Industry—Relevant Trends, Opportunities, Projections, and Resources," *a report presented by the Association of Energy Engineers*

MREA

It is interesting that solar is the only sustainable energy industry that has national certification standards. Across the United States, however, there are regional organizations that have developed their own certifications for renewable energy workers. One such organization is the Midwest Renewable Energy Association. Despite the organization's regional name, MREA Site Assessor certifications are valid across the United States.

This group offers certifications for Site Assessors in five different fields: Photovoltaic, Solar Hot Water, Wind, Non-Residential Photovoltaic, and Non-Residential Solar Hot Water. Each of these positions involves assessing building sites to evaluate the best locations for renewable energy systems, cost analysis, and creation of site assessment reports.

Candidates for MREA Site Assessor certification must complete an MREA course or have documented proof of on-the-job experience. They must then pass a multiple-choice test and submit two practice assessment reports.

For further information on MREA certifications, visit www.the-mrea.org.

Section 2: Colleges

In the past few years, the number of colleges offering four-year degrees in the fields of environmental studies and sustainable energy has exploded. The 13 colleges and universities described on the following pages offer some of the most esteemed green-centric educational programs in the United States, preparing students for a range of environmentally conscious professions, from business to engineering to public policy. Visit the schools' websites for more information on how you can apply.

A note about Environmental Studies: many of these schools offer generalized environmental degrees, such as Environmental Studies or College of the Atlantic's Human Ecology major. As with any other liberal arts degree, these degrees are not necessarily formulated to train students for specific job titles, as opposed to, say, engineering or chemistry degrees. However, Environmental Studies and similar majors are great preparation for students hoping to work in nontechnical green fields, such as policy, advocacy, business, or environmental law.

Public Schools

Appalachian State University

Location: Boone, North Carolina
Since 1991, Appalachian State University has allowed students to concentrate or minor in Sustainable Development, and in 2008, the school established undergraduate degrees in this discipline. The school's program emphasizes the interaction of "environment, economics, and social equity" to prepare students for careers in the sustainable energy economy. Its Bachelor of Science degree in Agroecology and Sustainable Agriculture is one of the premier sustainable agriculture programs in the country, and it also offers a concentration in Appropriate Technology where students can study the technology behind renewable energy sources like solar, wind, and hydropower.

Cost: Tuition and fees run about $2,000/year for in-state students and $7,600 for out-of-state students.

Claim to fame: Appalachian State University has been rated one of the 50 best values for public colleges and universities by *Consumer's Digest*.

Website: susdev.appstate.edu/

Arizona State University School of Sustainability

Location: Tempe, Arizona

Established in 2007, ASU's School of Sustainability is the first school in the United States to offer dedicated degrees in Sustainability. The school is an outgrowth of ASU's Global Institute of Sustainability, a research and education center that was established in 2004 to study environmental issues in urban areas. ASU's SoS offers undergraduate and graduate degrees in Sustainability with the goal of "creating and sharing knowledge, training a new generation of scholars and practitioners, and developing practical solutions to the most pressing environmental, economic, and social challenges of sustainability—especially as they relate to urban areas."

Cost: Yearly tuition and fees cost about $3,400 for residents, and $9,800 for nonresidents.

Claim to fame: In 2009, ASU was named one of the top 20 "coolest schools" in the United States for their environmental efforts and policies.

Website: schoolofsustainability.asu.edu

Evergreen State College

Location: Olympia, Washington

Located just west of picturesque Olympia, Washington, Evergreen State takes full advantage of its natural setting in its well-respected environmental studies and sustainable energies programs. The school enrolls about 4,400 students from around the world on its 1,000 acre campus, the largest of any public four-year school in Washington. Their environmental studies program offers classes in a full range of environmental-related concentrations, from economics to land-use planning and policy. Evergreen's commitment to the environment extends beyond the classroom; the school is working toward having a "climate-neutral" campus, and 100% of the school's energy is already being generated from sustainable sources.

Cost: Tuition, room, board, and assorted costs for a year at Evergreen State come to about $17,500 for Washington residents and $28,500 for nonresidents.

Claim to fame: In 2005, Evergreen State was ranked #15 on *U.S. News and World Report*'s list of schools whose graduates leave with the lowest amount of debt.

Website: www.evergreen.edu

University of Colorado at Boulder

Location: Boulder, Colorado

UC Boulder has been one of the leading universities for environmental studies since it created the Conservation Education major in 1951. It is consistently given high marks for its on-campus sustainability efforts, including the first college recycling program in the nation. The school even has a dedicated Environmental Center to educate students and the community about environmental issues. UC Boulder offers a range of environmental majors, including Environmental Design, Environmental Engineering, and Environmental Studies.

Cost: Tuition, fees, room, board, and books at UC Boulder come to about $20,000 for in-state students and $40,300 for nonresidents.

Claim to fame: UC Boulder was ranked #1 on *Sierra* magazine's 2009 list of "coolest schools" in the U.S. for their environmental efforts and policies.

Website: www.colorado.edu

Did You Know?

As universities have been looking at ways to increase efficiency, many have found one culprit in particular that generates a lot of waste: lunch trays. A survey by the Sustainable Endowments Institute found that 126 of the 300 colleges with the largest endowments have banned lunch trays in their cafeterias, as of 2009. After banning the trays, schools have seen shorter lines and less beverage consumption. West Virginia University reported a 41% reduction in waste at cafeterias that did not use trays.

University of Illinois

Location: Urbana, Illinois

University of Illinois' Department of Civil and Environmental Engineering (CEE) has long been a world leader in training students for civil and environmental engineering jobs. CEE graduates have worked on some of the most well-known structures in the United States, including the Golden Gate Bridge, the Hoover Dam, and the New York subway system. The college offers seven areas of study: Construction Management, Construction Materials, Environmental Engineering and Science, Environmental Hydrology and Hydraulic Engineering, Geotechnical Engineering, Structural Engineering, and Transportation, with an emphasis on sustainable practices.

Cost: In-state students pay about $30,000/year for tuition, fees, books, and room and board, while nonresidents can expect to pay more like $44,100 each year.

Claim to fame: U.S. News and World Report ranked the University of Illinois #2 on its 2009 list of the country's 10 best Environmental Engineering programs.

University of Washington College of the Environment

Location: Seattle, Washington

University of Washington's College of the Environment is "committed to creating future leaders, steeped in basic science and critical thinking, and focused on developing sustainable solutions to the critical challenges of our time." The college concentrates on the science of environmental studies, with departments in Forest Resources, Climate Change, Marine Affairs, and more. Their esteemed faculty includes members of the American Academy of Arts and Sciences and the National Academy of Sciences, a MacArthur Foundation Fellow, and five Fulbright Fellows.

Cost: For books, room, board, tuition, and transportation, at the University of Washington, Washington residents pay about $24,400, and out-of-state students pay about $42,000.

Claim to fame: The University of Washington was given special recognition as an Overall College Sustainability Leader by the Sustainable Endowments Institute.

Website: coenv.washington.edu

Private Schools

Aquinas College

Location: Grand Rapids, Michigan

In 2003, Aquinas College became the first college in the nation to offer an undergraduate major in Sustainable Business. Sustainable Business majors study business practices that "concurrently build profitability and economic stability, restore the health of natural systems, and promote prosperous communities." An internship is a requirement for all Sustainable Business majors, so students are assured the opportunity for real world experience that can help when it's time to search for a job.

Cost: Room, board and fees at Aquinas College come to about $29,300 per year.

Claim to fame: Aquinas College began life in 1886 as a teaching school for nuns.

Website: www.aquinas.edu

College of the Atlantic

Location: Bar Harbor, Maine

If you're looking for the stereotypical college experience where classes are conducted in lecture halls and you're surrounded by other students, College of the Atlantic probably won't be up your alley. There are only about 300 students at College of the Atlantic, and all share the same major—Human Ecology. However, the college's excellent environmental studies and marine science programs have made it one of the country's best schools for green studies. Although all students graduate with degrees in Human Ecology, they may specialize in a number of ecologically minded focus areas, including Field Ecology and Conservation Biology, Sustainable Business, and Ecological Policy and Planning.

Cost: Tuition, room, board, and fees at College of the Atlantic cost $41,550/year. The college offers financial aid to about 80% of its students.

Claim to fame: In 2008, College of the Atlantic was ranked one of the "best education values in the country" by *The Princeton Review.*

Website: www.coa.edu

Green Mountain College

Location: Poultney, Vermont

For students looking to get a full immersion in green education, Green Mountain College is as green as they come. In addition to their chosen concentrations, all Green Mountain students are required to complete a 37-credit Environmental Liberal Arts (ELA) General Education Program with an emphasis on field studies and community service. The ELA program is composed of four core courses that study environmental aspects of literature, culture, philosophy, and science. The school also offers majors in Environmental Studies, Environmental Management, and Natural Resources Management.

Cost: Tuition, room, board, and fees at Green Mountain College cost about $36,500 per year.

Claim to fame: In 2009, Green Mountain College was one of three schools in North America to receive a Sustainability Innovator Award from the Sustainable Endowments Institute.

Website: www.greenmtn.edu

Middlebury College

Location: Middlebury, Vermont

In 1965, Middlebury became the first school in the country to offer a degree in environmental studies. Today, Middlebury remains a leader in environmental education, offering environmental studies concentrations ranging from Conservation and Environmental Policy to environmental nonfiction. The Environmental Studies Center is headquartered in a recently renovated 1875 farmhouse that was retrofitted for energy and water efficiency. Middlebury is located in the basin of Lake Champlain near the Adirondack and Taconic mountain ranges, providing students with the opportunity to get real world experience with a wide variety of climates and topographies.

Cost: An education at Middlebury isn't cheap—a year's tuition, room, and board will run you $50,400—but the school is generous with its financial aid. In 2008, Middlebury gave financial assistance to more than 43% of its student body.

Claim to fame: Middlebury was ranked #2 on Grist's 2009 list of 15 Greenest Colleges and Universities.

Website: www.middlebury.edu/academics/ump/majors/es/

Eco-Quiz

Which school was the first carbon neutral college in the United States?

a. *Evergreen State*

b. *University of Washington*

c. *College of the Atlantic*

d. *Tufts University*

Answer: c. *College of the Atlantic. College of the Atlantic became completely carbon neutral in 2007. They accomplished this by producing its electricity from hydropower, increasing efficiency of campus buildings, and even offsetting emissions generated by the travel of prospective students.*

Northland College

Location: Ashland, Wisconsin

Northland's stated mission is to "integrate liberal arts studies with an environmental emphasis, enabling those it serves to address the challenges of the future." The school offers a variety of environmental-minded classes, such as Sustainable Business, Sustainable Agriculture, and the physics of Renewable Energy. Students can choose to major in a variety of different concentrations, including Natural Resources, Sustainable Community Development, and Environmental Science.

Cost: Tuition, fees, room, and board at Northland cost about $30,800 per year.

Claim to fame: Treehugger.com ranked Northland #1 in its list of 10 Best College Environmental Programs in the United States.

Website: www.northland.edu

Oberlin College

Location: Oberlin, Ohio

Oberlin College has received a lot of praise from environmental leaders for its Adam Joseph Lewis Center (AJLC), an "integrated building–landscape system" that is the center of Oberlin's Environmental Studies department. Since its opening in 2000, the AJLC has provided a hands-on workshop for Oberlin's Environmental Studies majors in sustainable design, energy consumption, and the interrelationship among building systems. Oberlin's Environmental Studies program focuses on the concept of "ecological design," which seeks to find ways to "remake the human presence in the world in ways that are both socially just and environmentally sustainable."

Cost: A year of tuition, room, board, and fees at Oberlin costs about $50,500.

Claim to fame: The AJLC was named one of the 30 milestone buildings of the twentieth century by the U.S. Department of Energy.

Website: new.oberlin.edu

Tufts University

Location: Somerville, Massachusetts

Established in 1984, Tufts University's Environmental Studies program is one of the oldest multidisciplinary environmental studies programs in the country. Environmental Studies majors can choose to concentrate in one of three tracks: Environmental Science, Environment and Technology, or Environment and Society. In addition, the school offers several highly regarded graduate programs in topics like urban planning (Urban and Environmental Policy and Planning), water conservation (Water: Systems, Science, and Society), and agriculture (Agriculture, Food, and Environment).

Cost: As with most other private universities, enrollment at Tufts isn't cheap; one year of tuition, fees, room, board, and books will run you about $50,000.

Claim to fame: Tufts University was listed by Treehugger.com as one of the 10 greenest schools in the United States.

Website: environment.tufts.edu

Section 3: Other Educational Opportunities

Read enough articles and studies about the future of the green jobs and you'll see one word repeated again and again: *training*. Everyone agrees that we need to train workers to do green jobs. But where does someone go to get this training? Apprenticeships and four-year college programs are great for people who are interested in moving into an entirely new field, but what if you'd like to take the skills you already have and apply them to a green career?

The answer depends on where you live and what you do. The good news is that, since the passage of the Green Jobs Act in 2007, there has been a nationwide effort to create green job training programs. The bad news is that in order to find out about training programs in your area, you will have to do a little bit of research. The funding for green job training hasn't gone to one particular program; instead, it's been distributed to a variety of sources, such as community colleges, job advocacy organizations, and state unemployment agencies. Listed on the following pages are some resources to learn about green training programs near you.

Community Colleges

According to the American Association of Community Colleges, there are about 1,600 community college campuses in the United States, offering convenient higher learning opportunities for Americans in almost all parts of the country. In a report by the National Council for Workforce Education and the Academy for Educational Development entitled "Going Green: The Vital Role of Community Colleges in Building a Sustainable Future and the Green Workforce," the authors concluded that

> *Community colleges—with their connections to local and regional labor markets and the flexibil-*

Green Quotes
2.3 million people have in recent years found new jobs in the renewable energy sector alone, and the potential for job growth in the sector is huge. Employment in alternative energies may rise to 2.1 million in wind and 6.3 million in solar power by 2030.
—"Green Jobs Facts and Figures," a report by the International Labour Organization

ity to respond to emerging industries and their changing skill needs—are the perfect gateway to good green jobs, preparing workers with the skills and competencies needed for green industries, and ensuring that these industries do not face a shortage of adequately trained workers.

Community colleges all over the country are getting into the act. At St. Louis Community College, administrators are using a $500,000 grant from the EPA to teach a training program in cleaning up brownfield sites. At California's community colleges, the California Clean Energy Workforce Training Program is funding classes that are teaching 5,600 students how to install solar panels, maintain electric vehicles, and research fuel cell technologies. As the ARRA funds are being distributed, green training programs are cropping up at community colleges across the country; similar programs are likely available at a school near you. To find a list of community colleges in your area, visit www.aacc.nche.edu.

The Workforce Investment Act

The Workforce Investment Act (WIA) was passed in 1998 to provide training for "job seekers, laid off workers, youth, incumbent workers, new entrants to the workforce, veterans, and persons with disabilities" over the age of 18. The Act set up a series of One-Stop Career Centers around the country that provide free or inexpensive training and job search and placement services. To find a list of WIA job training services near you, visit www.careeronestop.org/WiaProviderSearch.asp

Green Corps

For recent college graduates interested in moving into environmental activism, Green Corps is an "intense, one-year experience for recent college graduates that includes eight weeks of classroom training in the tools of environmental activism, rotating field assignments, and placement after graduation." Over the course of a year, Green Corps teaches students the ins and outs of environmental activism, from recruiting and training volunteers to speaking with the media. Although the competition for spots can be fierce, Green Corps pays its trainees ($23,750 for the year) and assists with job placement after the year is done. For more information on Green Corps, visit www.greencorps.org.

Veterans Green Jobs Academy

The Veterans Green Jobs Academy is a new program that trains military veterans to "lead America's transition to energy independence, ecological restoration, community renewal, and economic prosperity." The program incorporates classroom work and on-the-job training, with concentrations in topics like Energy Efficiency and Weatherization and Green Construction and Retrofit. The program is free for veterans, with a living stipend included. At the time of this writing, the Veterans Green Jobs Academy has programs only in Colorado, but they're planning to expand to four additional states by the end of 2010 and all other states thereafter. For more information on the Veterans Green Jobs Academy, visit veteransgreenjobs. org.

Solar Energy International

Solar Energy International (SEI) was founded in 1991 to provide workshops and online courses in renewable energy and sustainable building technologies. SEI teaches hands-on courses in 22 different cities and online courses year round. In spite of the name, the organization is not just committed to solar energy; it also teaches courses on topics like sustainable building and electric vehicle conversion. For more information about Solar Energy International programs, visit www.solarenergy.org.

CHAPTER FIVE

BUILDING A GREEN RESUME

Chapter Overview

How do you stand out in the crowded field of job applicants that you're likely to encounter as you begin your job search? Having the skills and experience to do the job are great, but your abilities won't mean anything unless you can sell yourself to an employer. In this chapter, we take a look at the basics of building resumes and cover letters that will get you hired.

Section 1: Writing a Resume

So you've decided what job you want and you've spent some time learning how to do it. Only one hurdle remains: convincing employers that they should hire you. In this section, you'll learn how to write resumes that will give you the edge on the competition.

Section 2: Writing Cover Letters

In many cases, your cover letter will be the first contact you'll have with a potential employer. If you're going to break through the clutter, you should plan to wow them from the minute they open your letter or e-mail. This section will give you some helpful tips for crafting cover letters that introduce you in style.

Section 3: Greening Your Resume and Cover Letters

When you are applying for a green job, your commitment to the environment should be clear to your future employer. This section will cover some different ways for putting your green experience front and center in your resume and cover letters.

Section 4: Sample Resumes

In Section 4, we look at some basic examples of resumes that you can use to guide your writing process.

In Their Own Words: Tom Savage, Founder and Managing Partner, Bright Green Talent

Bright Green Talent is an executive recruiting firm that specializes in placing workers in green jobs. Tom Savage cofounded Bright Green after starting three successful social businesses in the United Kingdom, including Blue Ventures, an organization that leads volunteers on marine conservation expeditions. In 2007, Savage was named the New Statesman Edge Upstarts Young Social Entrepreneur of the Year. For more information, visit www.tomsavage.co.uk.

I'd love to hear about how Bright Green started. You were formally at Blue Ventures, correct?

Yeah, that's right. I was at Blue Ventures, but just before I started Blue Ventures, I was at Oxford University doing a master's course. One of the lecturers was this guy called Paul Hannam, who'd previously been a very successful recruiter. He had an environmental epiphany one day while he was reading a book, and at that moment he decided to change the pace and the outlook of his life and move toward being somebody who tried to have an impact on the environmental space.

Prior to that, I'd been at Blue Ventures, where we were taking groups of people to Madagascar to work in conservation. But the real focus was using those resources—the people and the knowledge that we had and the money that they paid for the projects—to fund a conservation program that was actually incredibly successful. So [Paul came to me and] said, "Look, I've been looking for someone to start a new recruitment business that's focused on the environment, and I think you're my man. We put a business plan together, he funded the business, and we started it about $2\frac{1}{2}$ years ago.

One of the things that we both feel is that there's a lot of money and great ideas floating around, but really the key to the whole sector is the ability for organizations to capture and utilize the right people in order to make the changes necessary.

You started Bright Green in the United Kingdom, right?
Yes, and about six months later we started in the United States.

And you're in San Francisco now?
Yes.

How did that move happen?
I moved about eight months ago, in February of this year. Recruitment is one of the first things to get hit during a recession, so we made the tough economic decision to focus our attention on the United States for now. We're still working in the United Kingdom, however. I've actually got a few jobs on the docket at the moment that are U.K.-based.

Does it seem like it's promising here? Does it seem like there are jobs coming up?
It's certainly promising. I would say it's still quite bleak at the moment, [but] I think we've got signs of life, and I think everybody feels the green movement is going to be a really exciting, really dynamic, interesting movement. But, you know, the world has gone through a big economic shock, and people are quite cautious. I think people are slow to jump on the bandwagon and start hiring again. Workers are slower to look for new jobs, because they want that job security. Things are coming back online, but I think it's still going to take some time.

Are there any positions you're seeing more demand for?
Yeah, there are a lot of things like environmental engineering and electrical engineering positions. The main growth areas that we're seeing are in HVAC systems, which are air-conditioning, heating, and ventilation

systems within buildings, and so on. There's sustainable transport, particularly companies like Tesla, that are starting to hire people in fuel
cell design and so on. And then there's energy efficiency and clean tech.
There's a lot of work going into smart grid energy efficiency and clean
technologies like renewable energy. Those are the areas where, I think,
engineers and people with very specific training are doing fairly well at
the moment and it's starting to pick up.

**What are some of the things happening out there that you're most
excited about?**
I'm excited about the potential that Copenhagen presents for the various countries of the world. With Copenhagen coming around, we have
another example of awareness coming online. Right now, the govern-
ments of the United Kingdom and the United States are definitely saying
the right thing, but that doesn't always translate into reality.

There's a lot more enlightened thinking around sustainability and corporate social responsibility now, but I think the recession has essentially
forced people back into their shells, rather than allowing them to be bull-
ish, and therefore people are being more protective than perhaps they
were. But I'm an optimist; I think businesses have a huge part to play
in the environmental movement. The private sector is a great lever for
change. I think we're seeing a slight delay in that because of the way the
markets are, but I have hope that they're going to turn around.

**Are you seeing self-regulation in the companies you work with? Has
the culture moved to such a point that companies want to be seen as
environmentally conscious?**
Oh, for sure. All companies want to be seen as environmentally conscious.
You won't find very many companies that don't. I think it has yet to be
seen how deep that environmentalism goes within these companies.

What levels of workers do you try to place?
Up until now we've placed more senior level folks, but that's set slightly
against where we really want to be in maybe five years' time. I think the
real change is going to be seen at lower levels, at putting people back to

work, but traditional recruitment models don't necessarily support that. Now, at Bright Green Talent, one of the things my business partner and I have done is to develop a new way to try to place people at the lower end of the income level. We've come up with something that we're pretty excited about, and, although I don't want to count my chickens, it looks like there's a potential that we might raise some money for that.

What sort of jobs do you see that involving?
I think that would be the "shovel ready" jobs. So, people on the unemployment registers, people who are lower skilled, people who are unemployed, we'd be trying to get them back to work more quickly.

In a perfect world where everyone was hiring, what would you say to someone who was looking to get a green job?
Well, it's kind of hard to project, but the key thing we've found among businesses, is that people are looking for this quite rare combination of business savvy coupled with an environmental leaning. So there are a lot of people who have either an environmental leaning, but don't understand how that fits into the bottom line, or people who are very business-like, but don't know how to translate that into environmental-speak. So if you can tweak your resume to a point where you really get the symbiosis of those two fields—environment and business—that's where companies are most excited about hiring people in the long term. That being said, in terms of candidates for jobs of the moment, they tend to be people with specific skills that maybe they spent five or ten years honing, like engineering or electronics.

Section 1: Writing a Resume

The first step in securing the green career of your dreams is creating a resume. Whether you're looking for a manual labor job or a CEO position, an impressive resume can go a long way toward getting your foot in the door. As Susan Briton Whitcomb writes in *Résumé Magic*, "Writing your resume is an opportunity to write your future."

Before we get to work on crafting your resume, let's examine some popular misconceptions about what resumes should look like.

Misconception #1: It's okay to lie on your resume.
Absolutely 100% false. Your resume should be a true account of your experiences and skills. Filling your resume full of lies is a recipe for disaster; eventually, someone will ask you to prove that you can do what your resume claims you can do. Besides, if you have to lie to get a job, you're probably not qualified for that job in the first place.

This is not to say that your resume should include an extensive list of your faults and weaknesses. You should definitely put your best foot forward in your resume. However, there is a big difference between putting your best foot forward and lying. The key is finding dynamic, interesting ways to describe your accomplishments—even accomplishments that you, yourself, may not find particularly remarkable. Any adult of job-seeking age, just by virtue of having life experience, has accumulated skills that would make that person attractive to an employer if presented in the right way. Granted, it can be difficult to convince someone you can do a job you've never held before; however, you'd be surprised how many employers are willing to take a chance on someone who shows confidence in his or her abilities.

Misconception #2: Resumes should be only one page long.
This one is partly true. If you're just out of school, or you have less than five years of work experience, you should keep your resume to one page. At your age, you probably haven't accumulated the kind of extensive experience that would need to be spread out over two pages. If you've been working for awhile, though, you'll probably find that it's difficult to fit all of your important information onto a single page. In this case, it's far more important to include all of your pertinent qualifications on your resume than to stick to some arbitrary page limit that was

determined in the days before the majority of resumes were sent and received via e-mail. That being said, no employer is going to wade through a complete autobiography of your life; unless you're aiming to be the CEO of a Fortune 500 company, you should be able to fit your resume to a succinct two pages.

Misconception #3: There is a single, universally accepted way of writing a resume.

Actually, there are two different types of resumes—chronological and functional—and each can be tailored to fit your purposes. A *chronological* resume is an ordered list of your past work experience, from most recent job held to oldest. You should create a chronological resume if you have a clear work trajectory that you'd like to highlight; for instance, if you started at one company and moved up the ladder to better positions in the same field. A *functional* resume is a list of work experiences by category, such as Administration, Customer Service, or Sales. Functional resumes are best for employees who have gaps in their work record, or who have a range of experiences in different industries. You can combine elements of each of these formats to suit your purposes; for example, you can begin with a functional list of your skills and end with a chronological list of recent positions held.

Misconception #4: You should have only one resume.

Most career guides and books about resume writing take it for granted that you know exactly what job you're trying to get, and once you get it, you're going to remain in that industry for the rest of your work career. Unfortunately, in today's job market, the ability to have a focused career is becoming a rarity. Unless you've apprenticed in a specific trade or have a specialized degree, it's more likely that you will be looking for a range of different jobs in your field of interest. For this reason, it can be useful to have a few different resumes that emphasize different aspects of your experience.

Green Quotes

The best way to address an employment gap depends on how long you've been out of work. Shorter time frames of up to a year or so aren't absolute necessities to explain on a resume. Hiring managers understand job candidates will have date gaps from time to time, especially when factoring in the jobs lost during this recent recession.

—Teena Rose, director of ExpertResumes .com, as quoted on Monster.com

For instance, as a writer, I split most of my work between educational writing—test prep materials, textbooks, and career guides, like this one—and public relations/advertising work—ad pitches, press releases, marketing materials, and so on. Even though both of these jobs involve writing, most employers want to see that you have concentrated experience in the field for which they're hiring. My advertising clients could not care less that I wrote a spelling book, because they aren't looking for someone to teach spelling. Likewise, my educational clients aren't interested in knowing that I can write press releases, because that isn't what they're hiring me to do. So I have two different resumes: one emphasizing my educational work and one emphasizing my advertising work. If more than one career path fits your skills and interests, you might need to tailor your resume to showcase the skills that are most appropriate to each path.

Misconceptions all cleared up? Good. Then let's get to work!

The Art of Successful Selling

When you start working on your resume, it's important to remember who the audience will be. More likely than not, the person looking at your resume has seen or will see a lot of other candidates with skills similar to yours. With job competition tight all over the country, employers can see hundreds or even thousands of applicants fighting for the same positions. It's an employer's market right now, and if you hope to rise above the fray, you're going to need a resume that tells employers you can do the job better than anyone else.

A resume is more than just a chronological list of your skills and accomplishments. A resume is an advertisement, and *you* are the product. And as any successful salesperson will tell you, you can't sell a product until you know what you're selling. Now, I'm not saying you need to take some kind of soul-searching journey around Europe to get to know yourself before you can write a proper resume, but you do need to have an idea of what sort of image you wish to present. What skills do you have that set you apart from others? What accomplishments are you most proud of? Most important: What makes you the employee that an employer is looking for?

A great resume will distill your career experience, your skills, and your positive traits into a concise and readable format. It will be both a record of your past accomplishments and a definitive statement of where you would like to be in the future. Most important, it will be a dynamic sales tool that will convince employers that they'd be lucky to have you on their staff.

Did You Know?

Landscaping companies in Arizona and North Carolina have recently come up with an eco-friendly alternative to landscaping machinery: goats. When the city of Mesa, Arizona, wanted to build a new wastewater treatment plant, they brought in a herd of 80 grazing goats to clear the land for construction. Goats will eat pretty much any plant they encounter—including poison ivy—and their attention to detail cannot be recreated with industrial machines. A Seattle based company named Rent-a-Ruminant has gotten in on the act, offering "herds for hire" composed of rescue goats.

Focus, Focus, Focus

The importance of having a focused resume cannot be overstated. Even if your career hasn't shown a linear progression, a well-crafted resume will make it seem as though you've been on a continual upward path since you began working. If you're just coming out of school, you can emphasize highlights of your academic career, internships, part-time jobs, and/or volunteer work that show you'd be a responsible, motivated employee. You may think your experience is scattershot, but it won't necessarily appear that way to an employer, as long as you frame it correctly.

To start with, you should create a focus statement for your resume. A focus statement can take two different forms: *Objective or Summary*. Which you choose mainly depends on how much experience you have.

- *Objective:* An Objective statement is useful for someone who is just entering the workforce, or someone who is entering an entirely new field. The objective statement should be a simple and direct explanation of the type of job you'd like to have. For example, someone who would like to get a job in marketing might have an Objective statement that simply reads "A position in marketing." Alternatively, you could use the objective as an opportunity to showcase your positive qualities: "A position in marketing that will benefit from my creative writing abilities and knowledge of identity branding." Other terms you can use to describe an objective statement are *goal* or *target*.

- *Summary:* A Summary is a brief description of your professional experience. If an interviewer asks you to describe what you've done, the Summary is the statement you give. For example: "Experienced mechanical engineer with a history of team leadership and a strong knowledge of energy-efficient materials and design principles." Other terms that can be used in place of Summary are Executive Summary, Overview, or Synopsis.

Whichever type of focus statement you choose for your resume, you should view every other piece of your resume through the framework of that statement. If your objective is to get a position in marketing, what skills or experience do you have that prove you can handle that position? Likewise, if you're an "experienced mechanical engineer with a history of team leadership and a strong knowledge of energy-efficient materials and design principles," your resume should support this focus.

Format

Once you have a focus, it's time to choose your format. As I mentioned in the section on misconceptions, your resume can be chronological, functional, or a combination of both. A chronological resume is a list of past job positions, from most recent position held to oldest. A functional resume is a list of skills, supported by details from previous positions or experiences. For examples of the three different types of resumes, turn to the end of the chapter.

Layout

As a writer, I'd love to believe that people decide to buy my books because I hook them in with my engrossing writing style. But the truth is, even though we're told that we "shouldn't judge a book by its cover," plenty of books are sold every day because they have cool cover designs. Similarly, a nice-looking presentation can move your resume to the top of the pile before a single word has been read.

A well-formatted resume will be full of information without looking cluttered. There should be enough white space to keep the lines from running together, yet not so much that the page looks empty. Bullets are always a useful way to highlight significant information. It's important to convey a sense of symmetry in your layout; if you have bullet points under one job description, you should have bullet points in every job description.

Green Quotes

The majority of recruiters spend less than three minutes reviewing a resume, according to a survey conducted by the Society for Human Resource Management. That's why resumes need good organization. A well-organized resume allows recruiters to quickly find what they're looking for. Bullet points help organize information into nuggets and make resumes more manageable.

—Christopher Jones, "Why Bullet Points Matter" on Yahoo! hotjob

You should use only one font in your resume, preferably a simple font that is easy to read, like Times New Roman or Garamond. The font size for the body text should be no smaller than 10 points and no larger than 12. It's okay to use a larger font for your name at the top of the resume, but don't go overboard; disproportionately large fonts can make it look like you're trying to fill space. Job titles and section headings can be in a combination of bold and italics, as long as they look good. It's okay to underline important information in your resume, but be consistent and don't go overboard. Whatever you do, don't go for a wacky font like Comic Sans or Impact; they'll just end up making your resume look unprofessional.

The typical layout for a résumé looks like this:

Name and contact information (including e-mail, phone number, and address)

Objective/Summary

For a chronological resume:

- Employment history: Company, job title, dates of employment.

- Job tasks (example: "Managed a team of researchers at a sustainable energy lab.")

- Job highlights (example: "Increased efficiency of PV cells by 5%.")

For a functional resume:

- Qualifications: Skill titles such as Leadership, Sales, or Finance.

- Job highlights (example: "Managed $300,000 operating budget. Wrote grants to secure $2.5 million in funding.")

Education

Training

Additional information (awards, professional memberships, etc.)

Writing Style

Okay, so you've hooked the employer in with your beautiful layout and formatting. Now comes the most difficult part: describing your accomplishments. Many people have trouble striking the right tone on a resume; unless you're a politician, you probably don't spend much time telling people about all the great things you've done in your life. You might be tempted to downplay your skills to avoid coming across as arrogant. Well, don't worry about that. No one is going to hire a candidate who holds back on emphasizing his or her accomplishments out of self-consciousness. Remember: Your job is to prove to employers that they can't live without you. You need to fill your resume with unique, impressive accomplishments that prove you are a candidate of value. To accomplish this, you must:

Be Specific

The more specific your information is, the greater an impression it will make. For example, say your last position was as an administrative assistant for a sales department at a major company. You could describe your job as "assisting a group of salespeople at a major company," but any administrative assistant could write that sentence. Instead, pick out specific things about your job that made it unique, such as: "Oversaw all internal and external communications among six sales consultants responsible for $14 million of annual business." By tying your job into the $14 million of business, it connects your work directly to a specific and impressive figure.

Did You Know?

According to a report by Mark Z. Jacobson in the journal Energy and Environmental Science, *wind, concentrated solar, and geothermal are the cleanest forms of technology. The report examines various types of renewable energy according to efficiency of energy production, and impacts on global warming, human health, energy security, water supply, space requirements, wildlife, water pollution, reliability, and sustainability. If we wanted to generate all of our electricity from wind power, Jacobson estimates that we would have to cover .5% of the country with wind turbines.*

Be Brief

As important as it is to include specific information, it is equally important to know what information should be left out. If your resume is filled with 300-word-long paragraphs, those paragraphs will probably never get read. Use bullet points, and keep your job descriptions short but informative.

Also try to eliminate redundant or unnecessary language. Many people use the phrase "responsible for" in job descriptions; for example, "Responsible for repairing and maintaining electrical systems." Ninety-nine percent of the time, the phrase "responsible for" is just wasted language; in this case, it's more to the point to simply say, "Repair and maintain electrical systems."

Use Keywords

Often, your resume will only be skimmed quickly upon first pass. If you want to give an employer an immediate impression of your experience and skills, you should make use of *keywords*. Keywords are important terms and phrases that leap out at a reader during a quick scan. Proper nouns, such as job titles, schools attended, certifications earned, computer programs learned, and major companies worked for, are all keywords that will stand out on your resume. Industry-related terms, like "photovoltaic cells" or "HVAC systems" also make great keywords. You don't have to go crazy with the keywords, but you should have enough specific terms in your resume that someone can get a good idea with just a quick scan of who you are and what you can do.

Use Dynamic Verbs

The majority of creative writing in resumes lies in the use of verbs. You should try to fill your resume with strong verbs that paint an image in the reader's mind. For example, if your last position was as a sales associate at a clothing store, you shouldn't say you "worked in sales." You should say you "generated sales of more than $25,000 per day at a popular clothing store" (or whatever that realistic sales figure might be). A dynamic verb like *generate* can make it sound like you're leading the action, while a passive verb like *worked* sounds like your job happened to you.

Ignore Proper Sentence Structure

Resumes are one of the few places in the job search where it's okay to ignore rules of grammar. Take a look at the sample resumes at the end of this chapter and the astute English speaker will notice something strange: The typical resume has no complete sentences. There is no need to write complete sentences in a resume, because every sentence has an implied subject: *I*. For example, you wouldn't write, "I tested systems to ensure compliance with safety regulations. I supervised construction of a generator that came in $10,000 under budget." You'd write: "Tested systems to ensure compliance with safety regulations. Supervised construction of a generator that came in $10,000 under budget." This might leave all sorts of nasty little squiggly green lines under your sentences in Microsoft Word, but don't worry: As far as resumes go, grammatically incorrect is perfectly correct.

Text Resumes versus Attachments

When you're applying for a job online, it is useful to have a text resume that you can paste into the body of the e-mail. Some employers even specifically state "no attachments" in their job listings. For this reason, you should develop an attractive looking text resume that you can cut and paste into the body of an e-mail.

The easiest way to create a text resume is to copy and paste your resume from Word (or whatever word processing program you're using) into a text program like Notepad (included on all Windows PCs) or Apple NotePad (a similar program for Macs). After cutting and pasting, you should spend some time reformatting your resume; formatting options like tabs, bold, italics, and bullets won't translate over to a text program. In some cases, you may need to change your spacing; for instance, you won't be able to align your dates of employment on the right-hand side of the page. Whatever you do, *don't* type a succession of spaces to make it look like the dates are aligned on the right side. E-mail programs format spaces differently, and the lines might cut off at a different place on someone else's e-mail program than they do on yours, moving your carefully spaced text to a new line. This can render your resume unreadable, all but guaranteeing it will be ignored.

You can still keep the basic formatting that you've developed on a text resume, you just might have to get creative. Instead of bullets, use the "+" sign or an asterisk ("*"). Take another look at the line spacing; any adjustments you made to the spacing between paragraphs in the Word version of your resume won't carry through to the text program. A single blank line between different sections of your resume should be enough. Once you have finished reformatting, send your resume to yourself as an e-mail to make sure that everything looks all right. And make sure to save a copy of your text resume so you won't have to go through the whole process again!

For most jobs, attachments are acceptable and expected. The standard word processing program across platforms right now is Microsoft Word, and almost all businesses will be able to read resumes that are saved in the Word 97-2003 format.

And that, in a nutshell, is how to write a resume. Of course, this is just the tip of the iceberg; if you want to know more, there are lots of books in the career section at your local bookstore or library that can give you in-depth advice on how to best present your skills and experience to employers. The following websites are also excellent resources for resume and cover letter samples:

http://hotjobs.yahoo.com/RÉSUMÉ

http://career-advice.monster.com/résumés-cover-letters/careers.aspx

http://owl.english.purdue.edu/owl/resource/681/01/

One last thing: Before you send your resume out to anyone, make sure to *double-, triple-, and quadruple-check for errors.* There is nothing that will get your resume tossed into the trash quicker than spelling or grammatical errors. Even if your job has nothing to do with writing or spelling, your resume should still be impeccable. When employers look at an error-filled resume, they see one thing: a lazy employee. It's easy to overlook mistakes in our own work, so be sure to have someone else check your resume for errors, too.

Eco-Quiz

How many miles per gallon does the average long-haul tractor–trailer get?

a. *6 mpg*

b. *9 mpg*

c. *13 mpg*

d. *17 mpg*

Answer: a. *6 mpg. A report by the Rocky Mountain Institute found that the trucking industry could easily double the energy efficiency of their trucks using technology that already exists.*

Section 2: Writing Cover Letters

In some ways, writing a good cover letter is even more difficult than writing a good resume. You can get by with having a stock resume that you send to many different companies, but every cover letter you send should be tailored directly to your target company. A standardized, impersonal cover letter will come across as just that: standardized and impersonal. If you want to stand out, you should take the time to let a company know that you're applying to work for *them*, not for any faceless corporation that's fool enough to hire you.

Of course, in reality, you'll probably be sending out dozens if not hundreds of résumés before you land the perfect job. It would take all of your time if you did in-depth research on every company to which you applied. You shouldn't send the exact same letter to every employer, but there's no crime in having a standard template that you use over and over. The key is creating a stock cover letter with areas that can be modified to make it seem personal.

The cover letter gives you a chance to show your personality and creativity in a way that resumes do not. Don't go informal; it probably isn't wise to pepper your cover letter with words like *dude* and *'sup*—unless you're applying for a job at a surf magazine, that is—but you can and should use the cover letter to showcase information about yourself that might not come across in your resume.

The Basic Components of a Cover Letter

Every cover letter should contain three basic parts:

1. A brief opening sentence introducing yourself and explaining why you are sending your resume. Example:

   Dear Ms. Davis:

   I'm submitting my resume in response to the energy auditor position advertised on Craig's List.

   Alternatively, if you are sending a blind resume to a company that isn't advertising any specific positions, your opening sentence should leap right into why you're a good candidate for the job.

   Dear Ms. Davis:

   As a licensed energy auditor, I believe my skills could make me a valuable addition to the [company name] team.

2. A paragraph discussing the skills that make you a good candidate for the position. This paragraph is the most important paragraph in the cover letter; if you haven't

hooked the reader's interest by the end of this paragraph, they may never get to your resume. You should use this space to highlight one or two achievements from your past experience that would pique an employer's interest. You should also include some targeted information in this paragraph that lets the employer know you've done your research on the company.

As you're writing, try to include some intriguing personal details in this paragraph that will give the employer a sense of who you are. You don't need to list your measurements or talk about your fondest childhood memory, but a little hint that there's an actual person on the other end of the e-mail will draw employers in and turn you into someone they'd like to meet. Example:

> *For the past 10 years, I've managed construction crews on a variety of high-profile projects, including the Avett School and the Spencer award-winning Tullhouse Building in Montgomery, Alabama. As a builder, one of my key interests has always been using technology to increase energy efficiency, so over the summer, I returned to school to pursue LEED certification. Now that I'm LEED certified, I would like to bring my extensive experience to a leading company in energy-efficient building. I've been impressed with the research I've done on [company's name here], and I look forward to using my skills to help enhance your firm's reputation as an industry leader.*

3. A request for a meeting and a note of appreciation. Example:

> *I welcome the opportunity to meet with you and discuss how I could put my skills to work for [company's name]. I appreciate your taking the time to review my credentials and I look forward to meeting with you at your convenience.*
>
> *Best regards,*
>
> *[your name]*

Did You Know? *A 2009 report by McGraw-Hill Construction found that by 2014, green building retrofits will account for between 20%–30% of all commercial construction projects.*

A cover letter should never be longer than one page. If you're sending your cover letter via e-mail, keep it to three brief paragraphs. If your cover letter is being printed, use the same font for your cover letter that you used for your resume. If it is being sent via e-mail (the majority of cases), use the standard e-mail font.

Letters versus E-mail

Since the advent of the Internet, it's become increasingly rare for people to send hard copies of their cover letters and resumes through the mail. Although some employers still prefer getting hard copies, unless they specifically state that you should send your resume through the mail, you should assume they would like you to e-mail it. This is doubly true for green jobs; many companies will see a hard copy of a resume as a waste of paper.

If you are asked to send a hard copy of your cover letter and resume, stick to a basic paper weight and an unobtrusive color, like cream or white. You want to stand out, but most employers will see fancy-colored papers as trying too hard. It can be a nice touch to print your cover letter on a personal letterhead, but it is not necessary. Also, if you're sending the cover letter through the mail, handwrite the address on the envelope. A printed label runs the risk of looking like a form letter.

Addressing Your Cover Letter

If possible, try to find out the name of the person who will be receiving your letter and resume. Many Internet job listings will tell you the name of the contact person. Address that person at the beginning of the letter as either "Mr." or "Ms." If the person has a generic name like "Chris" or "Mel," *don't* make a blind guess. You can often find out whom you should be addressing by calling the company and asking the receptionist. If all else fails, you may open the letter with "Dear Sir/Madam." Avoid "To whom it may concern" at all costs.

Salary

Do not include your desired salary unless the listing specifically asks for it.

Section 3: Greening Your Resume and Cover Letters

Since you're looking for a green job, it's important to include information in your resume that shows your dedication to efficiency, sustainability, and/or conservation. You don't want to go "all green," focusing your resume entirely on your environmental experience; as we've discovered, green jobs require many skills that would fit into any industry. However, you should tailor your resume and cover letters to include information about what you've done to promote environmentally friendly efforts in past positions and to show the employer that you would be committed to such efforts in whatever job you take.

In some cases, your commitment to efficiency, sustainability, and/or conservation will speak for itself. For instance, if you majored in environmental studies and your past jobs included work at environmental nonprofits, your commitment to the environment will be self-evident. If you're transitioning from a job in a traditional industry to one in a green industry, however, there are a few things you can do to highlight your desire to become a valuable contributor to the green economy.

Eco-Quiz

What city was ranked the least toxic major city in the United States according to a 2009 report by Forbes *magazine?*

a. *New York, New York*
b. *Las Vegas, Nevada*
c. *Atlanta, Georgia*
d. *San Francisco, California*

Answer: b. *Las Vegas, Nevada. The* Forbes *report ranks cities according to number of Superfund sites, number of facilities releasing toxic chemicals, pounds of toxic chemicals released, and air quality. Surprisingly, New York beat San Francisco; New York was ranked #9, while San Francisco came in at #15. Atlanta came in dead last on the list, making it the #1 most toxic city in the United States.*

1. When listing your successes at past jobs, include anything you've done to increase energy efficiency, decrease waste, encourage recycling, and so on. Include specific facts and figures to show that your efforts met with success. Example:

   Started a recycling program that eliminated 30% of company waste and lowered waste collection bills by $30,000/year.

   If you are working right now and would like to transition to a green job in the future, look around your workplace to find areas that you feel could be improved and take it upon yourself to make those improvements. For instance, you can ask your IT department to set up the company's computers to print double-sided instead of single-sided, automatically decreasing paper waste by 50%. You'd be surprised how much your employer would be willing to change if you can demonstrate that it would save money and increase efficiency.

2. List any classes or training you've had in sustainable tech, environmental studies, or energy efficiency.

3. List any volunteer positions you've had with environmental organizations. (Unless they're radical organizations like the Earth Liberation Front . . . probably best to keep your past efforts at blowing up SUV dealerships out of the public eye.)

4. Include an Interests section at the end of your resume that includes any personal experience you have with environmental issues.

5. Include a sentence in your cover letter that explains why you'd like to transition into a green job. Example:

   In my job at ConAgra, I became interested in the advances being made in sustainable agriculture and decided my skills would be better served at a company that was committed to environmentally friendly farming practices.

Section 4: Sample Resumes

FIGURE 5.1   Chronological Resume

Mark Clavier

(123) 456-7890   7070 East Bay Street
MClavier@udragon.net   Peachtree, Georgia 12345

Summary of Qualifications

- Over 10 years of team leadership experience as an HVAC Technician, with a focus on improving energy efficiency of HVAC systems in commercial and residential properties.
- Outstanding commitment to customer service. Skilled at communicating with vendors, team members, and customers to deliver projects on time and under budget.
- Strong knowledge of Georgia state building codes.

Experience

THE BORDEN'S GROUP, Peachtree, Georgia   January 2006–Present

Lead HVAC Technician
Led a team of contractors in installation, maintenance, and repair of heating, ventilation, air-conditioning, and steam distribution systems at residential and commercial facilities. Analyzed blueprints and diagrams to gauge areas of strength and weakness in building construction. Performed extensive testing to determine most efficient placement of ducts, pumps, and piping.

- Retrofitted HVAC systems in all Peachtree government buildings to comply with new energy regulations. Retrofits increased energy efficiency of buildings by 55% and lowered city energy bills by approximately $45,000/year.
- Designed and oversaw installation of HVAC systems in Spencer Park, a housing development for low-income families that won the 2008 Begley Award for Socially Conscious Design. Holistic approach to HVAC system design saved average Spencer Park resident $800/year on electricity bills.
- Implemented new electronic billing procedures that dramatically decreased paper waste and saved company approximately $5,000/year in supply costs.

ANDERSON BUILDERS, Temescal, Georgia   March 2003–January 2006

HVAC Technician

Installed, maintained, and repaired components of HVAC systems including compressors, evaporators, VAV boxes, temperature controls, fans, and other mechanical equipment for residential and commercial buildings. Coordinated installation schedules between in-house team and subcontractors to ensure timely installation of systems.

- Attended the 2005 and 2006 International Builders Conference. In 2006, represented Anderson Builders in panel discussion on "The Future of Green HVAC Design."
- Brought in new revenue streams that helped Anderson Builders increase billing by $3 million/year.
- Achieved 100% satisfaction rate in customer reviews.

BIVOUAC CORPORATION, Newbury, Georgia   August 1999–March 2003

HVAC Installer

Installed, maintained, and repaired ductwork, air-conditioning systems, and forced air equipment at commercial properties. Managed subcontractors and in-house team on projects ranging from public utilities to big box retail stores.

- Introduced efficient employee practices that saved company up to $20,000/year in overtime payments.
- Started at Bivouac as part of the apprenticeship program; was the only member of my program to be offered full-time employment.

Education and Credentials

DADE COMMUNITY COLLEGE, Newbury, Georgia   1997–1999

AAS Degree, HVAC System Design and Installation
- HVAC team leader on a project that won second place in 1999's Georgia Community College Building Design competition.
- Graduated with honors.

Accredited LEED Green Associate

Seminars
- Principles of HVAC Design
- Air-Conditioning Repair, Troubleshooting, and Maintenance
- HVAC Implementation in Holistic Housing Systems
- Advanced Air Flow Management

FIGURE 5.2   Functional Resume

Mark Clavier

Home: 123.456.7890 • **Cell:** 123.789.0456
7070 East Bay Street • Peachtree, Georgia 12345
MClavier@udragon.net

OBJECTIVE

Grant-writing position at environmentally focused nonprofit organization that draws upon my 7 years of experience winning major funding awards for nationally recognized philanthropic organizations.

SKILLS SUMMARY

- Research
- Team Leadership
- Project Management
- Presentations
- Report Preparation
- Brand Marketing
- Client Relations
- Strong Computer Knowledge

PROFESSIONAL EXPERIENCE

Fundraising/Development

- Wrote grant applications that secured an average of $30 million per year for environmentally focused organizations such as the Green Brigade and Water Watch.
- Keep up-to-date on new developments at nonprofit funding organizations to ensure maximization of funding opportunities.
- Liaison with major donors to encourage involvement in fundraising activities and enhance donor familiarity with ongoing projects.
- Oversee creation of grant applications through all stages of development.

Managerial

- Manage writers' schedules to make sure that grants are finished before due date.
- Combine work from several sources to ensure compatibility of information and seamlessness of reading experience.
- Oversee all contact between freelance writers and nonprofits including invoicing, pay-outs, and rate agreements.

EMPLOYMENT HISTORY

2006–Present   **Clavier and Associates**, Macomb, Georgia; Freelance Grant Writer
2003–2006   **The Atlanta Philharmonic**, Atlanta, Georgia; Senior Grant Coordinator
2002–2003   **Eco-Adentures**, Laramie, Georgia; Grant Writer

EDUCATION

1997–2002   **University of Michigan**, Ann Arbor, Michigan; B.S., Political Science

FIGURE 5.3   E-mail/Text Resume

Mark Clavier

7070 East Bay Street
Peachtree, Georgia 12345
(123) 456-7890
mclavier@udragon.net

SUMMARY OF QUALIFICATIONS

+ Over 10 years of team leadership experience as an HVAC Technician, with a focus on improving energy efficiency of HVAC systems in commercial and residential properties.
+ Outstanding commitment to customer service. Skilled at communicating with vendors, team members, and customers to deliver projects on time and under budget.
+ Strong knowledge of Georgia state building codes.

EXPERIENCE

THE BORDEN'S GROUP, Peachtree, Georgia   January 2006–Present
Lead HVAC Technician

Led a team of contractors in installation, maintenance, and repair of heating, ventilation, air-conditioning, and steam distribution systems at residential and commercial facilities. Analyzed blueprints and diagrams to gauge areas of strength and weakness in building construction. Performed extensive testing to determine most efficient placement of ducts, pumps, and piping.

+ Retrofitted HVAC systems in all Peachtree government buildings to comply with new energy regulations. Retrofits increased energy efficiency of buildings by 55% and lowered city energy bills by approximately $45,000/year.
+ Designed and oversaw installation of HVAC systems in Spencer Park, a housing development for low-income families that won the 2008 Begley Award for Socially Conscious Design. Holistic approach to HVAC system design saved average Spencer Park resident $800/year on electricity bills.
+ Implemented new electronic billing procedures that dramatically decreased paper waste and saved company approximately $5,000/year in supply costs.

ANDERSON BUILDERS, Temescal, Georgia   March 2003–January 2006
HVAC Technician

Installed, maintained, and repaired components of HVAC systems including compressors, evaporators, VAV boxes, temperature controls, fans, and other mechanical equipment for residential and commercial buildings. Coordinated installation schedules between in-house team and subcontractors to ensure timely installation of systems.

+ Attended the 2005 and 2006 International Builders Conference. In 2006, represented Anderson Builders in panel discussion on "The Future of Green HVAC Design."
+ Brought in new revenue streams that helped Anderson Builders increase billing by $3 million/year.
+ Achieved 100% satisfaction rate in customer reviews.

BIVOUAC CORPORATION, Newbury, Georgia   August 1999–March 2003
HVAC Installer

Installed, maintained, and repaired ductwork, air-conditioning systems, and forced air equipment at commercial properties. Managed subcontractors and in-house team on projects ranging from public utilities to big box retail stores.

+ Introduced efficient employee practices that saved company up to $20,000/year in overtime payments.
+ Started at Bivouac as part of the apprenticeship program; was the only member of my program to be offered full-time employment.

EDUCATION AND CREDENTIALS

DADE COMMUNITY COLLEGE, Newbury, Georgia 1997–1999
AAS Degree, HVAC System Design and Installation

+ HVAC team leader on a project that won second place in 1999's Georgia Community College Building Design competition.
+ Graduated with honors.

Accredited LEED Green Associate

SEMINARS

+ Principles of HVAC Design
+ Air-Conditioning Repair, Troubleshooting, and Maintenance
+ HVAC Implementation in Holistic Housing Systems
+ Advanced Air Flow Management

CHAPTER SIX

NETWORKING AND
MAKING CONNECTIONS

Chapter Overview

As any advertising account executive knows, there is no better advertising than word-of-mouth. Studies show that 93% of consumers believe that word-of-mouth advertising is the most reliable way to learn information about a product. This statistic is equally true of employers. Your chances of getting an interview with a company improve dramatically if someone within the company is willing to vouch for you. In this chapter, we learn some tips for making connections and using the connections you already have to find a job. We also examine how the social networking website LinkedIn can help you meet the people you need to know.

Section 1: Networking Basics

Networking comes more naturally to some than to others. If you feel hesitant about reaching out to people in your job search, it may be because you have some misconceptions about what it means to network. In this section, we examine what it means to network and the crucial differences between business relationships and personal relationships.

Section 2: Targeted Networking

How many people do you know who have jobs? Now how many people do those people know? When you consider all of your friends, acquaintances, and friends of friends, you probably already have a wide pool of contacts to draw from in your job search. Your friends will probably be eager to assist you in your job search, but eventually you will have to add some new connections to your network. In this section, we learn that the best place to begin networking is your own address book, and then we offer some tips on how and where to meet people who can put you on the inside track to your desired job.

Section 3: Using Social Networking Sites

It started with Friendster. Then MySpace was all the rage. Facebook soon threw its hat into the ring, with LinkedIn following shortly thereafter. Whoever ends up dominating the increasingly crowded field, one thing's for certain: Social networking sites are here to stay. In this section, we take a look at how you can use social networking sites to get the jump on the competition, with an emphasis on the professional networking site LinkedIn.

In Their Own Words: Elizabeth Sullivan, Cofounder, City CarShare

In 2001, Elizabeth Sullivan, with the help of partners Gabriel Metcalf and Kate White, launched a nonprofit in San Francisco called City CarShare. For $45/ month, City CarShare members can reserve one of hundreds of cars that are parked in convenient locations around the San Francisco area. The cars are available 24 hours per day and can all be operated with a single electronic key. City CarShare estimates that its 10,000 members remove 25 million pounds of CO_2 from the atmosphere and save up to $700 per year over the cost of owning a car.

How old were you when you started working on City CarShare?
I was 26.

And what did you do before that?

When I got out of college, I was hoping to go into community organizing, but I couldn't find a job. I took one as an assistant at an ad agency, and it sucked. [Laughs.] I finally got a job as a community organizer with a group called the Neighborhood Parks Council.

How did you get started with City CarShare?

I was at the Neighborhood Parks Council for $2\frac{1}{2}$ years. And while I was there, at night, I was going home and working on City CarShare with Gabriel and Kate. We were planning it, writing grants, figuring out how to plan budgets, trying to get press. It basically started as an organizing project after our day jobs.

At 26, how did you have any idea how to start doing something like that?

Well, we all worked at various nonprofits, and we were getting a lot of training during the day about how to talk to foundations, how to submit grants, and learning about different companies that give money to nonprofits. We were learning as we went. I remember spending two months writing a grant for $2,000 which we didn't even get. I feel like if I started now I could organize City CarShare in about half the time. [Laughs.] It took forever!

When did you start to feel like City CarShare might become a reality?

The moment when we actually got the funding. Car sharing is an expensive project because you have to lease cars. It's not like finding a room somewhere that someone donates and saying, "okay, we're open for business!" We needed to raise a million dollars to get started. After about two and a half to three years of working on it in our spare time, a connection directed us to a fund in the Federal Highways Bill that supported innovative car projects. It took a long time for us to get our information together, but they ended up giving us $750,000.

Wow. Were you even asking for that much?

Oh yeah, we asked for more! We asked for a million dollars. I mean, it's federal highway money. That's like what they find under the couch in the hallway.

How were you able to convince them that you, this small group of three people, would be able to pull this off?

We did tons of networking to get other organizations to recognize us in various ways and to write letters on our behalf. Groups like the Bay Area Air Quality Management District and the Municipal Transit Authority wrote letters to the Federal Highway Administration for us. Meanwhile, we were also getting involved in local politics and doing things like speaking to neighborhood groups to get people excited about the idea.

Basically, networking and legitimizing ourselves as an idea and then getting that local support. And when we submitted our grant to federal highways, we had a letter from the mayor of San Francisco saying it was a great project. [U.S. House of Representatives Speaker] Nancy Pelosi wrote us a letter, too. I would say that was the most important part of the submission, actually. All the beautiful prose we worked on for months, of course they didn't read; they probably just flipped to the section of supporters, and they said, "Pelosi? Okay, fine." *[Laughs]*

So what did you have to do to get it started?

We wanted to build up a group of people who were going to join right away, so we wouldn't start up and then sit around for a few months while people thought about it. So we did a lot of reaching out and getting press, and just trying to raise the consciousness about what we were doing. And then we had to build an online reservation system, which was just crazy because we didn't know anything about how to put that together. Once it got started, I left the Neighborhood Parks Council and started working at City CarShare full time.

Were you giving yourself a salary?

Yeah, I had a salary! It was modest *[laughs]*, but fantastic. And then at some point a little later Kate quit her job, and we became co-directors. At that point it sort of started to feel like we were working at a small business. We were running a fleet of vehicles, a reservation system, we had customer service, troubleshooting, we cleaned the cars and got them maintained. It wasn't that different from working at Avis.

Was there any thought given to the sustainability of the company itself and how you treated your employees?

Yeah, there was a lot of thought about that. It was a big deal to us at the time that we give everybody healthcare right away, and we tried to be generous with vacation time, where you could take time whenever you wanted. We were pretty flexible and open. It's hard to find people who can work for so little money, so you do what you can to give people a fulfilling career in other ways. We were lucky to find some really amazing people.

How many employees did it grow to?

After we got started, I was there for another three years. When I left, there were maybe 50 employees.

Are any of the founders there anymore?

No, we've all gone. Kate just quit the board last year. From the beginning, we wanted to avoid "founder's disease," which is when the founder of a nonprofit becomes really controlling, walking around with the checkbook in her pocket. You know, if you got hit by a bus, the organization would just die. Nonprofits can sometimes become less about the mission and more about the founder. So we really wanted to hand it off.

If you were to talk to someone who was interested in starting their own nonprofit, where do you think would be a good place for them to start? Or what are some necessary skills that you feel they should have to develop?

For me, networking ended up being the most valuable part of the process. That and perseverance. The first day that we went out and talked to people about City CarShare, people didn't respond to it. But after we had the conversation over and over and started to get support from the community, we developed more confidence in what we were doing.

When you're starting something new, you really need allies and mentors and lots and lots of help. Find a community group you're interested in joining, and look for mentors, people who can give you advice. Our mentors were so valuable to us in the beginning, and they introduced us to a lot of people who ended up staying involved for the long haul.

After leaving City CarShare, Elizabeth Sullivan went back to school and is working today as a psychologist in private practice. City CarShare continues to supply San Francisco drivers with a convenient and inexpensive alternative to owning a car.

Section 1: Networking Basics

In *How to Win Friends and Influence People*, author Dale Carnegie, the godfather of the networking movement, wrote, "Dealing with people is probably the biggest problem you face, especially if you are in business. . . . Even in such technical lines as engineering, about 15 percent of one's financial success is due to one's technical knowledge and about 85 percent is due to human engineering—to personality and the ability to lead people."

Although *How to Win Friends* was written in 1936, Carnegie's observation is still just as relevant today. The ability to develop strong relationships with people is crucial to success in the workplace—and even more so during the job search. It is important to have good work experience and a strong knowledge of your field, but the best resume in the world won't get you hired if no one can stand talking to you. To increase your chances of getting a job, you will have to learn the basics of networking.

Green Quotes

The biofuel market is a magnet for start-ups, which tend to hire in waves as they launch. Interested applicants should join networking groups to keep up to date on company debuts and try to slip in by wangling an internship.

Just get into any company and get some experience on any level. Don't worry too much about whether the company is going to succeed or blow up, because all those people will create your network.

—Riggs Eckelberry, chief executive of OriginOil Inc., a Los Angles-based biofuel company, as quoted in the Los Angeles Times

What Is Networking?

At heart, *networking* is the act of using old social relationships and making new social relationships to increase your chances of getting a job (or, in the business world, making a sale, finding new clients, etc.). For many people, the idea of finding a job by networking is much more frightening than the act of sending out an unsolicited resume and cover letter because it involves doing something that many of us find difficult: talking to strangers. And not just talking to strangers, but asking them for help. No one wants to come across like a telemarketer, disturbing others while they're trying to eat their dinner. We like to think we can get a job based on the quality of our work and experience, not because we know somebody.

While those concerns are absolutely valid, they are based on a misconception of what it means to network. Even though you may be asking for the help of others, networking is not a one-way street. Once someone is in your network, you are also in that person's network. And even if you don't have a lot to offer that person right now, you may be a good person to know in the future.

Here's a little secret about human nature that you should keep in mind during your job search: *People really like helping others.* If you knew of a job opening at your company, and you knew someone who was qualified to fill that job, wouldn't it make you feel good to connect the job with the person? As you begin building your network of connections, it's helpful to remember that many, if not all, the people you will be interacting with have gotten to where they are with the help of their connections. These people won't see you as a pest, because they know what it's like to be in your position. If you treat people with courtesy and respect and can demonstrate that you are capable of doing the kind of job you're trying to get, most of the people you encounter will be happy to lend you a helping hand.

There is a difference between how we communicate in business relationships and how we communicate in our personal relationships. Interactions that might come across as pushy or forward in the personal world are often perfectly acceptable in the business world. For instance, if you met someone at a party whom you wanted to get to know better, it might seem a little odd to send that person an e-mail the next day listing the reasons why you would make a good friend. If, however, you met someone at a party who offered to help you find a job, it would be perfectly acceptable to send that person an e-mail telling them why you'd make a good employee. What is seen as pushy in real life is often seen in the business world as having the drive to succeed. Although you don't want to come across as a braggart, humility isn't always the greatest attribute when you're trying to convince someone of your value as an employee.

Eco-Quiz

What proportion of job seekers find their jobs through networking?

a. $\frac{1}{4}$

b. $\frac{1}{2}$

c. $\frac{2}{3}$

d. $\frac{3}{4}$

Answer: c. $\frac{2}{3}$. *According to Anne Baber and Lynne Waymon's book* Make Your Contacts Count, *two out of every three job seekers, or 67%, find their jobs through networking.*

Using Your Contacts

Unless you live by yourself in a cave, you already have a network in place; you just might not normally think of it as such. Everyone you know is in your network, from your mother to your pastor to your next-door neighbor. You never know what kinds of connections these people have until you start asking. For example, when I started telling people in my network that I was writing this book, I was surprised by how many people knew someone who was working in a green job, going to school to learn how to do a green job, or running a green business. The majority of people interviewed in this book, in fact, were found through a friend, a friend of a friend, or other members of my social and professional network. And what worked for me in the search for interview subjects can work just as well for you in your job hunt.

Once you've decided what kind of job you're looking for, your first step in building your network is to start going through your contacts. Look through your personal address book and e-mail contact lists. If you volunteer anywhere or belong to any clubs, think about the people you've met there who might be good sources of information. If you take any classes, your teachers and classmates are often excellent resources.

As you're compiling your list of names, try to narrow down the list to people who work in a field similar to the one you'd like to be involved in, or whom you think may be connected to someone who works in this field. Anyone directly connected to the field you'd like to get into should go on your "A" list of contacts. It's also good to add connectors to this list, that is, extroverted friends or relatives who know a lot of people and make connections easily. Even if they don't have green jobs themselves, connectors are often one or two degrees removed from people who can help you, and people who know a lot of people often enjoy helping others make connections. The rest of your network shouldn't be forgotten. Connections sometimes turn up in the most unlikely of places, but in the beginning, it's best to concentrate your energy on the most obvious targets.

Now that you have your list together, it's time to get in touch with your A-listers. E-mails and phone calls are a great way to start. Your relationship with each person will determine your tone, but it's important to be clear about what you are looking for. If you think it would be helpful to have a longer conversation, consider inviting that person out for lunch or coffee. Don't send a mass e-mail; you're much more likely to get quality information if you contact someone directly. However, you *should* try to spread the word to everyone you know that you're looking for a job, even your B-listers. Connections are sometimes found in the most unlikely places. Of course, you should show *some* restraint; your current boss probably doesn't need to know that you're planning on leaving, until you have the next job lined up.

When you talk to your contacts, make notes about any information that might help you in your job search, and keeps these notes organized. If they tell you that they know someone else whom you should get in touch with, try to get that person's contact information on the spot or follow up soon afterward. And even if someone turns out not to be much help, be sure to show gratitude for his or her time, and send everyone a thank-you card or e-mail. There's no telling whom that person will meet in the future, and they'll be more likely to think of you right away if they have positive memories of your interaction.

Moving Beyond Your Circle

On the first episode of Season 3 of *Mad Men*, AMC's television series about advertising executives in the 1960s, protagonist Don Draper meets an older gentleman at a wedding and has a pleasant, if unremarkable, conversation with him. A few episodes later, Don receives a call from this gentleman, who turns out to be Conrad Hilton, founder of the Hilton chain of hotels. Hilton, it turns out, was impressed enough in the few minutes he spent talking to Don that he hires Don's firm to create a multimillion dollar advertising campaign for the Hilton hotel chain—even though he's never seen any of Don's work.

The point of this story is not that you should be watching *Mad Men* but that any social event can be an opportunity to expand your network of connections. Going to industry-specific networking events can be a good way to make connections, but networking can really happen anywhere. You never know who will be standing in front of you at the grocery store, sitting next to you on a plane, or standing beside you on an elevator. I'm not saying you should start handing your resume out to people on the street, but the more conversations you have with strangers, the greater your chances will be of meeting someone who can help you in your job search.

Of course, for most of us, talking to strangers is easier in theory than in practice. As children, we were warned that we should "never talk to strangers," a practice that many of us continue to abide by in our later years. You'd still be well-advised to avoid the guy standing in front of his van with a sign reading FREE CANDY, but for the most part, starting conversations with strangers is nothing to be afraid of. The truth is, *everyone* is self-conscious to some degree. And at the same time, *everyone* is looking to make a connection with other people. If you can become that person who connects with others easily, the world will be your oyster.

There is no magic secret to opening a conversation; sometimes, a great conversation can arise from simply asking someone how they're doing. Just gathering the courage to approach someone is 99% of the battle; you'll often find that people are happy to have a conversation with someone who has something interesting to say and treats them with respect.

If the thought of building your network seems intimidating, here are 10 tips for talking to people at social events or networking parties that will leave them with a good impression.

Tip #1: Be Complimentary

It's a rare person who doesn't like to be complimented. If you'd like to talk to someone wearing an interesting tie, you can easily say something like, "That's a great tie; where did you get it?" Try to be honest; a compliment with an obvious ulterior motive could easily backfire. And you should probably avoid complimenting people on their body parts, no matter how great their legs look. But a sincere compliment delivered in a positive way can be an excellent icebreaker.

Tip #2: Ask Questions

If there's one thing I've discovered in my experience as an interviewer, it's that people love it when someone shows interest in their lives. Everyone has an interesting story; your job is to figure out what that story is. Ask open-ended questions; you won't get too far in a conversation if all of your questions can be answered with a "yes" or "no." There's nothing wrong with asking tried-and-true conversational questions like, "What do you do?" but it

Did You Know?
According to the American Wind Energy Association, well-placed wind turbines in North Dakota alone could supply more than 25% of the energy needed in the United States. Add to that the wind power potential in four additional states—Texas, Kansas, South Dakota, and Montana—and wind power could theoretically produce 100% of our energy.

can make for a more interesting conversation if you can frame your questions in ways that can't be responded to with stock answers. For example, instead of asking someone what he or she does, ask, "How do you fill your days?" And remember to express an interest in the person's answers; simply peppering them with a barrage of questions can quickly grow tiresome.

Tip #3: Prepare Your Elevator Pitch

The phrase *elevator pitch* is used in the entrepreneurial world to describe a brief, 30-second pitch for a product or idea. If you had only the span of an elevator ride to sell your product or idea to someone, what would you tell them? In the case of job hunting, your elevator pitch will be a short statement about who you are and what kind of job you're trying to find. If, for example, you were to get involved in a networking conversation and someone were to ask you what you do for a living, you might say something like, "Well, my background is in carpentry, but I recently got my LEED certification, and I'm hoping to become a consultant for a green architecture firm." At the same time:

Tip #4: Don't Have an Agenda

Treat your networking opportunities the same way you treat any conversation. If you go into a networking event with a set of prewritten lines that you're planning to deliver, people will assume you are talking to them only because you want something from them. The point of networking isn't to get one piece of information out of someone and then drop that contact; it's to forge a mutual relationship in which you could eventually both benefit.

Tip #5: Don't Limit Yourself

Say you're interested in working at a geothermal plant, and you find out the person you're talking to works at a wastewater treatment facility. Just because this person isn't in the exact industry you're looking to get involved in doesn't mean he or she has nothing useful to offer. The perfect job opportunity might not present itself right away, and it's good to keep your options open when you're looking for a job.

Tip #6: Know Your Industry
If you're going to an industry-specific event, you should know enough about the industry to have an intelligent conversation with others about it. Read books, keep an eye out for mentions of your industry in the news, and feel free to bring your information into any conversations you may have, if the situation presents itself. If you can demonstrate that you have an inside scoop on industry information, the chances of people's getting back in touch with you when they have useful information increases.

Tip #7: Don't Get Trapped
There's no reason to stick with a conversation that doesn't seem to be going anywhere. You don't want to discount people right away, but after a few minutes, you should get a good idea of whether you're hitting it off with someone. The goal of a networking event is to meet as many new people as time allows; if you don't have anything to say to someone, there's no shame in excusing yourself and finding someone new to talk to.

Tip #8: Get Contact Information
If it seems as if the person you're talking to might be a good resource in your job search, make sure to get that person's contact information. If you don't have a personal business card, get some printed with your e-mail and phone number, which you can hand out. Business cards don't have to cost an arm and a leg; you can either design and print your own cards at home using software like Microsoft Word, or, for a more professional looking job, you can get them done through an online printing service like Vista Print (www.vistaprint.com) or 123 Print (www.123print.com).

Tip #9: Be Yourself

After reading all this advice, you might get the impression that you have to assume a persona to make an impression on people. This is far from the truth. Phoniness will get you nowhere. Just as you shouldn't lie on your resume, there's no reason to lie when you're meeting new people. If you don't have much experience in the industry, it's okay to be upfront about it. As long as you're knowledgeable and eager to learn, people will respect you. Sometimes, your naivete can even work to your advantage; if there's one thing people like more than talking about themselves, it's telling people what they know.

Tip #10: Be Patient

When you are just starting to build your network, it may feel as if things are moving slowly. It would be great to attend one event and walk away with a new job, but the chances of that's happening are slim. Don't lose hope! You are building a network of people that you will keep for the rest of your professional life, and that takes time. If you keep a positive attitude and keep trying, the work you put in is certain to pay off in the long run.

The Follow-Up

Once you've met someone whom you think could be a good addition to your network, following up with that person is crucial. Unless that person specifically told you to get in touch with them about a job interview, don't ask for anything from your first follow-up conversation or e-mail. Instead, drop them a note to tell them it was nice meeting them and you hope to run into them again at future events. If you've read any industry-related news that you think they might find useful, sending them a link to the article is also a great way to keep your name in front of them. As at the beginning of any other relationship, it's good to demonstrate your value. If you just want to take without giving anything in return, you won't stay in that person's contact list for long.

Did You Know?
In November 2009, the International Energy Agency, an energy policy think tank, predicted that oil consumption would hit its peak in 2030. The surprising findings indicate a slower rate of growth in oil usage than earlier predictions. According to the IEA, the energy-efficiency and sustainability measures taken by developed nations have had a larger impact on oil demand than previously thought.

Section 2: Targeted Networking

The Informational Interview

If you're trying to get into a new industry, an excellent way to build your network is by setting up informational interviews. This is just what it sounds like: a short, information-gathering interview with someone about his or her industry. The goal of the informational interview is not to find out about particular job opportunities, but to learn more about the industry in which you're interested. It is also a good way to show people who are already working in your industry of choice that you're serious about making the transition. Once you've spoken with them and have found out more about what they do, people will be likely to keep you in mind if any opportunities come up.

Informational interviews are pretty easy to set up; you'll find that most people are willing and eager to discuss what they do. Be courteous and respectful when asking to interview someone, and make sure to find out whether they'd be more comfortable doing the interview at the office or over lunch or coffee. Go into the interview prepared with a list of questions, but don't feel tied to your list if the conversation takes a different turn. Here are some questions to get you started.

- How did you get started in your job?
- What sort of responsibilities do you have?
- Is there any job-specific training I should get?
- Do you see a lot of opportunities in this field in the future?
- Where do you see your industry headed?
- What are some of your likes and dislikes about your job?
- What kind of prerequisites would I need to be qualified for this job?

Networking Parties

Industry-specific networking parties are another good place to start building your network of connections. Many industries have free, regular parties or get-togethers to make it easy for people to meet others in the same businesses. You'll have to do a little bit of detective work to find out about these get-togethers, but once you're in the loop, there are usually mailing lists you can sign up for that will keep you updated on upcoming opportunities. A list of places to look for network parties is provided in Chapter 9.

Industry Associations

There are associations for every kind of industry, from food packaging (Foodservice Packaging Institute) to chain manufacturers (The National Association of Chain Manufacturers). Green industries are no different. Often, the websites for these associations will have event calendars that list upcoming events. You can find a list of associations for many types of green industries in Chapter 9.

Conventions

With the hype surrounding green jobs, conventions are being held around the country on an almost-weekly basis geared toward green job seekers. It usually costs money to register for these conventions, but it can be money well spent when you're building your network. I discuss some of these conventions in the Entrepreneurial section of Chapter 3; these conventions and others are listed in Chapter 9.

Job Fairs

Job fairs don't always provide the best opportunities to build your professional network; they tend to be filled with more job seekers than job providers, but they can be

Green Quotes

I've been waiting a long time for that tipping point, when politicians and the public recognize the threat of climate change and act to avert it. But I think we're closer than ever. Reality does have a way of knocking on the door.

—*Al Gore, in an interview with Newsweek November 9, 2009*

a good way to learn about the different businesses and opportunities that are available in your area. Some states have even started holding green job fairs that target environmental and sustainable career opportunities. To find a list of upcoming job fairs near you, visit the website for your state's department of employment or career development.

Section 3: Using Social Networking Sites

If you spend any time using the Internet, chances are you've already had some experience with social networking. Although the Internet has been used as a social tool since its inception (people have been connecting with others through chat rooms, message boards, and e-mail for years), it wasn't until the introduction of Friendster that one could actually use a single program to build and maintain a network of friends. When Friendster was launched in 2002, it ushered in a wave of programs that allowed users to post pictures, send messages, connect with new people, and announce their likes and dislikes to the world. (Actually, a social networking website called SixDegrees.com predated Friendster by five years; however, the site was unable to attract many users and went out of business in 2001.)

Friendster's success was immediate, attracting three million users in the first few months of its existence. A year later, MySpace was released and quickly made Friendster a relic of the past. Where Friendster was clean and targeted toward adults, MySpace was messy, irreverent, and targeted toward the younger users, who were raised online. Although MySpace reigned as the supreme social networking site until 2005, it was primarily used for posting pictures and party invites, and did not have much use as a business tool.

And then came Facebook. Originally created as a site to connect students at Ivy League colleges, Facebook opened its doors to users of all ages in 2006. Facebook was the first networking site with mass appeal; its look was professional enough to appeal to adults, yet not so stodgy that it turned off younger users. As of this writing, Facebook looks like it's here to stay; however, if past experience is any indication, something newer and better just may come along before this book even goes to print.

So which program is the best for developing your professional network? You can discount Friendster right off the bat, since it's basically a ghost town at this point. MySpace still has its place for artists and musicians, but it probably won't help you find a new green career.

Facebook can be useful in some respects, mostly because its popularity far exceeds any of the other social networking sites. When I have to find interview subjects for articles or books, for instance, Facebook is the first place I turn to, sending out a message to my network of friends. If you're an entrepreneur, Facebook has a lot of features that make it a useful promotional tool. As a management system for your professional network, however, Facebook is not really appropriate; you probably won't want your professional contacts to be reading your every random thought or looking at those old pictures of you and your college friends doing body shots in Cabo San Lucas.

That's where LinkedIn (www.linkedin.com) comes in. LinkedIn does one thing and does it well: It manages your professional profile. Since 2003, the site has quietly been building a dedicated user base of employers, employees, job seekers, and recruiters. Although it shouldn't take the place of face-to-face networking, LinkedIn is a useful and powerful site that is becoming a necessary part of the modern job searcher's tool kit.

Eco-Quiz
What percentage of people surveyed in a 2009 Pew Research Poll had never heard the term cap-and-trade?

a. *15%*

b. *30%*

c. *55%*

d. *80%*

Answer: c. 55%. *The poll found that only 23% of respondents even knew that cap-and-trade was related to the environment, while 29% thought it was related to health care, banking reform, or unemployment.*

Getting the Most Out of LinkedIn
Step One: Register
Before you can start developing your profile and making use of LinkedIn as a networking tool, you have to register. Signing up for LinkedIn is free; although there are paid subscriptions available for LinkedIn power users, a free account provides you with all the tools you'll need to develop your network.

If you don't already have a profile, visit www.linkedin.com to set one up. Follow the steps to go through the registration process and confirm your e-mail address.

After that, you'll be taken to your LinkedIn homepage (see Figure 6.1).

On the left-hand side of the screen, near the bottom, you'll see a box that reads "Your profile is 25%." As you add information to your profile, this percentage will increase. Now, click on the link at the bottom of this box reading "Edit," to go to your profile page. (You can also access this page by clicking on the "Profile" link in the preceding box.) This is where you'll fill in your experience to start building your personal profile. You can either retype information from your resume in the appropriate boxes, or upload your resume and let LinkedIn do it for you. Uploading your resume is the fastest option, but you may need to do some editing to make sure LinkedIn put everything in the right place.

FIGURE 6.1   Sample LinkedIn Homepage

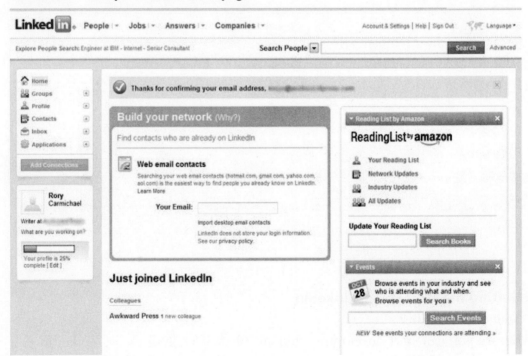

Step 2: Build Your Network

Once you have your profile information completed, it's time to start adding people to your network. At the top right-hand side of the page you'll see a search box with a dropdown menu next to it (see Figure 6.2). By default, the box reads "Search People." The dropdown menu allows you to do a few different kinds of searches: people, jobs, companies, answers, inbox, and groups. For now, let's stick to searching for people and companies.

If you currently have a job, a good place to start is by doing a search for your company. LinkedIn has a database of thousands of companies; it's likely that you will find your company listed. Click on the company name and you'll be taken to a company profile page with listings of your coworkers who already have profiles on LinkedIn. (Don't worry; LinkedIn is widespread enough at this point that no one at your company will assume you're looking for a new job just because you're building a profile on the site.) When you find one of your coworkers, (preferably a coworker with whom you have a good working relationship), click on the link on the right-hand side of the page that reads

FIGURE 6.2   LinkedIn Search Box

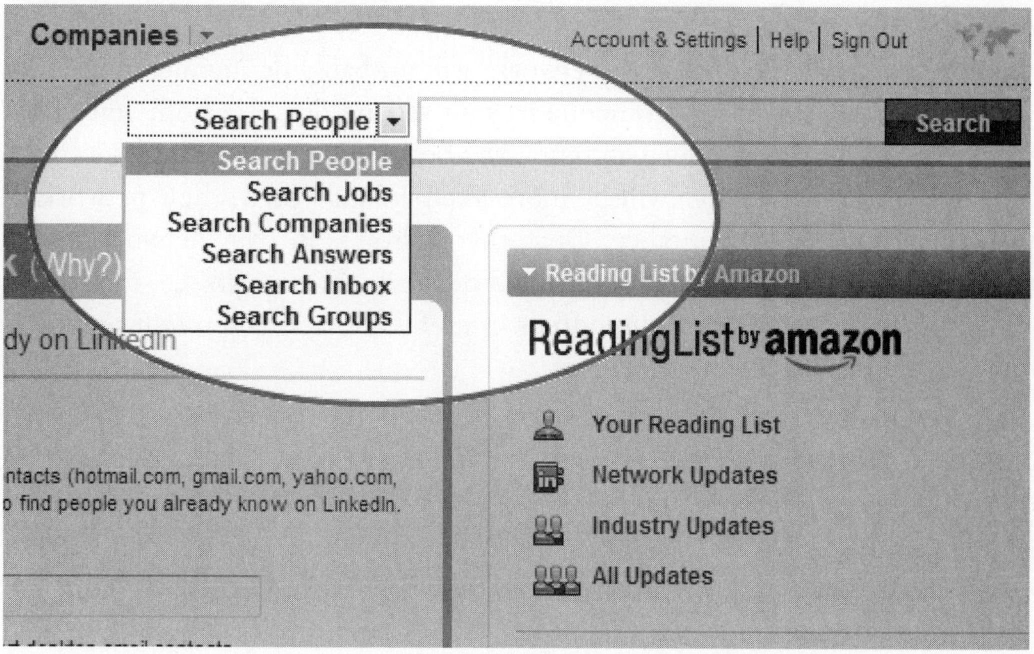

"Add [coworker's name] to your network." This will take you to another page where you are asked to describe your relationship with that coworker and add a personal note, if you wish. After you've filled in the necessary information, click "Send Invitation." When your coworker responds to your invitation, they will be added to your network. You can also use the search box to look for for friends whom you know outside your work world. Feel free to add these people to your network as well; however, keep in mind that the goal of LinkedIn is not to collect friends; it's to develop a network of professional contacts who can help in your job search.

One of the most useful innovations of LinkedIn is the *relationship degree* function. Everyone to whom you are directly connected is in your "first degree" network. When you click on the profile of someone in your network, you will see a circle with the number 1 next to that person's name. Your second-degree network is composed of people who are connected to your contacts but are not directly connected to you. Third-degree connections are people who are connected to contacts of your contacts. For instance, if Bob is your first-degree contact, and Mary is one of his contacts but not one of yours, then Mary is your second-degree contact. If Mary is connected to Sam, but neither you nor Bob is connected to Sam, then Sam is your third-degree contact.

Your first- and second-degree networks will probably be the most useful in your job search. If you find someone in your second degree whom you think would be a good contact, you can request to be introduced to that person. Just as in the real world, people will be more likely to add you to their network if you have a mutual acquaintance. Once that person is in your network, *all* of their contacts will now be in your second network. As you can see, this could quickly put you in touch with hundreds of useful contacts you might not have discovered otherwise.

Step 3: Get Recommendations

One of the great features that helps make LinkedIn a powerful promotional tool is that it enables you to collect and display recommendations, which are pre-written references from clients or coworkers. Having quality recommendations can be as, if not *more*, impressive than having a strong resume. It's easy to make your work experience sound good when you're the one writing it, but a recommendation is proof that others find your work valuable as well.

To get recommendations on LinkedIn, you must request them from members of your network. You access the Recommendations page by clicking on the plus sign next to the Profile link on the left-hand side of the page (see Figure 6.3). At the top of the Recommendations page, you will see three tabs: "Received Recommendations," "Sent Recommendations," and "Request Recommendations." As you may have guessed, the link you will want to click on is "Request Recommendations."

When you're deciding whom to request recommendations from, it goes without saying that you should concentrate on people whom you believe will give you a good endorsement. Limit your recommendation requests to people you have worked with or for; your friends may have wonderful things to say about your personality, but if you have too many recommendations, the important ones will get lost in the shuffle. Don't just limit your requests to

FIGURE 6.3   LinkedIn's Recommendations Page

bosses, either; positive recommendations from coworkers show that you work well in teams, while recommendations from people under you demonstrate your management abilities. At the same time, be conscious of not requesting too many recommendations. A handful of excellent ones are more powerful than 30 mediocre ones.

It can be okay in some situations to send the stock message when asking someone to connect to your network, but you should always send a personal message when you're requesting a recommendation. It takes time to write a recommendation for someone, and you should acknowledge your gratitude to whomever you are making the request of. It can also be helpful to write a recommendation for that person before you make your request.

Also, keep in mind that you are not required to display all of the recommendations you receive. All are sent to you for approval before they are viewable by others, and even after you've accepted a recommendation, you are allowed to hide it from display. If you're unhappy with what someone has to say about your work, simply hide the recommendation and no one will be the wiser.

Green Quotes

We are working to rebuild our economy in a more equitable manner, one that is inclusive of all Americans regardless of socio-economic background or gender. Together we can help individuals enter career pathways leading to economic self-sufficiency. The new foundation green jobs can provide long-term security for the economy as a whole, and bring security to a family to help pay their mortgage, get their children health care, and put food on their table.
—U.S. Secretary of Labor Hilda Solis

Step 4: Find Jobs

LinkedIn is not just a networking tool; it's also become one of the premier job search engines on the Internet. To start your job search, click on the "Jobs" link at the top of the page (see Figure 6.4). This will take you to the job search page, where you can search for jobs in your ZIP code using keywords. You can also click on the "Advanced Job Search" tab for more specific searches.

It is in the area of job searches that the power of LinkedIn's networking approach to employment is most apparent. Once you have a network of contacts, the job search page will display a list of companies to which you are con-

FIGURE 6.4   Jobs Link on LinkedIn

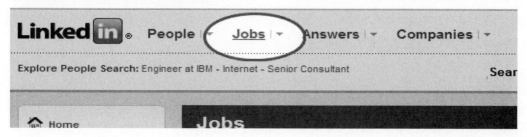

nected (see Figure 6.5). Click on any of these companies, and you can see how you are connected to them.

You can perform additional searches within your network of companies by clicking on the "See more" link at the bottom of the box. This will take you to a page where you can search using keywords, industry, location, and company size. On the bottom right-hand side of the page there's a checkbox; click on it and you can see which companies in your network are hiring. These search options are what put LinkedIn a cut above other job search engines; instead of sending a blind resume that will end up in a pile with those of hundreds of other applicants, you can use your network connections to make a targeted appeal to the people you'd like to know.

Step 5: Learn More

I've covered the basic steps of building your network and searching for jobs, but LinkedIn offers many other features to help you find, build, and maintain your career. To learn additional tips and tricks, visit the LinkedIn Learning Center at learn.linkedin.com. There are also many books available that can

FIGURE 6.5   LinkedIn's List of Companies

help you take advantage of LinkedIn's features, including Jan Vermeiren's *How to REALLY use LinkedIn*, Jason Alba's *I'm on LinkedIn—Now What???* and Steven Tylock's *The LinkedIn Personal Trainer*.

As the Internet continues to evolve and ingrain itself into every aspect of our lives, our online networks are becoming just as crucial as our off-line ones. If you don't want to be left behind in your job search, you should start building your online network today. When it comes to looking for jobs, there is no such thing as having too many resources.

CHAPTER SEVEN

MASTERING THE INTERVIEW PROCESS

Chapter Overview

The interview is your final chance to prove your value to the company you'd like to join. Everything you've been working on up to this point—crafting your resume and cover letters, networking, searching for jobs, and contacting companies—has been leading up to this moment. How should you dress? What information should you convey? How can you answer the tough questions that are likely to come up? In this chapter, you learn how to "close the deal" by convincing your interviewer that you're the right person—nay, the *only* person—for the job.

Section 1: Interview Dos and Don'ts

Do: Impress the heck out of your interviewer. Don't: Embarrass yourself. In this section, we look at a list of dos and don'ts that will give you a leg up on the competition.

Section 2: Research as a Preparation Tool

If you show up to your interview knowing nothing about the company but the address, you're going to be in trouble. When you really want to make a great impression, you have to do some research. This section explores where to do corporate research and what you should be looking for as you get ready for your interview.

Section 3: Typical Interview Questions

One of the most impressive traits in a job interview is the ability to answer questions quickly and intelligently. Taking the time to practice the most common questions before the interview will help you come across as thoughtful, well-spoken, and confident. In this section, we look at some tips for answering the most popular interview questions. In addition, we talk about questions you can ask the interviewer that will help you learn more about the job and leave a great impression.

In Their Own Words: Frank Cozza, Siemens Building Technologies
Frank Cozza is a project manager at Siemens Building Technologies. He is based in Michigan.

What do you do?
My primary job is working for Siemens Building Technologies. Last summer I got LEED certified. We're trying to get as many people in Siemens Building Technologies LEED certified. The division I work for is Siemens Government Services. That's simply a proxy company that allows Siemens to do business with the federal government.

How long have you been at Siemens?
This is my second tour of duty with them, since 2005. But I've been within this industry for awhile. All of my jobs have been energy related, in terms of energy reduction—doing things in buildings to reduce their energy load. Primarily that has involved cutting back their usage of gas, electricity, and water. But one of the new ways to cut that demand is by going to alternative sources of energy.

And what exactly are you doing there?

I'm kind of a highfalutin sales guy. *[Laughs]* I'm a program manager on a program we have with the army that involves energy reduction. I help Siemens win contracts to do work with the federal government in that area.

What was the LEED certification process like?

To get LEED certified you have to take a very, very difficult test. Studying for the test was quite onerous, to say the least. I probably put in . . . I would say, probably close to 400 hours studying last summer. You can't use any resources or anything. They could just make it open book and say, "Here's a project. Get it LEED certified."

So there was a lot of memorization?

Yeah. A lot of rote memorization.

Did you learn a lot during that process?

Oh, absolutely. I knew the control world and energy reduction, but [I also learned a lot about] new types of materials that are being used in buildings, and all the things that could be done when you're retrofitting a building or you're building a new one; things you want to do to lessen the amount of debris you have going into landfills.

Are you looking at your job in a different way now that you know all that stuff?

Absolutely. And it's good for my customers, who are mainly federal agencies. We try to get them to do things more efficiently. As a taxpayer, I'm concerned about that.

Are there a lot of things we can do that actually save money?

I would say so. Let me just pontificate for about two minutes here. *[Laughs]* The whole green movement, what it's based on is getting us off fossil fuels, which is a great thing. Around that core of getting us off fossil fuels is energy reduction, cleaner uses of energy, and methods to lower the cost of energy. Eventually solar power could be very inexpensive. It's not right now, because the cost to make photovoltaic cells is still more expensive, unfortunately, than electricity made in a coal plant.

It seems like there's no single magic bullet solution.
Yeah. It's a combination of things. Now, I don't have a good understanding of geothermal, in terms of how expensive it is, and how much sense it makes, or how practical it is. I know people are doing it and seem to be doing it quite successfully. But one area I do know well that I've worked with on five or six big projects over the past few years, is landfills. Using the methane that comes off the decomposing landfills to provide natural gas for, say, an automobile plant. That's very efficient. You're going to have garbage no matter what. Why not put it to use?

Are you hopeful? Do you feel like a lot of good progress is being made?
Yeah. I think the arrow is definitely pointing upward. I'll tell you what I was building up to, though, and that is the greenest energy out there is nuclear.

That's a touchy political subject.
It is, but it's the greenest energy out there.

Do you think that's coming around?
We've seen signs of it slowly coming around. We're starting to see a resurgence of interest around the United States. Obviously you have to control it, but if you want to get off foreign oil, I think it's a good way to go. It's at the far right end of green energy, but I'd say it's definitely green.

It seems like a lot of the immediate demand is in construction, building, retrofitting, that sort of thing. But are you seeing any other places that you feel could really use workers?
[Before you can] get to the construction, you have to have somebody engineer and design the system. And I don't think there are enough of those guys out there. Once that starts to take off, you'll see more middle-income construction jobs in things like building windmills, working for companies that manufacture solar panels.

The potential is big. That's why you have [Michigan governor] Jennifer Granholm and everybody in the state here going after alternative energy companies. But there's still a lot of research and development that needs to be done. The federal government must be better about funding these projects, as they were during the Manhattan Project. When we wanted to build a bomb, we found the funding for that.

Section 1: Interview Dos and Don'ts

In Japan, it is very important to demonstrate the proper amount of respect to your peers and superiors. When talking to one's superiors or meeting business associates, Japanese businesspeople use a form of language known as *keigo* that is built around the usage of honorifics. There are three different forms of *keigo* which are used in specific circumstances: *sonkeigo* (respectful language), *kensongo* (humble language), and *teineigo* (polite language). Each form of language involves unique verb conjugations, forms of address, and noun prefixes, all of which are governed by rules of social behavior that can be learned only through years of practice.

Although business relations aren't quite as complicated in the United States, the business world still requires us to behave and communicate differently from how we would in other social settings. In some ways, business relationships are even trickier in the United States; at least in Japan, everyone is operating under the same set of rules. Here, you have to size up every person you meet to determine what form of communication will work best. This is difficult enough when you're meeting people in your own peer group in a social setting; it becomes even more difficult when you're trying to convince someone to hire you. You want to come across as confident but not cocky; resolute but adaptable; knowledgeable but willing to learn. Some people will judge a too-polite demeanor as phony, while others will see a too-familiar approach as disrespectful.

Every interview is different, and there is, unfortunately, no single template you can follow to guarantee a great interview every time. An interview is similar to a first date; sometimes you'll hit it off immediately, and at other times you'll have a difficult time finding anything to say. You can't really prepare for every aspect of the interview process, but there *are* some things you can do to create a good impression and improve your chances of making it on to the next round. Over the next few pages, we take a look at interview Dos and Don'ts, from deciding what to wear to the ever-important follow up.

Green Quotes
The environment unites us in ways that transcend religious and philosophical differences as well as political and cultural differences. Paradoxically, the more we harm the environment, the more the environment proves that we are all connected. . . . It is not too late. God's world has incredible healing powers. Within a single generation, we could steer the earth toward our children's future. Let that generation start now.

—Ecumenical Patriarch Bartholomew of the Eastern Orthodox Church, speaking before the Brookings Institute

Before the Interview

Do *Dress Appropriately*

Contrary to popular belief, this does not mean that you have to wear a business suit to every interview. You might be expected to wear a suit if you were interviewing to work for a financial company, but in a creative job, a suit might come across as too stuffy. Before you go in for your interview, do a little research to gauge the accepted style of dress at the company you're interviewing for. On the day of the interview, wear the nicest outfit you would ever have to wear on the job. (Note, however, that if you're not sure what to wear, it is better to dress too well than not well enough. In this case, a business suit is a good default outfit.)

If you're interviewing for an industry where you would normally be allowed to dress ultracasually—construction, for example—you should still dress up for the interview. A business suit probably won't be necessary, but a nice pair of pants or a skirt and a button-down shirt would show that you made an effort to look professional.

Don't *Try to Showcase Your Personal Sense of Style*

When you're assembling an interview outfit, the goal is to show that you can fit in with the rest of the team. Unless you're interviewing to be a clothing designer, it is more important to outshine the other candidates with your experience and personality than with your outfit. If you normally have a distinctive way of dressing, downplay it for the interview, even if you feel that it is the ultimate expression of your personality. There will be plenty of opportunities for you to establish your individuality once you have gotten the job; for now, you should play it safe.

Do *Look Clean and Tidy*

Shave, brush your hair, take a shower, wear deodorant. Tuck in your shirt. Nothing will get you shuttled out the door faster than looking like you just crawled out of bed.

Don't *Wear Heavy Perfume or Cologne*

Some people are more sensitive to smells than others, and you don't want to risk offending someone with your odor. A scent can leave a powerful psychological impression, and if your interviewer dislikes your perfume, that's what will stick in his or her mind. Don't take the risk; wear a minimal scent or nothing at all.

Do *Take the Time to Practice*

Find a friend or family member and do some role-playing. It's not enough to practice by yourself; you need the input of another person to truly get a sense of what it's going to be like in the interview situation. Go over some of the common questions included in this chapter and practice giving your answers. Try practicing with several people. Every interviewer has a different interviewing style; if you practice with only one person, you may get comfortable with one type of style and discover that your actual interviewer has a much different style.

Don't *Memorize Answers*

If you've made it to the interview stage, the interviewer already knows you're qualified for the job. The point of the interview is to test skills that can't be seen on a resume: your communication skills and your ability to think on your feet. The interviewer does not want to hear you repeat information from your resume; she wants to see how you handle yourself in the moment. You can't really determine ahead of time what questions an interviewer is going to ask, and even if you could, it would be a bad idea to memorize your answers. As any professional speaker will tell you, it is much easier to engage your audience with a speech that is improvised from a general outline than a speech that is written out, memorized, and delivered word-for-word. You can practice ahead of time to get an *idea* of how you're going to respond to questions, but if you walk into an interview with specific answers memorized, you're likely to waste a lot of mental energy trying to work your answers into the conversation.

Did You Know?

The EPA manages a voluntary program called the Green Power Partnership, in which companies are allowed to offset their usage of nonrenewable energy sources by generating renewable energy onsite and purchasing Renewable Energy certificates. By purchasing 1,301,300,000 kilowatt hours of green energy in 2009, Intel was the largest buyer of renewable energy in the country. As large as this figure is, it was only equal to 48% of Intel's total energy usage. PepsiCo, the #2 purchaser of green power, offsets or generates 100% of its energy from renewable sources.

During the Interview
Do *Arrive Early*

Try to be at the office (or wherever the interview is taking place) 10 minutes before the interview begins. If you encounter a problem and won't be able to make it on time, let the interviewer know as soon as possible. Make sure to bring the interviewer's contact information with you when you leave the house in case you get stuck in traffic or find that you're running late. Chances are the interviewer has other interviews scheduled, and if you show up 10 minutes late you're likely to throw off the entire schedule. This is not the first impression you want to make, so get there early.

Don't *Bring Anyone with You*

Bringing someone with you to an interview is like bringing someone along with you on a date without informing the person you're dating. Even if your friend is planning on sitting quietly in the hall during the interview, it's still considered unprofessional. If you have kids, arrange for a babysitter.

The Power of "Yes, And"

People who perform improvisational comedy or acting have a rule for scenes known as "yes, and." When you say "yes, and" in a conversation, you are agreeing with what the person is saying and adding something on top of that. The opposite of "yes, and" is "no, but." When you say "no, but," you reject what the other person is saying and replace his or her ideas with your own. The best improvised scenes come from "yes, and" conversations.

For example, say you are in an improvised scene where you and another actor are camping in the woods. The other actor looks up and says, "Oh my gosh, is that a bear?" If you respond, "Yes, and he's coming right at us!" then you have an action that will move the scene forward. If you respond, "No, that's just a garbage can," there's nowhere for the scene to go.

"Yes, and" is not just useful in improvisation; it's also a good conversational tool. People love feeling appreciated, and making use of "yes, and" sentence structures is a good way to make people feel that you are on the same page. Now, it's impossible to say "yes, and" for everything; you shouldn't say "yes" to a yes or no question if the correct answer is "no." But an easy way to get into an interviewer's good graces is to say things like "I agree," and "that's a good point" when they offer opinions, and then add on to what the interviewer is saying. It's difficult to reach any sort of understanding in a "no, but" conversation, because you're constantly refuting each other. Look for opportunities where you can *agree* with ech the interviewer is saying and *add* your own unique perspective.

Do *Be Friendly to Everyone You Meet*

There may be only one person who makes the final decision on whether you will get hired, but everyone you encounter from the moment you step into the office can be a potential ally. Assistants and receptionists, in particular, have a lot of influence. If you're rude to the receptionist, the interviewer is bound to hear about it after you have left. And even if the interviewer doesn't hear about it, remember that, if all goes well, you'll be working at this company soon. There's no reason to start out on a bad foot with anyone.

Don't *Try to Be Everyone's Friend*

If the interviewer introduces you to people, you should be polite and friendly. But if not, don't go around introducing yourself to people who are trying to do their work. There will be plenty of time for that after you get the job.

Do *Shake the Interviewer's Hand*

Give the interviewer a firm (but not overbearing) handshake and look him or her in the eye when introducing yourself. While you're shaking his or her hand, be sure to smile. A smile creates an instant impression of warmth that can have a positive effect on the tone of the entire interview.

Don't *Get Too Familiar*

It's good to create the impression of familiarity in an interview, but you don't want to be presumptuous. Treat the interviewer as you would a respected teacher, even if he is younger than you. Call the interviewer by the name he uses when he introduces himself. Don't assume that nicknames are okay, no matter how common they may be; if he introduces himself as "Charles," it's disrespectful to assume he likes to be called "Charlie."

Do *Come Prepared*

Bring a copy of your resume and a list of references with you—even if you think the interviewer already has this information. Bring contact numbers and dates of employment from your old jobs in case you have to fill out an application form. It's also helpful to bring along a pen and a notebook to take notes during the interview. You may not have to use them, but just the act of bringing these materials shows that you are good at planning ahead.

Don't *Bring Too Much Stuff with You*

A small bag, briefcase, or portfolio should be plenty. This isn't show-and-tell; there's no reason to bring anything other than the essentials.

Do *Show Enthusiasm*

Note that I said *enthusiasm*, not *excitement*. Enthusiasm indicates a positive attitude, while excitement indicates that you are anticipating something. A half-hour conversation with someone who is enthusiastic can be inspirational, while a half-hour conversation with someone who is excited is just exhausting. Speak clearly and distinctly when responding to the interviewer's questions, and let her know that you'd be a valuable addition to the team. Your enthusiasm should give the interviewer the impression that you can't wait to be hired and start making a difference, *not* that you can't wait for the interview to be over!

Don't *Downplay Your Accomplishments*

There are many times in life when you should be humble: after you've won an Olympic medal, for instance, or when receiving a Humanitarian of the Year award. A job interview is not one of these times. You don't want to come across as arrogant, of course, but there is nothing to be gained by telling an interviewer your past accomplishments were "no big deal."

This can be tricky at times during an interview, because many interviewers love to throw in questions that seem to be begging for a negative answer (i.e., "What are some of your weaknesses?") Don't fall for their trap. As we'll see in Section 3, questions like this really test your ability to turn negatives into positives.

Eco-Quiz

How many energy efficiency jobs are middle-skill, requiring less than a bachelor's degree?

a. $\frac{1}{5}$

b. $\frac{2}{5}$

c. $\frac{1}{4}$

d. $\frac{2}{3}$

Answer: d. $\frac{2}{3}$. *According to the Workforce Alliance, 66%, or $\frac{2}{3}$ of all energy efficiency jobs require less than a bachelor's degree. Of these jobs 21% are low-skill, requiring no education, and 13% are high-skill, requiring a bachelor's degree or higher.*

Do *Listen to the Interviewer*

When the interviewer is speaking, you should be listening. If you accidentally start talking before she finishes, apologize and ask her to continue. Don't interrupt while the interviewer is speaking, and try not to formulate your answers until the question has been asked; it's easy to miss important information when you're preoccupied with what you're going to say next. It's also important to make sure you're answering the questions that the interviewer is asking. They're not interested in your ability to spew nonsense; they want to see that you are able to interpret what they are saying and give a well-considered response.

Don't *Just Wait for the Interviewer to Ask Questions*

You should let the interviewer lead the discussion, but a certain amount of give-and-take can make the conversation feel more natural. Do what you would do naturally; if you have a question that is sparked by something the interviewer says, you won't be penalized for asking it. Also, if you have information you think could help you get the job that you have not had a chance to address during the interview, there is nothing wrong with bringing that information up before you leave.

Do *Ask Questions Yourself*

At the end of the interview, the interviewer will usually ask if you have any questions. Even if all of your questions have been answered, you should take advantage of the opportunity. It doesn't matter what you ask, (within reason—try to avoid asking questions like, "Do you ever fall asleep listening to yourself talk?"), just as long as your questions demonstrate that you've been listening during the interview and that you did your research before you came in. The question period of the interview puts the ball in your court. You've already told the interviewer why you are right for the company; this is your chance to find out why the company is right for you.

As the interview is coming to an end, be sure to ask the interviewer when she expects to come to a hiring decision. This will help you plan the proper timeline for your follow-up strategy.

Don't *Be the First Person to Discuss Salary*

Salary is the most sensitive part of the hiring process, and you should avoid talking about it for as long as possible. If you bring it up too early in the process, your salary requirements could get you taken out of consideration. If you wait until you're offered the job, you know they want to hire you, and you'll have a better chance of getting the salary you want.

Do *Stay Calm*

The interviewer is just a person, and the interview is just a conversation. True, interviews tend to be somewhat more one-sided than many other conversations, but we've all spent plenty of time in our lives meeting new people and talking about ourselves. If you appear shaky and nervous, your body language is going to overshadow the quality of your answers. On the other hand, if you're confident, relaxed, and well-spoken, you will impress the interviewer at once.

Don't *Forget What You're There for*

As much as you want to make sure the conversation flows naturally, remember: Your goal is to get hired, not to make a new friend. It's good to have a pleasant, likeable demeanor, but it's also crucial to show that you are the right person for the job. Go into the interview with specific examples of past successes that illustrate a variety of different strengths. If you can demonstrate that you're capable, experienced, likable, and confident, then the job is as good as yours!

And finally:

Don't *Chew Gum*

I mean, come on.

After the Interview

Do *Know When the Interview Is Over*

The interviewer might not always announce that the interview is over, but you should be able to gauge when things are wrapping up. Don't make a pest of yourself; thank the interviewer for his time, shake his hand, and show yourself out. If the interviewer has an assistant who sits near his office, you should smile and say good-bye to the assistant on your way out. You never know who's going to put in a good word for you after you have left.

Don't *Rush It*

The last thing you want is to look like you can't wait to get out of there. You shouldn't overstay your welcome, but you shouldn't be too eager to leave, either. Keep an eye on the clock and pay attention to the interviewer's cues and you should be just fine.

Do *Follow Up*

After you have left the interview, write down everything that happened. Make a special note if the interviewer mentioned any particular interests or news topics; just as with networking, it's always good to follow up with specific information that is of interest to the other party, when possible.

The follow-up does not need to be elaborate. Send the interviewer an e-mail thanking him for his time and telling him you're available to answer any questions. You can also use this chance to reiterate any important points you feel may have gotten buried during the interview.

If you haven't heard anything in a week, send another follow-up e-mail. You can keep following up once a week until you hear something for certain. Keep in mind what the interviewer told you when you asked for the estimated decision date; this will give you a good idea of when to just give up. For the majority of jobs, you should get an answer one way or the other within a few weeks.

Don't *Apologize*

When you're sending follow-up e-mails, it's tempting to say something like, "I'm sorry to be a pest, but . . ." *Don't* do it. If you apologize for being a pest, the interviewer is more likely to see you as a pest. Interviewers expect you to follow up. It shows you're interested in the job.

The best salespeople know that it sometimes takes a lot of follow-up to close the deal. And be patient: Sometimes the hiring process takes longer than you might think. Remain positive and courteous in all your correspondence with the interviewer. And don't burn any bridges: Even if you don't get the job, you should let the interviewer know that you'd appreciate being considered for any other positions that arise.

Section 2: Research as a Preparation Tool

Before you go into the interview, it's important to know what you're getting into. When you speak with the interviewer, you should be able to demonstrate that you have an understanding of what the company does, how they function, and what your job requirements will be. Your chances at making a good impression will increase if you show a genuine interest in the company and what they do. It's not enough to just reread the job description posted in their HELP WANTED ad; the savvy job seeker will take the time to learn about the company through research. The more information you have when going into the interview, the easier it will be for you to ask informed questions and to demonstrate your interest in the company.

Questions to Answer

You know that you should research the company to prepare for the interview, but what exactly should you be researching? Following is a list of questions to keep in mind while researching the company.

- What does the company do?
- When was the company established?
- What are the circumstances behind the company's founding?
- Who are the company's clients? Do they make a product or provide a service?
- Are they privately owned or publicly traded?
- How is the company organized? What are its divisions?
- Approximately how many employees work at the company?
- Who are the company's competitors?
- What sets the company apart from its competitors?

- Has the company been in the news for any reason? If so, what for?
- How has the company been performing financially?
- What do outsiders think of the company's financial prospects?

Where to Research

In the old days, researching a company meant spending the day at the library poring through microfiche newspaper collections, government archives, and stock reports. Today, in-depth information about practically any company you can think of is available to anyone with a home computer and an Internet connection. In fact, it's so easy to find information today that it's easy to become overwhelmed before you even begin. Not to worry; if you limit your search to a handful of important sources, you can learn all you need to know to impress your interviewer with your knowledge. These sources include the following.

The Company's Website

The company website has become a necessary marketing tool for any new or established business. It's doubtful you'll interview at a company that doesn't have an online presence of some sort. (If you do find a company without a website, there are still ways to research them. Read on to the end of the section to find some tips for doing old-school offline research.)

Most corporate websites contain a wealth of information that will come in handy during your interview. Go through the About section of the website. Read up on the company's history. Look at the employee directory to get an idea of whom you may be working with. Take a look at their job listing pages to get an idea of whether they're growing. Read their recent press releases. (Note: Frequently, sections like About and Press will be located at the bottom of the homepage, in text links.)

Pay special attention to annual reports. All publicly traded companies are required by the Securities and Exchange Commission (SEC) to file an annual report featuring information on things like earnings, goals, and projections. Annual reports can often be found in the Investor Relations section of the company's website.

LinkedIn

As I discussed in Chapter 6, LinkedIn offers a number of different functions that make it a useful tool for job seekers. Thousands of companies now have profiles on LinkedIn that provide company information, including employee lists, subsidiary information, and news. When you look a company up on LinkedIn, you can also see if you're connected to anyone who works there. This is useful information to know when you're interviewing, as your connections can often put in a good word about you to the interviewer.

Green Quotes

"When you're speaking sustainability with business people, you have to speak the language," said Richard Goode, head of climate change programs for Alcatel-Lucent, a global telecommunications company. "The language has always been profitability."

—"More Corporations Are 'Greening' Supply Chains"—Quoted in Reuters, September 28, 2009

Corporate Information Aggregators

Corporate information aggregate sites are a good place to get an overview of what companies do and how they're doing. These websites contain listings of tens of thousands of companies, with information about stock prices, financial statements, and lists of competitors. Most of these sites provide some useful information free but require users to pay for in-depth reports. (Note: Unless you're thinking about buying stock in the company, it's probably not worth your while to buy a report.)

www.hoovers.com

www.corporateinformation.com

www.standardandpoors.com

www.dnb.com

Business News

Some websites focus on business news; a search on these sites is a good way to find out how the company is viewed in the media.

www.bloomberg.com

www.businessweek.com

money.cnn.com

www.forbes.com

www.bizjournals.com

Print Resources

If you're having a difficult time finding information online, there is always the traditional way of researching: going to the library. A few different publications that list information about corporations can help you in your research. Some of these publications have moved to CD-ROM; ask your librarian to help you find the latest edition.

Business Periodicals Index

Dun and Bradstreet Regional Business Directory

Lexis Nexis: Director of Corporate Affiliations

Ward's Business Directory of U.S. Private and Public Companies

One more important *don't* when it comes to research: *Don't research the individuals at the company*. In the age of the Internet, it's easy to find out way more information than we need to know about people. If you walk into an interview knowing the names of your interviewer's pets, you've gone too far. You want to look informed, but you don't want to look like a stalker. Limit your research to the company and keep any information you have about the individuals who work there to yourself.

Section 3: Typical Interview Questions

Every interviewer has his or her own style. Some interviewers will come prepared with a list of questions they ask of everyone, and other interviewers will just wing it. Unless you're interviewing at a company with a permanent staffing department, you probably won't be talking to someone whose main job is interviewing new hires. You're likely to encounter a mixed bag of interviewing abilities, from the ultraprofessional to the barely experienced.

Types of Job Interviews

It's impossible to predict ahead of time what questions will be asked, but there are some questions that are more common than others. On the next pages, you will find some of the most common questions you can expect, and some strategies for answering them.

TYPE	WHAT TO EXPECT	TIPS
Telephone Screening Interview	A call from an employer to screen you and other candidates for essential criteria.	Have your job search records organized and handy. Refer to your resume as needed.
In-Person Screening Interview	An in-person screening for initial impressions of your attitude, interest, and professional style.	You may not be meeting with the final decisionmaker, but don't slack off. Sell yourself as you would in a regular interview.
Selection Interview	In-depth questions on your qualifications used to evaluate your ability to fit in.	Establish rapport with everyone you meet (before and after the actual interview). Sell yourself as a natural addition to the team.
Work Sample Interview	An opportunity to demonstrate your specific skills. It may be a display of your portfolio or a demonstration of your skills.	Run through different ways to describe the projects in your portfolio. Practice your presentation until it is smooth.

TYPE	WHAT TO EXPECT	TIPS
Peer Group Interview	A meeting with your prospective coworkers, who will evaluate how well you fit in.	Don't forget to smile. It shows confidence.
Group or Panel Interview	Three or more people who will ask you questions on your qualifications and evaluate how you fit in.	Direct your answer to the person who asked the question, but try to maintain eye contact with all group members.
Luncheon Interview	Interview conducted in a restaurant to assess how well you handle yourself in social situations.	Pick easy things to eat so you can answer questions and pay attention to the conversation.
Stress Interview	Questions intended to make you uncomfortable. This is usually a test of how you will handle stress on the job.	Keep your cool and take your time in responding to the questions. Don't take anything personally.
Video Conference Interview	A person-to-person interview by video.	Practice before a video camera or mirror if facing a camera during an interview makes you nervous.

Source: Creative Job Search Guide, Minnesota Department of Employment and Economic Development. Copyright © 1994–2008. Used by permission.

Question #1: Tell me about yourself.

If you were conducting a journalistic interview for a newspaper or magazine, this would be a terrible question. First of all, it isn't actually a question. Second, it's too open ended. Ironically, this is exactly what makes it a great question for a work interview because the way you choose to answer the question can tell the interviewer as much as the answer itself.

The best strategy for answering this question is to give a basic overview of your work experience. If you have a Summary statement on your resume, this is basically what they want to hear. "I am a [blank], and I am looking to get involved in [blank]. Some of my skills are [blank], [blank], and [blank]." You can include some personal details to establish a sense of familiarity, but keep it light; the interviewer doesn't need to know how you felt when your dog passed away. Since you'll presumably be interviewing for a green job, you should also include information about any environmental work you've done. Keep your answer short and broad, though; there will be plenty of time in the rest of the interview to get into specifics.

Question #2: What are some of your strengths?

The key to answering this question properly is providing specific examples. It's not enough to say, "I'm smart, responsible, and efficient"; you should come prepared with specific stories from your previous experience that will demonstrate these qualities to the interviewer. Two or three strengths with specific examples should be plenty.

Question #3: What is your greatest weakness?

The strategy for answering this question is to choose a *positive* negative. For example, you might say your greatest weakness is perfectionism, because you don't like doing shoddy work. Or your greatest weakness is your inability to leave a project unfinished. Whatever you do, *never* give an answer that would cause the interviewer to doubt your competence. If you tell the interviewer that you're habitually late, or irresponsible, or that you have a difficult time getting along with others, you can kiss your job offer good-bye.

Eco-Quiz

How many components does the average wind turbine have?

a. *8*

b. *80*

c. *800*

d. *8,000*

Answer: d. *8,000. In terms of complexity, assembling a wind turbine is comparable to assembling a car. Wind turbines have a lot of parts that need to be designed, manufactured, assembled, and maintained, which will create new jobs at all levels of the economic spectrum.*

Question #4: Why do you want to work here?

This is where your research pays off. This question really deserves two answers. First, you should tell the interviewer why you want the position for which you're interviewing. For example: "I've always been interested in environmental studies, and this position is a great match for my skills." Next, you should give the interviewer specific information that you've learned about the company. For example: "I did a lot of research about solar panel developers, and it seems like your company creates great products that I'd be proud to work on."

Question #5: Why did you leave your last job?
(Or: Why do you want to leave your job?)

Much like the "greatest weakness" question, this question requires you to turn a negative into a positive. A great answer for this question is a variation on "I needed a new challenge, and your company seems to offer a lot of opportunities." The best answers will say something positive about the company at which you're interviewing, without speaking ill of your previous job. For example: "I am looking to transition into a more environmentally conscious field." If you were laid off from your previous job, you should be honest but positive: "I made it through three rounds of layoffs, but my company ultimately decided they could not afford to keep my department fully staffed." Corporate layoffs are common enough that no one will consider it a reflection on your work performance, as long as you word this properly.

It's harder to give a positive answer if you were fired from your previous job for poor performance. The most important thing to do is be honest and accept responsibility for your mistakes. Don't try to blame others or come up with excuses. However, if you were fired for a long list of reasons, you don't need to bring them all up. Pick the reason that is easiest to spin positively. For instance, if you were fired because you lost a big sales account, and your clients were constantly complaining about your rude attitude, you should focus your answer on losing the sales account. Whichever way you end up spinning it, you should work out the answer to this question ahead of time so that you are not caught off guard. (And while you're at it, take some time to figure out why all of your clients were complaining about your rude attitude!)

Question #6: What were some of your likes/dislikes about your last job?

For this question, you should focus on answers that relate to the work you were doing and the way the company functioned. Don't say that you liked the free ice cream bar in the cafeteria but you hated everyone you worked with. For your likes, you should concentrate on things that helped you do your job and that you would like to make a part of your new job. For instance, you could say that projects were given reasonable deadlines, or that the company helped pay for continuing education. For your dislikes, you should focus on minor annoyances: The commute was long, some of the meetings felt unnecessary. You should never speak ill of your former coworkers or bosses. Even if you thought they were all a bunch of jerks, you don't want the interviewer to think you are difficult to get along with.

Question #7: What are your career goals?

With this question, you should concentrate on career goals that could be accomplished at the company for which you're interviewing. If you're interviewing to work for an environmental law firm, for example, don't say that your ultimate goal is to be a real estate tycoon. Focus on answers that show why you would want to work at this company. For example: "I would eventually like to have an upper management role at a company that cares about the environment, because I think we have a remarkable opportunity right now to change our world for the better."

Question #8: What do you like to do in your spare time?

It may seem like this is a throwaway question, but it actually provides another opportunity to focus on why you would be a good candidate for the position. If you do any volunteer work, now is a good time to bring it up. Any of your hobbies are fair game to talk about, as long as they are things that paint you in a good light. If your hobbies include "sleeping, drinking, and breaking things," you should probably keep that information to yourself.

Question #9: How much do you expect to make?

Before you go into the interview, you should do some research and figure out what the typical salary is for the position. If you're asked this question in an interview, you should respond by asking another question: "How much do you typically pay someone in this position?" The general rule of thumb in salary negotiations is that you should avoid stating an exact figure for as long as possible; you don't want to lowball yourself, nor do you want to be rejected because you're asking for too much. If the interviewer still refuses to state a figure, you should respond with a range, i.e., "between $45,000 and $55,000." Be reasonable in your expectations, and make the low end of your range a figure you would actually be happy with. Surprisingly, employers don't automatically take the lowest number; often, they just want to make sure that your expectations aren't wildly over their budget.

Question #10: Why should we hire you?

Your answer to this question should demonstrate why you are uniquely qualified to fill the position. Why should you be hired for the job over everyone else they're interviewing? What can you contribute to the company? Don't just treat this question as another opportunity to describe your past successes; explain to the interviewer what you can do for the company. For example: "My combination of technical knowledge and demonstrated leadership abilities can help your company run more smoothly and increase profits."

Behavioral-Based Questions

A growing number of employers are beginning to incorporate *behavioral-based* questions into their interviews. These are questions that ask you to discuss how you dealt with issues in the past that you might encounter if you get hired. You can recognize a behavioral-based question, because it will begin with a phrase like, "Tell me about a time when you . . ." or "Give me an example of a way you have . . ."

There is an infinite number of variations on behavioral-based questions, and for this reason, they can be difficult to prepare for. Although you won't be able to come up with your answers ahead of time, you can take some time to remember incidents in your past when you've had to overcome challenges. Often, one experience can be used to answer more than one question.

As with the more traditional questions, behavioral-based questions will sometimes seemingly be asking you to admit something negative. For example, an interviewer might say something like, "Tell me about a time when you were disappointed with your performance." The best answer will be one that hinges on a mistake that anyone could make and ends on a positive note, such as "I once had to ask for a two week extension on a project because I hadn't budgeted enough time into my schedule. Although the client was happy with my performance and continued to hire me for contracting jobs, I still know I could have done even better if I had been more realistic about the schedule ahead of time."

Questions You Should Ask

At the end of the interview, the interviewer will typically ask if you have any questions. It's a good idea to bring a list of questions with you so that you don't have to think on your feet. Listed next are some questions to get you started.

- What would my main responsibilities be in this position?
- Whom would I be working with most closely? What departments would I interact with?
- What kind of benefits package do you offer?
- Do employees here get regular performance reviews? Are raises tied to the reviews?
- How much of my job will include routine work?
- How much time do employees here spend working independently?
- What are some of your favorite things about working here?
- What is a typical day like here?
- How would you describe the culture here?
- Where do you see the company headed?

The quality of your questions in this portion of the interview isn't going to make or break you. Obviously, don't ask any questions that you should already know the answer to (i.e., "What kind of work do you do here?"), but other than that, there aren't really any hard and fast rules about the types of question you should ask. This is your chance to get greater clarity about what your life will be like if you take the job.

CHAPTER EIGHT

CHANGING CAREERS: ADVICE FOR EXPERIENCED JOB SEEKERS

Chapter Overview

According to the U.S. Department of Labor, people change jobs an average of 10 times between the ages of 18 and 38. Although the Department of Labor does not take keep track of how often people change careers, it's reasonable to assume that a portion of those changes are among industries. Consider your friends and family members, for example; how many of them have held the same career for more than 20 years?

The fact is, most people enter the workforce before they're old enough to know what they really want to do with their lives. We all change over time, and a career that seemed fascinating at 18 might not seem so lustrous at 30. There are many things that can prompt the desire for a career change: a bad experience with a specific company, the need for more money, lack of interest in your daily tasks. No matter what the catalyst is, if a voice inside is telling you to pursue a new career, that's a voice worth listening to.

The work world has changed a lot in the past 20 years. The employment model that most of us grew up with was the *ladder*; that is, you start at the bottom rung and climb up in a vertical line until you reach the top. For most professions, that model just doesn't make sense anymore. Companies are constantly shutting their doors, downsizing, or moving departments to new countries, making job security about as difficult to find as a winning lottery ticket. The model that workers follow today could be more aptly described as a web than a ladder: We start in one position at one company, move to another position at another company, move up in that company, then move again to another position at an entirely different company. This model may seem frustrating to people who grew up with the vision of moving up the ladder, but if you are able to change your expectations, you can learn to embrace the new model and use it to your advantage. In this chapter, I give you some tips for how to do just that.

Section 1: Identifying Your Transferable Skills

Even if you don't have experience in the profession you hope to move into, if you've been in the workforce for awhile, you have definitely accumulated *transferable skills*. Transferable skills are job skills from your current profession that also relate to the job you're hoping to get. This section will help you identify the transferable skills that you can use to position yourself in your new career.

Section 2: Leveraging Your Skills

Transferable skills are useless unless you know how to mention them in your resume, cover letters, and networking. In this section, I discuss how to use your transferable skills to your best advantage.

Section 3: Gaining Experience

As useful as transferable skills can be, they sometimes won't quite be enough to land your dream job, because many jobs require specialized experience that you can get only from on-the-job or classroom training. In this section, we look at some ways to gain experience in your field of choice.

Section 4: Advice for Older Workers

No one has it rougher in the job search than older workers. Employers are often reluctant to hire older workers because they're seen as a poor investment. To counteract this stereotype, the older worker needs to demonstrate that they have something of value that can't be matched by a hundred younger employees: years and years of experience. In this section, we examine how older workers can think outside the box to sell their services in a competitive marketplace.

In Their Own Words: Joe Paolone, Recycling Coordinator for the University of Alabama at Birmingham

How did you get started on your career path?
I went into the Air Force right out of high school. The job I was assigned to was called Bioenvironmental Engineering. More or less, that's Occupational Health and Safety, radiation protection, and environmental protection rolled into one. It's a very broad career field. I finished my training in 1995 and got stationed in 1996 at Tinker Air Force Base in Oklahoma City.

What did you do after you left the military?
I got out in the fall of 1999 and went back home to Birmingham and lived with my parents for awhile. I enrolled in school at the University of Alabama at Birmingham and got a student job in occupational health and safety. I eventually picked an individually designed major called Environmental Studies. My minor was Environmental Science. For the minor, I took a lot of biology, chemistry, rainforest ecology, tropical ecology, regular ecology, things like that. For my major I had to take courses like solid hazardous waste, water and air pollution, environmental disasters, American environmental history . . . just, really, all across the spectrum.

Where did you hope to go after that?
I wasn't really sure. I never had a real well-thought-out plan. [*Laughs*] I was just seeing where it took me.

In the fall of 2004, I got a job offer from the VA Medical Center in Birmingham, working in Occupational Safety and Health at the hospital. I got to the end of my probationary period and I just really wasn't enjoying it. I didn't care for the hospital setting and for the numerous regs we had to deal with. They seemed like even more than in the Air Force.

I didn't really do much for awhile, just putzed around, and then in the summer of 2005 I got a job with the Alabama Department of Environmental Management. I liked that a lot better. But ultimately, that didn't really conform to my standards, either, and I didn't last beyond the probationary period. Then I ended up getting a pizza delivery job, just so I could have some kind of income.

Were you feeling discouraged at all about your chances of finding that job that you would really enjoy?

Yeah, I definitely was. Especially for awhile into the pizza delivery gig. I was really down on myself, thinking, Am I going to get into a decent career field, or am I going to be a pizza delivery guy for the rest of my life? I made decent money; I wasn't poverty-stricken by any means. But I was definitely overqualified to work at a pizza place.

So, fast-forward to January of 2008. I was still pretty active in some campus groups; kind of still in that quasi undergrad/graduate student mind-set. I got involved in a club called the Green Initiative at UAB. I went to some of their meetings and started to become active. We were starting to get a grassroots movement together to get a recycling program on campus. So we started pushing for a campuswide recycling program and Becky [the head of the program] recommended my name to run it. This was in January of 2008, while I was still doing the pizza job. They said they would be creating the position in a few months. Then, the state education budgets started getting cut left and right. They were having a hard time getting the position off the ground.

In the summer of 2008 I got two jobs, waiting tables and working at a recycling center run by a nonprofit group, the Alabama Environmental Council (AEC). It was four days a week, part-time. Very blue collar. I was helping people unload their recyclables, crushing cardboard and plastic, baling the plastic, keeping the center clean.

Did you enjoy doing that?

To some extent, yeah. I definitely liked the casual workdays. I liked being outdoors and doing stuff with my hands, not being in the office. And I definitely got to meet a lot of people, some of which led to friendships and later connections. So that aspect was good. But again, I still felt like I was overqualified for what I was doing.

So this whole time, the other job is sort of bubbling under the surface?

More or less. I kept calling them every couple of weeks to see how things were going. Finally, they opened the position up formally. I filled out my application, and actually I and my immediate supervisor [at AEC] were going for the same position. So they interviewed us and I got called back for the second interview and I finally accepted.

Interestingly enough, the fact that I had a degree and he didn't was the big deciding factor over why they chose me over him. He had run the recycling program for a couple of years at that place and had a little more experience in the managerial aspect than I had, whereas I was more ground level. But the position that they created called for a bachelor's degree.

What are your duties?
The official title is Recycling Coordinator for UAB. I coordinate and manage the recycling program. Really, I'm just managing all aspects of it. My immediate supervisor solves a lot of the budgetary issues, but as far as the actual program goes, I'm really the voice and the face of it for the university.

The program that I run has two halves. One is the collection program where I supervise my drivers who go out and collect the recyclables. The other part is the drop-off center, where people can come by and bring their stuff either from home or from work and drop it off. Another thing we're looking at is doing some composting with the dining halls. That's really still in the planning stages. I'm trying to manage a lot of other things, and it requires a lot of juggling right now.

Are you feeling like you've finally found the job you want to stay in?
Kind of. I like the position and it's cool working at my alma mater where I still see a lot of familiar faces. I like the variability of it. It's a little more white collar but it's loose enough where I can wear shorts to work if I need to. And I like getting out and about. I love recycling, I think it's great, and I think there's a need for it. But truly my heart is in more conservation and travel. I definitely want to stay in this position for at least a year or two.

I'm sure it's great experience.
Well, helping build the program from the ground up is going to be very translatable to other careers.

What would you tell someone who was looking for work in the green field right now?
I know it's a cliché, but it's not just what you know, it's who you know. Having connections absolutely helped me get this position. I still had to

have the degree and the experience, too. You can't discount that, but if I hadn't had the connections, I definitely don't think my chances would have been nearly as high.

I would say try to look at different opportunities. Get involved with a lot of different groups. The more groups you're involved with, especially professional-type groups, the more people you'll meet.

I've gotten a reputation for volunteering for many different events and projects, and that's a great way to meet people, too. I can't tell you how many different fundraising affairs I've done. There are usually nice benefits; you get to eat food and drink for free, and the connections you make are very, very valuable. Getting out in the community and volunteering, even if they're not directly connected to the career field, I think can be very helpful.

Section 1: Identifying Your Transferable Skills

It's easy to feel trapped if you don't like what you do. From an early age, most of us are told that we can all realize our dreams if we just work hard and believe in ourselves. (If this was true, our workforce would be entirely composed of movie stars, ballerinas, and astronauts.) When we end up in jobs that make us miserable, we feel as if we've personally failed. It often feels easier to just stick with the status quo than to start all over again.

Well, the good news is that you don't have to start all over again. If you've held a job for any length of time, then you've developed *transferable skills*. As discussed previously, transferable skills are useful skills that are not industry specific. For instance, if you've managed a retail store, the skills you've acquired will come in just as handy in any management position. Many jobs today require computer skills; if you know your way around a computer, you can do a lot of jobs that might seem unrelated to your current field.

Did You Know?

Sprint announced in 2009 that it would switch to recyclable packaging for its wireless accessories. The move was expected to save $2.1 million per year and remove 647 tons of waste from the environment.

Before you can sell yourself on your transferable skills, you first need to identify what those skills are. You should start by examining your current job duties and the skills that are at the root of those duties. For example, if one of your current job duties is *filing contracts*, the transferable skill behind that job is *organization*. Your new career choice might not include any filing, but it will almost certainly draw upon your ability to keep organized.

Your transferable skills don't necessarily need to be related to your 9-to-5 job, either. There are plenty of skills we develop in our spare-time activities that can be attractive to employers. You might not be a manager in your professional life, but if you're the president of your local PTA, then you have leadership skills.

Following is a list of universal skills that are necessary to perform a wide range of tasks. Fill out Worksheet 8.1, matching these skills with your current job duties and life activities. (If you think of skills that aren't on the list, feel free to include them.)

Universal Skills

analytic ability	interpersonal skills	public speaking
attention to details	leadership	reliability
clerical skills	meeting goals	sales ability
communication	multitasking	scheduling
computer skills	negotiation	teaching
creativity	organization	teamwork
customer service	presentation	technical knowledge
decision-making	problem solving	thoroughness
dependability	project management	time management

Worksheet 8.1   Transferable Skills

Duties/Activities   *Transferable Skill*

_____   _____

_____   _____

_____   _____

_____   _____

_____   _____

Once you've identified your transferable skills, the next step is identifying the skills that will be applicable to your desired job. Start by looking at job descriptions of your desired position and make a list similar to the one you made in Worksheet 8.1, with duties on one side, and applicable skills on the other side. Then, take a look at your list of transferable skills, and find places where they overlap with the skills needed in your desired job.

Hard Skills versus Soft Skills

Transferable skills are considered *soft skills*, that is, skills that can be developed through a variety of different experiences. Soft skills come in handy if you want to move into a position in a new industry that's similar to your current position. If you want to move onto a completely different career path, however, you may need to take the time to develop some *hard skills*. Hard skills are those that require specialized training and do not really match to your personal experience. For instance, no matter how great you are at debating, you're never going to get a job as an environmental lawyer unless you have the appropriate legal training.

Section 2: Leveraging Your Skills

Once you've figured out what your transferable skills are, it's time to use them to position yourself for the job you want.

Using Transferable Skills in a Resume

At this point, you should have a good idea of both your current skill set and the skills you will need in the job you hope to transition to. The next step is to develop a personal profile that shows why you are a good candidate for the new position. To do this, you should use your transferable skills, as well as any training or education you've had in your new field of interest, to rewrite your resume.

As detailed in Chapter 5, the first step in writing your resume is to develop an objective statement. What do you want to do, and what makes you qualified to do it? When you're changing careers, an objective statement is often a better choice on a resume than a summary statement. Summary statements generally position you to move laterally or to the next rung on the ladder, while objective statements position you to move to a place you haven't been before. Your 10 years of experience as a sales representative at a hardware store is impressive if you're going for another sales job, but it's not the best information to lead with if you're looking for a job as an energy auditor. It's a safe bet that whoever ends up looking at your resume will not take the time to read between the lines and figure out why you'd be a good match for the position; they will develop an image of who you are based on whatever information you give them. Hand them a resume that focuses on your sales experience, and they will assume you're a salesperson.

This doesn't mean that you should avoid discussing your previous experience. The mere fact that you have a work history gives you a leg up on younger workers, who have to convince employers not only that they can do the job for which they're being hired, but that they're responsible enough to hold a job, period. Most employers would rather hire someone with solid experience in a different field than someone with a great education and no job experience. You just need to reframe your experiences to fit the profile of the position you're looking to fill.

How you do this is dependent upon your transferable skills. In the preceding example of a sales representative at a hardware store transitioning to a job as an energy auditor, some of the overlapping skills between those two positions might be "analytic ability," "attention to detail," and "communication." For example, as a career salesperson, you might have this bullet point on your resume:

• Broke company sales record by generating $1,000,000 worth of sales in a single month.

While $1,000,000 is an impressive figure, it doesn't speak much to the skills you would use as an energy auditor. Instead, you should rewrite this bullet point to focus on skills that will be more pertinent to your desired job.

• Analyzed customers' hardware needs to recommend most suitable purchases for construction projects based on budget constraints, blueprints, and energy efficiency. Customer satisfaction with recommendations led to sales of $1,000,000 in a single month, a company record.

You don't need to hide the fact that you're a great salesperson; it's still an impressive career achievement that shows you're a hard worker. You should just rephrase it in a manner that is more relevant to the position you're seeking.

Green Quotes

According to John Farrell and David Morris,
authors of the report "Energy Self-Reliant States,"

All 36 states with either renewable energy goals or renewable energy mandates
could meet them by relying on in-state renewable fuels. Sixty-four percent
could be self-sufficient in electricity from in-state renewables; another 14 percent
could generate 75 percent of their electricity from homegrown fuels.

—"Energy Self-Reliant States: Second and Expanded Edition,"
* report published by the New Rules Project, October 2009*

Cover Letters

Career-changing cover letters, like resumes, should focus on your transferable skills and explain why those skills would make you a good candidate for the new position. Here are a few rules of thumb to keep in mind as you begin drafting your cover letters.

- **Make your previous career an asset, not a liability.** In your resume, you crafted the descriptions of your previous experience to show how your skills are applicable to the new position you're seeking. Still, anyone looking at your resume will be able to tell that you're transitioning into a new field. Instead of trying to hide the fact that you used to be in a different industry, use your work history to your advantage. For example:

  In my years as a sales representative at Molson's Hardware, I learned how to evaluate equipment and construction materials for energy efficiency. By working closely with contractors in the planning stages of construction projects, I was able to study how different construction firms design residential and commercial properties to maximize efficiency across systems.

- **Explain why you're pursuing a new path.** Although it may seem counterintuitive to draw even more attention to your lack of experience in the field, employers will be more willing to look upon you as a viable candidate if you demonstrate that you are passionate about your new career. Don't say that you're moving into the new field to make more money. Explain that you became interested in the new field while working at your previous job, and demonstrate the steps you've taken to prepare yourself for your new career.

- **Don't apologize.** Even if you don't feel confident that an employer will hire you over someone with more experience, you should never allude to these feelings in your cover letter. Your cover letter should demonstrate to the employer that you have complete confidence in your ability to do the job. You may be tempted to say something like, "Although I've never worked in this field before . . ." Don't. Instead, explain why your previous experience actually makes you *more* qualified for the job than someone who has worked in only one field for his entire career.

Networking and Informational Interviews

As an experienced worker, you've probably developed a network of previous coworkers, bosses, clients, and vendors. This network will prove to be a valuable asset when you're looking to change careers. The best resources when you're making a career change are people you've had a successful business relationship with in the past who are working in the field you'd like to move into. These people already know you're a competent worker and can help you get your foot in the door of the new industry.

As discussed in Chapter 6, an excellent way to connect with people in your new industry is by setting up informational interviews. If you find someone in your network who's working in your field of interest, ask that person if you can sit with them for a half-hour or so to learn more about what they do. An informational interview is a great way to gain valuable insight into your new career and to form connections with people who can help you make the switch.

Section 3: Gaining Experience

As important as it is to identify your transferable skills, they will be difficult to be taken seriously by employers if you don't have any experience in the field you'd like to get into. If you've been in the workforce for awhile, however, you're probably not very eager to start all over again in an entry-level position, nor to experience the salary cut that would likely accompany it. So how do you get experience in a new field without sacrificing all the things you've spent your career working for?

- **Take classes.** When researching your new field of interest, you should be aware of the kind of training you'll need. Many of the jobs discussed in the book require some form of specialized training. In many cases, however, you won't need to get an entirely new four-year degree; a class or two is often enough for you to qualify for employment. If your job doesn't require any specialized training, it can still be a helpful experience to take a few classes in sustainable energy or other green topics that relate to the job you're trying to get.

- **Get a part-time job.** You don't need to figure out how to get your foot in the door of a company if you're already inside. A part-time job in your field of interest will help you understand how the industry works and will give you an opportunity to evaluate whether that industry is really where you want to be. It may be difficult to find a part-time job in the exact position you'd like to move into, but any part-time job will give you an idea of how the industry works and will introduce you to people who can help you in your career goals.

- **Volunteer.** Volunteer positions are a good way to learn about new fields and to get free on-the-job training. Want to learn more about the construction industry? Volunteer for Habitat for Humanity. Hoping to get into conservation? Volunteer to work for the parks department. Most nonprofit volunteer organizations are eager for the help and will be glad to teach you as much as you'd like to learn. Besides, as anyone who's ever tried to beef up their extracurriculars for a college application can tell you, volunteer work looks great on a resume!

Another good option is to look for jobs similar to your current job in the industry you'd like to move to. It's much easier to switch jobs once you're in an industry than it is to leap right into an entirely new position in a new industry.

Eco-Quiz

In gasoline-powered vehicles, approximately how much energy is wasted as heat?

a. *20%*

b. *40%*

c. *60%*

a. *80%*

Answer: d. *80%. Only 20% of the gasoline in gasoline-powered vehicles is actually converted into motion. Electric-powered vehicles are exactly the opposite: 80% of the energy is converted to motion, with 20% lost as heat.*

For example, if you're an administrative assistant at a pharmaceutical company right now, you're probably not going to be able to move directly into an engineering job without going back to school. But if you can get an administrative assistant position at an engineering firm, you'll be surrounded by people who can help you make the transition to engineering. You'll gain inside knowledge of how an engineering firm operates that will be valuable experience to have on your resume. You'll still have to go back to school if you want to move into a specialized career, but if you prove yourself valuable enough to your new company, they may even be willing to help pay for your education.

Section 4: Advice for Older Workers

Older workers who are looking to change careers face a unique problem that younger workers don't have to deal with: ageism. Ageism can be a powerful force in the workplace. Older workers are often seen as expensive, set-in-their-ways, and unwilling to learn: in short, a poor investment. Unlike other forms of discrimination, ageism rarely goes challenged in courts, and it is often viewed as justifiable discrimination by corporations that are more interested in finding inexpensive workers than in building a knowledgeable, experienced workforce.

On the flip side, older workers have an easier time moving into positions of authority than younger workers. If a 50-year-old and a 25-year-old are interviewing for the same management position, the 50-year-old has a distinct advantage in terms of accumulated experience. In addition, older workers who are able to think outside the box are often taken more seriously than younger workers would be. If you display a little bit of creativity and initiative in your job hunt, you may have the opportunity to build the kind of career you've always dreamed of.

Create Your Own Position

Let's get one thing straight: Unless you're a high-powered executive, jobs for older workers don't really exist. No one is looking to hire an unemployed factory worker with low skills and high salary demands. If you're over 50, you can throw the want ads into the garbage; they're not going to be much help. You'll have much more luck targeting companies and contacting them directly than you will have applying for posted positions that are bound to attract a surfeit of resumes. If you know how to sell your life experience properly—and as an older worker, life experience is your greatest asset—you'd be surprised at how many companies would be willing to take a chance on you.

So how do you switch careers if there are no jobs out there for you? Simple: You create your own position. As an older worker, you have valuable experience that no younger worker can match. You've seen how companies operate. You know what works and what doesn't; and that is knowledge that many businesses, particularly small to midsize companies, would be anxious to have.

Green Quotes

Development of clean energy invests directly in people, substituting labor for fuel expenses. It is this fundamental fact that allows renewable energy technologies to provide, on average, three to six times as many jobs as equivalent investments in fossil fuels when manufacturing, installation and operations and maintenance jobs are taken into account.

—*"Building the Clean Energy Assembly Line: How Renewable Energy Can Revitalize U.S. Manufacturing and the American Middle Class." The Blue Green Alliance, 2009*

Research Is Everything

When you are creating your own position, the value of targeted research cannot be overstated. Begin by coming up with a list of companies that you would be interested in working for. Since you're relying upon your experience to sell yourself, it's probably best to concentrate on an industry that you know well. At the same time, you shouldn't limit yourself; if you've worked in a factory for 30 years, you may have learned the ins and outs of running an assembly line. The knowledge you've gained can be just as valuable in an automobile manufacturing plant as it is in a wind-turbine manufacturing plant.

After you've identified the companies you'd like to work for, the next step is to research their operations. Read through the companies' annual reports and make a list of common hurdles. Set up informational interviews with employees at the company and ask them what they would like to see improve at their company. Get in touch with anyone you know who might have inside knowledge about the companies on your list and interview them to determine what kinds of problems these companies face.

The next step is the most crucial: *Fix the problems.* Use your knowledge of what has worked and what hasn't worked at the companies you've worked for in the past to come up with solutions to the problems faced by the companies on your list. Concentrate on simple solutions. If you start by tackling a giant problem, you can quickly become bogged down in details. For instance, if you find out that a PV cell manufacturer you have targeted is having trouble meeting demand for their product, you don't need to design a completely new manufacturing system that is unlike anything the world has ever seen. Instead, focus on tackling manageable problems in their operations. Is the company ordering parts from its suppliers on a reasonable schedule? Are there areas where their manufacturing processes could be sped up? Would the company have an easier time meeting demand if they increased their hours of operations? In your analysis, consider things that you observed as an employee that would have increased efficiency. Is there anything your company could have done that would have made you more motivated?

Once you've determined solutions for the challenges faced by the company, the most crucial step is to *locate yourself within these solutions*. You're not just looking to give the company free advice. You're looking for a job. Figure out how you fit into the solutions you've devised. It could be by establishing a position within the company, or it could be by coming in as an outside consultant. No matter where you fit in, you shouldn't pitch your solutions until you know what you would like to get from the company in exchange for your expertise. Are you looking for a full-time position? Part-time? Freelance? What kind of benefits would you expect? Whom would you report to? What kind of compensation would you expect in exchange for your services? And most importantly, why are you worth the money they would pay you?

The Interview

When you feel like you have a handle on how the companies could improve their operations and you know how you could help, your next step is to secure a meeting with management. Don't bother with employees on lower rungs of the organization or the human resources department. Go directly to higher management. It's easier to set up a meeting if you can find a connection through a member of your network, but barring that, a direct phone call to the president is often a successful approach. You may find the approach intimidating at first, but remember: Your solutions are going to help the company improve. They *need* your expertise. And your age will entitle you to a certain amount of respect, assuming you have a pitch worth listening to.

The interview itself should be handled differently from the normal type of interview described earlier in this book because you're not trying to fit in with the company culture. You're selling your services as a professional, and to do that, you should look professional. Wear a business suit. And use your age to your advantage; although you don't want to come across as old and stuffy, you will be greeted with more respect if you sell yourself as a seasoned expert than if you attempt to pander to a younger audience.

The goal of this interview is to sell yourself—even more so than in a regular job interview. In fact, it's a bit of a misnomer to even call this an interview; it is actually a sales pitch. If you go into the discussion expecting the interviewer to be prepared with questions, you will be treated to a lot of awkward silences. Your job is to tell the interviewer what you've learned about the company's challenges, and explain how you are the only person capable of addressing those challenges. Presentation materials can be helpful; in addition to guiding the discussion, they are a nice item to leave behind to remind the interviewer of your meeting.

Don't put all your eggs into one basket. Interview with as many of your targeted companies as you can. If you've really done your homework and have devised worthwhile solutions to the companies' challenges, you're bound to have your choice of competing offers. At this stage in life, you're entitled to have the kind of job you've always wanted, and you can bargain with a lot more leverage if you are choosing among several offers. And finally, once you've settled on an offer, be prepared to roll up your sleeves and get to work. You just may find yourself more satisfied with your career than you've ever dreamed possible.

CHAPTER NINE ||||||||||||||||||||||||||||||||||||||||||||||||

ONLINE RESOURCES
FOR GREEN JOB SEEKERS

Chapter Overview

The green movement has spawned an entire cottage industry of green-related media. Turn on the TV, and you have your choice of green-related programs (The Sundance Network's *Big Ideas for a Small Planet*, PBS's *Building Green TV*) or an entire green network (Planet Green). There are magazines about green activism (*Yes!*), green style and fashion (*Boho*), and green parenting (*Kiwi*). Yet if you took all the magazines and TV shows and add them together, the result wouldn't equal a fraction of the green websites that have sprung up in the past 10 years. From green job search engines (greenbiz.com) to green news sites (grist.com), there are plenty of online resources that can provide valuable assistance during your search for a green job.

In this chapter, we look at the best sites for finding information about green jobs, green news, and green organizations. We also look at industry-specific resources, trade show information, and other job sites that will help you find the green job of your dreams.

Section 1: Green Job Search Engines and News Sites
Section 1 covers job search sites that are dedicated to green jobs and sites that feature news about the green economy.

Section 2: Professional Associations
In Section 2, we look at associations for professionals in several sectors of the green economy.

Section 3: Green Policy and Advocacy
Section 3 covers nonprofit organizations that advocate for environmental issues.

Section 4: Green Conferences
Reprinted from Chapter 3, Section 4 provides links to green conferences for green entrepreneurs and others interested in green-job networking opportunities.

Section 5: Reports
In this section, you find links to interesting reports about the state of the green economy.

Section 1: Green Job Search Engines and News Sites

Listed on the next few pages are the sites that I've found to be the most useful aggregators for green jobs; there are more green job search sites than I've listed here and new sites are cropping up every day. If you come across a green jobs site, be sure to take a look at where their jobs come from. Many search engines are powered by outside job collection services like Job Thread and Simply Hired. I've tried to find one example site that relies on each of the different job collection services; make sure when you find a new site that you're not simply searching the same jobs you're searching elsewhere.

Just Jobs

Clean Edge

jobs.cleanedge.com

Clean Edge, Inc., is a firm that researches and reports on the clean tech industry. Their job board lists clean tech jobs with major firms around the country.

CleanLoop

www.cleanloop.com

Although CleanLoop does not have a lot of job listings, the listings they do have are unique to the site. CleanLoop is a subsidiary of VentureLoop, a job search site that partners with venture capitalist firms to list jobs at start-up companies.

Commongood Careers

www.cgcareers.org

Commongood connects job seekers with nonprofit organizations that are looking for talent. Their site features an article center with news and helpful tips for nonprofit job seekers. Commongood also offers one-on-one services; for a small fee, they will help you write your cover letter and resume and advise you on the best ways to search for jobs in your field.

What percentage of Americans believe they are doing enough to save the environment?

a. *about 15%*
b. *about 30%*
c. *about 50%*
d. *about 65%*

Answer: c. *about 50%. In a September 2009 poll by Earthsense and Greenbiz.com, 52% of those surveyed said they were doing enough to help the planet. In the same poll, only 26.6% of respondents said the U.S. government is doing enough.*

EHSCareers

www.ehscareers.com

EHSCareers concentrates on jobs for environmental and occupational health and safety workers. The site collects listings from major employers including Tyson, Cargill, and PepsiCo.

Environmental Career

www.environmentalcareer.info

Environmental Career specializes in conservation and corporate jobs for workers with higher education degrees, such as environmental scientists and toxicologists.

Great Green Careers

www.greatgreencareers.com

Created by Ogden Publications, Inc., publishers of *Mother Earth News* and *Utne Reader*, Great Green Careers is a fairly basic site allowing users to search for jobs and post their resumes.

Green Career Central

www.jobtarget.com/c/search_results.cfm?site_id=7288

Founded by the author of *Green Careers for Dummies*, Green Career Central is "a complete online center for people who want to switch to a green career or find a green job." It features free job boards for job seekers and additional features for paid members.

Green Job Search

www.greenjobsearch.org

With an interface that recalls the clean look of Google, greenjobsearch.org is a no-nonsense search engine for green opportunities. The site provides easy links to help you search for jobs by category, keywords, or location.

Idealist.org

idealist.org

As one of the first job search sites to focus on nonprofit work, Idealist.org has a long track record of helping job seekers find positions at organizations that are making a difference in the world. Their site also includes helpful resources for nonprofit job seekers, including information about nonprofit career fairs.

Sustainjobs

www.sustainjobs.com

Sustainjobs lists positions around the world at renewable energy companies. Their listings tend to be for workers with higher education degrees and/or extensive experience.

USAJobs

www.usajobs.gov

USAJobs is the first place to check if you're looking to work for the federal government. Although not strictly a green jobs search engine per se, the government's investment in sustainable energy is creating new jobs in fields like clean tech, building, and policy every day; USAJobs is a great resource for these jobs and more.

Did You Know?

In 2009, Wal-mart announced an initiative to create a "sustainability index" evaluating the environmental impact of its supply chain. The company is surveying its more than 100,000 worldwide suppliers to create a report that will be viewable by customers and the general public. "Customers want products that are more efficient, that last longer and perform better," Mike Duke, CEO and president of Wal-Mart said in a press release. "And increasingly they want information about the entire life cycle of a product so they can feel good about buying it."

Jobs and News

Change.org

News: www.change.org/

Jobs: http://jobs.change.org/search

If you're a staunch Republican, you might want to skip the news page and go right to the job listings; Change.org is an activist site with a decidedly liberal bent. The jobs page lists plenty of politically neutral jobs in nonprofit organizations, though, such as Web Specialist at Green for All and Chief Development Officer at Habitat for Humanity.

Environmental Leader

News: environmentalleader.com

Jobs: energy-environment-jobs.environmentalleader.com/a/jbb/find-jobs

Environmental Leader is an excellent site for clean tech business news. Their job search page, powered by Simply Hired, lists a variety of different green business jobs from all over the country, from Energy Engineers to Energy Portfolio Managers.

GreenBiz.com

News: greenbiz.com

Jobs: jobs.greenbiz.com

GreenBiz.com calls itself the "business voice of the green economy." The site is updated daily with news about a variety of green business topics, from "energy and climate" to "marketing and communications." The job search engine, powered by JobThread, lists openings at nationally recognized companies like Zipcar and Stonyfield.

Green Guide Network

News: www.greenguidenetwork.com

Jobs: www.greenguidenetwork.com/job-board

Green Guide Network is primarily a green news site, but they have a section of green job listings that is well worth adding to your bookmarks. They also list green businesses by city, which can be a helpful way to find out about interesting businesses near you that may have job opportunities available.

Renewable Energy World

News: www.renewableenergyworld.com

Jobs: www.renewableenergyworld.com/rea/careers/jobseekers

The name says it all. Renewable Energy World concentrates on the world of renewable energy, with well-organized links to clean energy news, blogs, and multimedia presentations. They also host an excellent job search board with extensive listings around the world.

Sustainable Business

News: www.sustainablebusiness.com/

Jobs: www.sustainablebusiness.com/index.cfm/go/greendreamjobs.main

Sustainable Business features news about renewable energy, green building, sustainable investing, and organics, but its major attraction for job seekers is its Green Dream Jobs job board.

Sustain Lane

News: www.sustainlane.com

Jobs: www.sustainlane.com/green-jobs/jobs

Sustain Lane is a blog-style site that features user-generated opinion columns, advice, and reviews. It also hosts a Green Collar Jobs job board with special boards for jobs based in San Francisco, New York, Washington, DC, Portland, Denver, Seattle, and Los Angeles.

Treehugger

News: treehugger.com

Jobs: jobs.treehugger.com

Don't let the cutesy name fool you. Treehugger.com is a useful source of green job listings from around the country. In addition to the jobs board, Treehugger.com provides a wealth of information on all things environment-related.

Other Job Search Sites

CareerBuilder

careerbuilder.com

Indeed

www.indeed.com

Monster

www.monster.com

Yahoo! HotJobs

hotjobs.yahoo.com

Green Collar Blog

www.greencollarblog.org

Green Collar Blog focuses on advice for green job seekers. It is also home to a massive collection of links to other useful sites, including Job Boards, Job Fair information, Job Training sites, and Green Recruiters.

Green Options

greenoptions.com

Green Options is a network of blogs including Sustainablog, Planetsave, and CleanTechnica that report on environmentally related news for a range of different audiences.

Grist

News: www.grist.org

Established in 1999, Grist has been on the cutting edge of environmental news for more than a decade. Their motto, "gloom and doom with a sense of humor," is reflected in their opinionated stories about climate change, politics, and green living. Grist features a job board as well, powered by Simply Hired.

Mother Nature Network

www.mnn.com/

Mother Nature Network is an extensive news site that reports on all aspects of environmental living. Its content is updated often, and it includes lots of community features that enable readers to contribute to the site's content.

World Green

www.worldgreen.org

Created by the Leonardo Academy, an environmental education center, World Green offers tips on living green and links to green news and events.

Did You Know?
In 2007, there were 68,205 clean-energy businesses in the United States. That year, they patented 8,384 new clean-energy technologies.

Section 2: Professional Associations

Professional associations are a great way to learn more about the industries in which you are interested. Their websites usually contain links to member companies and organizations, which can be a good place to start compiling places to send your resume.

Renewable Energy

American Solar Energy Society

www.ases.org

The ASES website features news and information about the solar industry. They also host a useful job board with links to the biggest solar power organizations and providers.

American Wind Energy Association

www.awea.org

AWEA.org lists news and information about the wind-power industry, including links to industry events. The AWEA also sponsors a job search board, which can be found at www.careersinwind.com.

The Association of Energy Engineers

www.aeecenter.org

The Association of Energy Engineers is the largest worldwide professional society for energy engineers. Their mission is "to promote the scientific and educational interests of those engaged in the energy industry and to foster action for sustainable development." The website includes information about seminars, educational opportunities, and a job search board.

Eco-Quiz

Which household appliance consumes the highest amount of electricity over the course of a year?

a. *refrigerator*
b. *clothes dryer*
c. *television*
d. *dishwasher*

Answer: a. *refrigerator. Americans pay about $90 per year in electricity bills to run our refrigerators. Clothes dryers consume slightly less energy, costing about $80 per year to run. Televisions cost surprisingly little to run, coming in just above the electric blanket (!) at less than $20 per year.*

Geothermal Energy Association

www.geo-energy.org

The GEA website isn't much to look at, but it contains useful information for workers interested in geothermal energy. The site includes a listing of all geothermal plants by state, descriptions of, and links to all the major geothermal companies, and lists of projects that are currently in development around the country.

National Hydrogen Association

www.hydrogenassociation.org

The National Hydrogen Association was formed to promote the creation of a hydrogen energy infrastructure in the United States for providing energy to homes, vehicles, and industry. Their membership includes representatives from the automobile industry, energy providers, and the government. Their website includes information about government policy, press releases, and a job search board.

National Hydropower Association

www.hydro.org

The NHA website features news and information about hydropower. Click on the Hydro Facts link at the top of the page to find links to other useful sites for hydropower information.

Renewable Fuels Association

www.ethanolrfa.org

The RFA is the trade association for the U.S. ethanol industry. Their website features resources for information about the biofuel industry and useful links to member companies and organizations.

Building

Sustainable Buildings Industry Council

www.sidebaricouncil.org

The Sustainable Buildings Industry Council was founded in 1980 by "the major building trade groups, large corporations, small businesses, and individual practitioners who recognized that energy and resource efficient design and construction are imperative to a sustainable . . . environment." Since 2001, the SIDEBARIC has given an annual award called the Beyond Green Award that recognizes exemplary achievement in green building and design. The organization also sponsors training seminars and workshops for construction professionals and home buyers.

U.S. Green Building Council

www.usgbc.org

The U.S. Green Building Council is the leading organization for the green building industry. As the creators of the LEED certification system for green buildings, the USGBC has established the primary criteria for evaluating a building's environmental efficiency. On their website, the USGBC offers in-depth information about LEED requirements, test preparation tools for LEED certification exams, green building news, and tools for job seekers. Their extensive links page contains resources for many different subsectors of the green building industry. The USGBC also offers free online courses for website registrants, as well as their own job search engine at careercenter .usgbc.org/home.

Transportation

All Things Biodiesel

allthingsbiodiesel.com

Sponsored by the National Biodiesel Board, All Things Biodiesel is, as its name implies, a one-stop shop for useful biodiesel information. Their site contains news, forums, classified ads, and an immense collection of links.

Did You Know?

One of the most pressing problems for parents trying to lead an environmentally conscious lifestyle is what to do about all those dirty diapers. The average baby generates approximately one ton of dirty diapers before he or she is potty-trained. Cloth diapers are more environmentally friendly than disposable diapers, but they require a lot of maintenance that can be difficult to manage for today's on-the-go parents.

A company called Knowaste Ltd. is working to solve the dirty diaper dilemma with its Knowaste Nappy Processor, a machine that separates the recyclable components of diapers from the organic human waste. The recovered plastic is then used in products like roofing tiles and shoe insoles, while the organic waste is used to power the recycling facility.

American Public Transportation Association

www.apta.com

APTA is a public transportation advocacy and lobbying group. Their website contains reports about public transportation and links to public transportation organizations in all 50 states. They also have a cleverly hidden job board: To find it, click on the For Members link at the top of the homepage, then Member Programs and Services. On the right-hand side of the page you'll find a link to the Job Bank.

Electric Drive Transportation Association

www.electricdrive.org

The EDTA is the national advocacy organization for electric vehicles. Their website contains general information about electric vehicle technology, events listings, and links to other organizations dedicated to alternative fuel sources.

Natural Gas Vehicles for America

www.ngvc.com

NGVAmerica is "a national organization dedicated to the development of a growing, sustainable, and profitable market for vehicles powered by natural gas or hydrogen." Their website provides information about government policy concerning natural gas vehicles and links to natural gas-related businesses.

Food and Agriculture

National Sustainable Agriculture Information Service

www.attra.org

The National Sustainable Agriculture Information Service website contains information for farmers and others interested in many different aspects of sustainable farming, including soils, water management, and organic farming. It also features a calendar with links to sustainable agriculture conferences and education opportunities.

Organic Trade Association

www.ota.com

The Organic Trade Association is the major trade association for the North American organic business community. On its website, you can find news, links to industry events, and an extensive list of OTA's members that can come in handy during the job search.

Green Quotes

We've figured out how to achieve tripled-efficiency cars, trucks, and airplanes, laid many of the conceptual and practical foundations for electric and water efficiency and widespread renewable energy; reinvented energy strategy, superefficient engineering design, real-estate development, security, and (with Paul Hawken) a natural version of capitalism; and devised profitable solutions to climate change, oil dependence, nuclear nonproliferation, and critical-infrastructure vulnerability.

*—Amory Lovins, Chairman and Chief Scientist
of the Rocky Mountain Institute*

Recycling and Waste Management

Air and Waste Management Association

www.awma.org

The A&WMA is an organization that provides news, education, and information for professionals in the air and waste management industries. Their website contains links to education opportunities and a career center for aspiring air and waste management professionals.

National Recycling Coalition

www.nrc-recycle.org

The National Recycling Coalition is a nonprofit organization that represents recycling advocacy groups and state and regional recycling organizations. Its website features news, a search engine for local recycling centers, and a list of events and programs.

Section 3: Green Policy and Advocacy

The websites for green policy and advocacy organizations contain lots of useful information about the green economy that you can use when you're networking and interviewing. The following sites are also good sources of information for people interested in working in the nonprofit world.

American Council for an Energy-Efficient Economy

www.aceee.org

The ACEEE is a nonprofit organization founded in 1980 to study energy efficiency and make policy recommendations. They also have an employment page that lists jobs in energy-efficient organizations around the United States.

The Apollo Alliance

apolloalliance.org

Started in the wake of 9/11, The Apollo Alliance is a "coalition of labor, business, environmental, and community leaders working to catalyze a clean energy revolution that will put millions of Americans to work in a new generation of high-quality, green-collar jobs." On their website and blog, they offer news about the green economy and information about how The Apollo Alliance is working to build America's green economy. Visit apolloalliance.org/digest/ to sign up for their free, daily clean energy and green jobs newsletter.

The Blue Green Alliance

www.bluegreenalliance.org

The Blue Green Alliance is a partnership between environmental organizations and labor unions. Their website includes reports and press releases about the state of the green economy, as well as a news section for the latest information about green jobs.

The Environmental Protection Agency

www.epa.gov

The Environmental Protection Agency was founded in 1970 to provide a governmental response to the environmental dangers of pollutants in our air, land, and water. Their website is an invaluable resource for anyone looking to learn more about the issues that are facing our environment and the United States' response to these issues.

Green America

www.greenamericatoday.org

Green America is a nonprofit dedicated to growing the green economy to create healthy, sustainable communities around the world. Some of Green America's activities include soliciting donations for environmentally responsible businesses, lobbying corporations for environmental changes, and organizing consumer groups. The highlight of their website for green job seekers is the National Green Pages, a listing of thousands of green businesses across the country.

Intergovernmental Panel on Climate Change

www.ipcc.ch

The Intergovernmental Panel on Climate Change (IPCC) was established in 1988 by the United Nations and the World Meteorological Organization. The work of the IPCC is done on a voluntary basis by thousands of scientists from 194 member countries. To date, the independent scientific body has created four comprehensive assessment reports on the state of the environment. The IPCC does not make policy recommendations, but its well-researched assessments have been instrumental in helping policy makers understand how climate change is affecting our planet.

Did You Know?

In India, a company called Husk Power Systems is supplying electricity via biomass to villages that are too remote to be connected to the power grid. The energy is created by converting rice husks, a waste product, to a gas that runs modified diesel engines. Fifty villages currently get their electricity from HPS, with plans to expand to 2,000 villages by 2012.

Section 4: Green Conferences

Industry conferences are an excellent place to network with representatives from green companies and organizations. Although conferences usually charge an attendance fee, the connections you make can be well worth the price of admission.

Building Energy Conference

www.buildingenergy.nesea.org

Who it's for: Architects, engineers, planners, scientists, or anyone else interested in green building

Fortune Magazine's Brainstorm: GREEN

www.timeinc.net/fortune/conferences/brainstormgreen/
   green_home.html

Who it's for: Business leaders, environmentalists

Green Business Conference

www.greenamericatoday.org/cabn/conference

Who it's for: Green business owners or anyone interested in starting a green business

Green Jobs Conference

www.greenjobsconference.org

Who it's for: Community and business leaders, union members, environmentalists

Green Manufacturing Expo

www.devicelink.com/expo/gmx10

Who it's for: Energy consultants, energy software developers, green manufacturers

Greenbuild Expo

www.greenbuildexpo.org

Who it's for: Architects, contractors, developers, engineers, builders, students, urban planners

NAHB National Green Building Conference

www.nahb.org/conference_details.aspx?conferenceID=59

Who it's for: Architects, builders, land planners, energy-efficient product manufacturers

Opportunity Green

www.opportunitygreen.com

Who it's for: Business owners and anyone interested in starting a green business

West Coast Green

www.westcoastgreen.com

Who it's for: Green innovators, business leaders, and entrepreneurs

Section 5: Reports

The following free reports were extremely useful when I was writing this book. If you're interested in learning more about the green economy, these reports are must-reads.

"Careers for Colorado's New Energy Economy"

www.colorado.gov/energy/images/uploads/pdfs/6fb0cc18facf0526889704ca90
a6bd19.pdf

"The Clean Energy Economy"

www.pewcenteronthestates.org/uploadedFiles/Clean_Economy_Report_Web
.pdf

"Clean Energy Economy Fact Sheets"

www.pewtrusts.org/news_room_detail.aspx?id=53262

"Defining, Estimating, and Forecasting the Renewable Energy and Energy Efficiency Industries in the United States and in Colorado"

www.colorado.gov/energy/in/uploaded_pdf/GreenJobsReportFull.pdf

Green Quotes

This is the best time in history to buy solar. In California, homeowners can take advantage of utility company rebates covering 15 to 20% of the costs, as well as the 30% federal tax credit for solar. In places where electricity costs are high, the economics are unbelievable.

—*Danny Kennedy, president of solar power company Sungevity and former campaigns manager for Greenpeace, as quoted on Greenbiz.com*

"The Economic Benefits of Investing in Clean Energy"

www.americanprogress.org/issues/2009/06/pdf/peri_report.pdf

"Going Green: The Vital Role of Community Colleges in Building a Sustainable Future and Green Workforce"

www.greenforall.org/resources/going-green-the-vital-role-of-community
-colleges-in-building-a-sustainable-future-and-a-green-workforce

"Green Jobs Guidebook: Employment Opportunities in the New Clean Economy"

www.edf.org/documents/8489_Green Jobs Guidebook FINAL with cover.pdf

"Green-Collar Jobs in America's Cities: Building Pathways out of Poverty and Careers in the Clean Energy Economy"

www.apolloalliance.org/downloads/greencollarjobs.pdf

"Green-Collar Jobs: Realizing the Promise"

www.sightline.org/research/green-collar-jobs/green-jobs-primer/green-jobs
  -primer-pdf

"Green Jobs: Survey of the Energy Industry"

www.aeecenter.org/shows/PDFs/Survey%20of%20the%20Green%20Energy
  %20Industry%20.pdf

"High Road or Low Road? Job Quality in the New Green Economy"

www.goodjobsfirst.org/pdf/gjfgreenjobsrpt.pdf

"National Commission on Energy Policy's Task Force on America's Future
Energy Jobs"

http://ourenergypolicy.org/docs/20/NCEP_Task_Force_on_America_s_
  Future_Energy_Jobs_-_Final_Report.pdf